BUDDHIST REMAINS IN ANDHRA AND THE HISTORY OF ANDHRA

BETWEEN 225 & 610 A.D.

BUDDHIST REMAINS IN ANDHRA AND THE HISTORY OF ANDHRA

BETWEEN 225 & 610 A.D.

BY

K. R. SUBRAMANIAN, M.A.

Lecturer in History, Maharaja's College, Vizianagram, Sankaraparvathi prizeman for Research in Ancient Indian History 1927 (Madras University), Guntur District Board Fellow, 1927-28 (Andhra University), Author of The Origin of Saivism and its History in the Tamil land, The Maratha Rajas of Tanjore, etc., etc.

3 Maps and 6 Plates

WITH A FOREWORD
BY
DR. G JOUVEAU-DUBREUIL
Author of The Pallavas, Pallava Antiquities, Ancient History of the Deccan, etc. etc.

GYAN

Published by

Gyan Publishing House
5, Ansari Road
Daryaganj, New Delhi-110002
Phone: 011-47034999, 9811692060
E-mail: books@gyanbooks.com

Distribution Network
gyanbooks.com
India, USA, Canada, UK, Australia, France

ISBN : 978-81-212-4503-6 (HB)
First Published, 1932

2nd Impression 2020

Printed at: Gyan Press, Delhi.

Buddhist Remains in Andhra and The History of Andhra
Author: K. R. Subramanian

Buddhist Remains in Āndhra

AND

The History of Āndhra

between 225 & 610 A.D.

BY

K. R. SUBRAMANIAN, M.A.

Lecturer in History, Maharaja's College, Vizianagram, Śankarapārvathi prizeman for Research in Ancient Indian History 1927 (Madras University), Guntur District Board Fellow, 1927-28 (Āndhra University), Author of *The Origin of Śaivism and its History in the Tamil land*, *The Marātha Rājas of Tanjore*, etc., etc.

3 MAPS AND 6 PLATES.

WITH A FOREWORD

BY

DR. G. JOUVEAU-DUBREUIL

Author of *The Pallavas*, *Pallava Antiquities*, *Ancient History of the Deccan*, etc., etc.

MADRAS

PRINTED AT THE DIOCESAN PRESS, VEPERY

1932

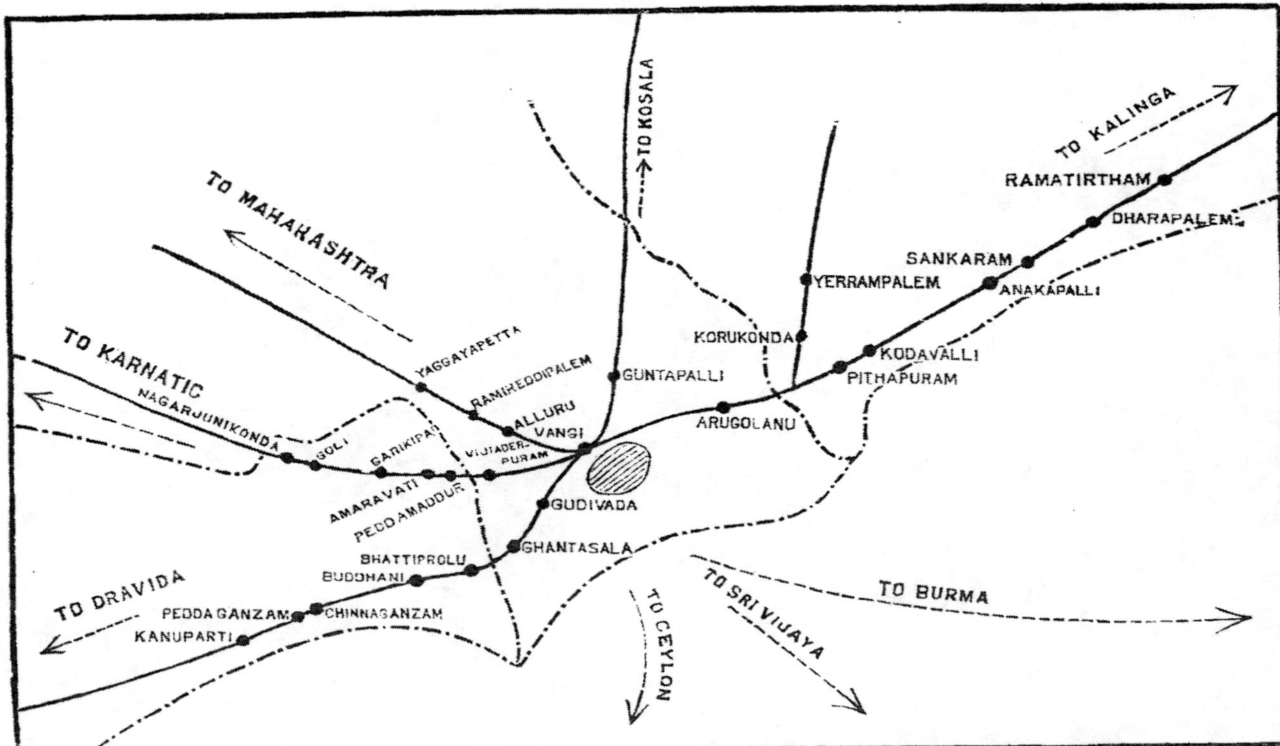
TO KOSALA
TO KALINGA
RAMATIRTHAM
DHARAPALEM
SANKARAM
ANAKAPALLI
YERRAMPALEM
KORUKONDA
KODAVALLI
PITHAPURAM
TO MAHAKASHTRA
YAGGAYAPETTA
RAMIREDDIPALEM
GUNTAPALLI
ARUGOLANU
ALLURU
VANGI
TO KARNATIC
NAGARJUNIKONDA
GOLI
GARIKIPA
VIJIADER-
PURAM
AMARAVATI
PEDDAMADDUR
GUDIVADA
GHANTASALA
BHATTIPROLU
BUDDHANI
TO DRAVIDA
PEDDA GANZAM
CHINNAGANZAM
KANUPARTI
TO CEYLON
TO SRI VIJAYA
TO BURMA

FOREWORD

THE work of Mr. Subrạmanian will give the reader very complete details concerning—

1. Archæology of the Āndhra country.
2. Its history during the Third, Fourth, Fifth and Sixth centuries.

I think that as Preface for this book it would be well that I fix—

1. in space (on the map) the archæological remains,
2. in time (chronology) the historical facts.

Section 1. Geographical position of Archæological remains in Āndhra.

In examining the map opposite, one will find the Buddhist sites placed along certain lines. The country of Vengi was a great meeting place of roads. Five great routes converged at that place :

1. The road to Kaliṅga (North-East),
2. The road to Dravida (South),
3. The road to Karnāṭic (South-West),
4. The road to Mahārāshṭra (North-West),
5. The road to Kośala (North).

These five roads converged towards the country of Vengi which lay along the coast. Some great ports existed in this country and from them ships used to start to Chryse, i.e., the country of gold, Burma and Śri Vijaya.

We have absolute proof of the fact that the country of Vengi had a preponderating influence on the civilisation of Burma, of Malaya states and of Indo-China. This proof is supplied to us by the alphabet of the inscriptions found there.

One would believe that Burma had close relations with Bengal and less relations with Vengi. It is quite the contrary. A Buddhist stupa discovered recently in old Prome contained inscriptions in Kanarese-Telugu script of the Sixth Century. We know that from early times the alphabet of Indo-China was derived from that of Vengi. Thus, these overseas countries were making use of the alphabet of Vengi and not of the alphabet of the Gangetic valley.

The commerce of India with the Far East was not carried, as one would think, through the port of Tāmarliptị (Tamluk) or the ports of Orissa. It is from the country of Vengi that Indian ships sailed to go to the Far East.

We are astonished at this; for, we are accustomed to consider the mouths of the Ganges as a great centre of maritime commerce. This illusion is produced by the importance of the big modern town of Calcutta.

But, we must understand that the valley of the Ganges is not a coastal region.

On the contrary, through the valleys of the Godāvarī and the Krishṇā, the big routes of the Deccan converge towards the sea in the country of Vengi.

Such being the case, let us consider the map of the Buddhist sites. These sites are numerous. There are some thirty of them. And all the Buddhist sites are along the five great routes that we have cited.

1. On the road to Kaliṅga, Vengi, Arugolu, Pithāpuram, Kodavalli, Anakapalle, Śankaram, Dhārapalem, Rāmatīrtham, Śālihundam.

2. On the road to the south, Guḍivāḍa, Ghanṭaśāla, Bhaṭṭiprolu, Buddhāni, Chinna and Pedda Gañjam and finally Kanuparti.

3. On the road to the Karnāṭic, the sites of Vijayadērpuram (Bezwāda), Peddamaddur, Amarāvatī, Garikipādu, Gōli, Nāgārjunikoṇḍa.[1]

4. On the road to Mahārāshṭra are found Allūru, Rāmireḍḍipalle, Jaggayyapēṭa.

5. Lastly, at the beginning of the road to Kośala which started from Vengi and followed the Godāvarī to go to the centre of India *via* Nāgpur, we find the site of Guntapalle. Another road towards the north lay through Korukoṇḍa and Yerrampālem. It was because the Buddhist monks lived on charity, they were obliged to live near the big towns and the great roads in spite of their love for solitude and meditation.

I think that it is necessary to mention these routes, for we are familiar with the present-day geography only. We must therefore say here what the old road map was.

1. Road to Kaliṅga. If you look at a modern map, you see that there is absolutely no road in the region comprised between the Kollēru lake and the sea. The whole right bank of the river Uppuṭṭēru is devoid of villages and roads.

[1] Dr. J. Dubreuil is of opinion that Chējārla is not Buddhist.

The Grand road, therefore, lay on the north of the Kollēru lake through Vengi and Arugolu and crossed the Godāvarī probably near Dowlēśwaram through the island of Bobberlanka. This place is precisely the one where the sacred river which, so far, was running in one stream divided itself into many branches. Dowlēśwaram situated near the source of the Gautamī must have been particularly sacred for the pious Buddhists. Thus, the Grand road to Kaliṅga lay far away from the mouth of the Godāvarī, and it is for this reason that no Buddhist site is found in the *delta* of the Godāvarī. From Dowlēśwaram the road led to Pithāpuram where there was a stūpa; then, towards the well-known site of Kodavalli; thereafter the road followed the coast through Anakapalle and Śankaram, Dhārapalem near Simhāchalam and, finally, Rāmatīrtham.

2. Road to Draviḍa. Guḍiyāḍa was a very important town. It was the capital of the Kūdūra country. A good road connects even to-day Peddavēgi (through Ellore) and Gudivāḍa. This good modern road continues as far as Pāmārru. It is probable that the island of Potarlanka favoured the passage across the Krishṇā; for, this place was surrounded by three famous sanctuaries: Śrīkākulam which was probably Buddhist in olden days and on each side of the river two big stūpas, Ghaṇṭaśāla on the left bank and Bhaṭṭiprolu on the right. Potarlanka is the biggest island in the Krishṇā. So, in the Roman epoch, the capital of the country was Mālanka (the big island). That is perhaps the reason why the inhabitants of Śrīkākulam say that the capital was in a place situated in the middle of the Krishṇā. It is there that Anantapāla the minister of Śimukha, the King of the Āndhras, lived.

It must be noted that even to-day the town of Rēpalle is isolated and a fine road connects Bhaṭṭiprolu with Bāpaṭla through Buddhāni where were discovered Buddhist statuettes. The road from Bāpaṭla to Ongōle is now followed by the rail and it is on that road that you find Chinna and Pedda Gañjam and Kanuparti.

3. Road to the Karnāṭic. It crossed the Krishṇā probably in its largest width between Vijayadhērpuram and Peddamaddur not far from Amarāvatī. More to the west is Garikapāḍu. Finally, the road crossed the Krishṇā near about Gōli and Nāgārjunikoṇḍa.

4. Road to Mahārāshṭra. It commenced probably in the environs of Allūru and passed near Rāmireḍḍipalle to join

Jaggayyapēta from where it turned towards Tagara (Tēr) and then towards Sopāra or Bharukkacha.

5. We know only of one site on the route from Vengi to Kośala and it is Guṇṭapalle. The road followed the Godāvarī for some distance and then turned towards Nāgpur and from there towards Northern India. A second road started from Rājahmundry and passed through the Buddhist sites of Korukoṇḍa and Yerrampālem.

Thus, we see that all the Buddhist sites known at present are found along the grand roads of communication.

Section II. The chronology from 150 to 610 A.D.

In 150 A.D. Rudradāman ruled over Aparānta. He was replaced in this country by Gautamīputra Yajña Śrī. In fact, we have found in the ruins of the stūpa of Sopāra constructed by Yajña a coin belonging to this king, quite different from the ordinary coins of the Āndhras. It is a silver coin and it bears the effigy of the king, Yajña. As this piece is evidently an imitation of the coins of Rudradāman it is not doubtful that Yajña reigned immediately after Rudradāman in Aparānta.

If we place Yajña towards 170 or 180 A.D., and, if we can believe the references of the Purāṇas that after Yajña, ruled the three kings Vijaya, Chandra Śri Śāntikarṇa and Pulomā, the last king should have lived towards 225 A.D., and the dynasty of the Śātavāhanas would have ceased to reign towards 230–240 A.D.

In the Mahārāshṭra the Śātavāhanas would have been replaced by the Ābhīras. In fact the inscription (No. 1137 of Lüder's list) at Nāsik the script of which resembles that of the Śātavāhanas is dated in the ninth year of the reign of the King Mādharīputra Īśvaraśēna an Ābhira, son of Śivadatta. In the Telugu country it was the Ikśhvākus who replaced the Śātavāhanas. I think it necessary to draw attention here to a detail which seems to have escaped the historian's attention till now. The Ikshvāku king bore the name of Purushadatta which has the same termination *Datta*[1] as the Ābhīra Śivadatta. Besides, there is a king with the surname Mādharīputra (same as Purushadatta's) in the Nāsik

[1] Vāsula*datta* nephew of Kāla the Nāga Rāja (in story), Captain Kumāra*datta* of Myakadōni ins. and Swami*datta* of Kotturu may be noted here. K.R.S.

inscription. Thus, these kings who were the successors of the Śātavāhanas and who must have been nearly contemporaneous, bore very similar names. They lived probably in the middle of the Third Century A.D. (250 A.D.)

These Ikshvākus seem to have had matrimonial relations with the Śakas of Ujjain.

The second half of the Third Century 250–300 A.D. seems to have been marked in the Deccan by a vast expansion of the Śakas of Ujjain. On the banks of the Krishṇā at Karad 31 miles south of Satāra a treasure was found containing coins of Vijayasēna, Damajadaśri III, Rudrasēna, Visvasimha, Bhartridāman and Visvasēna. This last king ruled from 296–300 A.D. Besides, a treasure discovered at Amarāvati in the Berars contained coins of Rudrasēna 256–272 A.D.

We may conclude that the Śakas of Ujjain were masters of Mahārāshṭra in the second half of the Third Century A.D. The treasure of Karad contained a coin of Rudragaṇa. This king ruled in Aparānta, for 500 pieces of silver of this king were found at Dāman. They tell us that Rudragaṇa was the son of the king Indravarman. This king whose name ends in *varman* reigned therefore in Aparānta towards the end of the Third Century. It is to be noted that in the same epoch there appears in the Karnāṭic a dynasty of Pallava princes whose names end in *varman*.

These Pallava kings who ruled over the countries of Banavāsi and Amarāvatī had their capital at Kāñchipuram.

They took the place of the Ikshvākus towards 275 A.D. Many hypotheses have been built as regards the origin of the Pallavas. The word 'Pallava' is nearly identical with the word 'Pahlava' which was the name of princely families in the kingdom of the Śakas. The ending *varman* is not met with anywhere in the Deccan before the Third Century, and it is in Aparānta that we find Indravarman whose name ends in this manner. It is not doubtful, in my opinion, that it was at the time when the Śakas ruled in the upper valley of the Krishṇā that the Pallavas succeeded in creating for themselves a kingdom south of that river at Banavāsi and Amarāvatī.

They could not, however, maintain their position there for a long time. In the country of Banavāsi the Pallavas were replaced by the Kadambas. In the country of Amarāvatī they were replaced by the family of the king, Kandara, of the *gotra* of Ānanda.

In my article *Amarāvatī from A.D. 100–700* (Q. J. A. H. R. S., vol. v, Part ii, Oct. 1930) I have shown that this family of Kandara reigned in the Fifth Century and was replaced during the second half of the Fifth Century by the Vishṇukuṇḍins who reigned up to 610 A.D.

The history of these epochs was for a long time very obscure. Little by little more light is thrown upon it.

The Āndhras seem to us a glorious race. To them we owe the school of Amarāvatī sculpture, the philosophical school of Nāgārjuna, and it is probably from the Āndhra ports that the vessels which have civilised Indo-China, Java and Sumatra started.

The excellent book of Mr. Subramanian will be, to the modern Āndhras, a powerful stimulant. A country which was so glorious in the past is destined to be glorious in the future.

November 29, 1931. G. JOUVEAU-DUBREUIL.

PREFACE BY THE AUTHOR

In the following pages is recorded the result of my work as Gunṭūr District Board Fellow during the year 1928–9. I beg to convey my respectful thanks to the Rajah Saheb Bahadur of Vizianagram for having granted me leave of absence from the College on half pay for one year and thus enabled me to take up the Fellowship. I am highly obliged to the Āndhra University for having chosen me as the first Guntur Fellow and financed my tour in March 1929 to study some of the Āndhra monuments *in situ*. It was in the course of that tour that I discovered an image of the Buddha in white marble in a deserted Hanumān temple in Jaggayyapēta. I have presented the image to the Āndhra University and written an article on the same (with its photo) in the *Hindu Illustrated Weekly* for July 27, 1930. Subsequently the University has arranged under its auspices for two courses of lectures by me on the subject of my study, at Cocanada and Vizagapatnam, in March 1930 and December 1931. My thanks are due to Mr. C. R. Reddi Garu for permitting me to dedicate this book to him as a token of my high regard for him. During the year of my Fellowship I worked under the late lamented scholar Mr. P. T. Srinivasa Iyengar (then Reader in the Madras University and subsequently Professor in the Annāmalai University), and I must acknowledge with gratitude his valuable guidance. I sorely feel his loss as he promised to go through the proof-sheets and write a Foreword. My sorrow has been assuaged to some extent by the ready kindness of Dr. Dubreuil of Pondicherry who has written the Foreword. The distinguished Doctor is the most competent person in the field covered by my book and, in fact, I wanted to work under him but could not do so as he went home during the year. But, I cannot easily forget his enthusiasm, encouragement and hospitality when I first met him at Pondicherry in June 1928. He has now placed me under a debt of gratitude which it is not easy to discharge. The Archæological department has been very kind in supplying me with the photographs reproduced in this book, and the Editor of the *Hindu Illustrated Weekly* has been so good as to allow me to utilise my articles to his valuable paper on *The Nagarjunakoṇda Excavations*

(2-3-30), *Nāgārjuna Bodhisattva* (16-3-30), *The Ikshvākus of the Deccan* (30-3-30), *Āndhra Culture Abroad* (13-4-30), *Early Āndhra History : The Telugus, their land and language* (18-5-30), *Jaggayyapeta* (27-7-30), *Sanghārāma* (12-10-30), *Goli with Nāgārjunakoṇḍa sculptures* (19-10-30), and *Amarāvatī* (21-12-30) and (28-12-30). My thanks are also due to Mr. V. Nārāyanan, M.A., M.L., Advocate, and Mr. A. V. Venkatarāman, M.A., L.T. (then Curator), for having read through some chapters of my book and offered a few valuable suggestions, and to Mr. S. Srinivas Acharya, B.A., Tutor in French, Āndhra University, for having given me, at my request, a free translation of the Preface written by Dr. Dubreuil.

It is desirable, in my opinion, to make a few remarks in this preface on the subject-matter of the book worked at nearly three years ago. My interest in the history of Āndhra Buddhism was roused some years ago by a visit to Rāmatīrtham (about 8 miles from Vizianagram), where one may study the various stages of our religious evolution, viz., Śakti worship (in the *Durgakoṇḍa*), Buddhism (in the *Bodikonda* corrupted into *Boḍikonda* as the hill is bald), Jainism (in the *Gurubhuktalukonda* and elsewhere), and Saiva and Vaishnava cults, the latter represented by traditions of Rāmānuja's visit and by the disciples of Maṇavāḷamahāmuni. My appetite for more knowledge was whetted by a study of the remains of *Lingālakoṇda* (a hill of stūpas actually) or *Bojjanakoṇda* (a corruption of Buddhannakoṇda) in Sanghārāma near Anakapalle. Fascinated by the subject, I collected together facts of the Buddhist remains in Āndhra as a mere hobby and delivered a lecture on the same on November 19, 1926, which was subsequently reproduced in the *Maharaja's College Magazine* (vol. vi., No. 2). Considerable impetus was given to my work in this field by the startling discoveries of Dr. Jouveau-Dubreuil, Mr. A. R. Saraswati and Mr. Longhurst in the district of Guntūr. I then applied to the Āndhra University for some help to enable me to study some of the easily-accessible remains in the Āndhra districts (May 1927).

So, when I was appointed to do some research work in July 1928, I naturally decided that the legacies of the age of Nāgārjuna and far-famed Amarāvatī should be collected together and presented as Part I of my book. Mr. Rea, Mr. Longhurst and Dr. Dubreuil have done a good deal of spade-work, and I was fortunate in making a personal study of their work on the spot besides utilising their interesting reports. Archæological remains are the main source for a study of this epoch of the history of Āndhradēśa. Curiously enough, there are only a few literary works extant from this period, and what little we know of them we owe to the Chinese. Sātavāhana coins have been found in large quantities and throw some light on Āndhra political, religious and economic history. The valuable epigraphs in Brāhmi and in Prākrit from the Buddhist *tīrthas* are another important mine of information of a reliable character. Āndhradēśa was saturated with Buddhism till long after the last Śātavāhana (225 A.D.) and the beginnings of Āndhra culture are coeval with the beginnings of Buddhism in the land. As Hiuen-Tsang testifies, the religion of the Buddha was not an insignificant factor to be ignored even after the close of the last scene of my book (610 A.D.).

No connected account of the Buddhist remains of Āndhradēśa has hitherto been written and, therefore, Part I of my book will be found supplying a gap in her history. A clear study of the location, character and value of the monuments and the deductions concerning ancient life and manners from the marbles of Amarāvatī may be found to possess an original character and special value. The data about Nāgārjuna, his life, works and age scattered in many works, have been brought together and he is given a setting in Nāgārjunakoṇda which is identified with Fahian's *Polo yu* and Hiuen-Tsang's *Polo molo kili*.

Part II of the book deals with the history of the various dynasties of kings that ruled over Āndhradēśa between 225 and 610 A.D. The available materials for the study of this epoch are meagre, and it is difficult to correlate them logically and chronologically. The utmost that could be pressed out of these sources was a dynastic skeleton or skeletons. A glimpse into some aspects of the original picture is given by a stray reference here or there. Here, again, we feel the lack of literary sources if we except the travels of Hiuen-Tsang, and archæological remains also fail us as early Hindu works are rare. We hear of Pallava gold pieces distributed to Brahmans and of Ikshvāku coins, but have not discovered even one of them. So we have to rely upon inscriptions, mostly copper-plates which do not seem to have been used in the Śātavāhana period. There are three copper-plates for the early Pallava, six for the Śālaṅkāyana, nine for the Later Pallava (including the Darśi fragment and the spurious

Udayēndiram grant), two for the Ānanda Gotra, five for the Vishṇukuṇḍin, nine for the Kaliṅga and two or three for the Early Chāḷukya dynasties. Besides, there are stone inscriptions of the Ikshvākus, the Ānanda Gotra and the Early Chāḷukyas. A few inscriptions of other dynasties like the Kadambas, the Gangas and the Vākāṭakas, the Allahabad Pillar inscription of Samudragupta and the Vāyalūr and Vēlūrpāḷaiyam inscriptions of the later Pallava dynasty of Simhavishṇu throw sidelights on the history of Āndhra. These epigraphs have been ably edited in learned journals by distinguished savants like Dr. Fleet, Dr. Hultsch and Mr. H. Krishṇa Śāstri. Fragments of unrelated information are derived from these evidences, and sometimes we have to build up a whole person out of his extant finger-nails, as it were. Our history is, thus, essentially fractional, and it is very hazardous to generalise. But, I thought that a thorough first-hand study of the extant sources, aided by a sound historic imagination, would have its own value, although facts hidden in the womb of Time may, when discovered, upset some of my conclusions. To cull out hard facts from indisputable quarries, classify them and interpret their general laws, and thus make them glow with life, is the task of a historian. While he is responsible for his erroneous conclusions, the vagueness of the picture must be held as due to insufficiency of facts.

The subject-matter of Part II may be summarised in a few words. The bulk of Āndhradēśa or the Telugu-speaking country of to-day has been a separate linguistic belt from very early times. The first independent dynasty that ruled over almost the whole area was the Śātavāhanas who were masters also of some neighboring kingdoms. After their decline (225 A.D.) there was division of Āndhra under two or more dynasties. Roughly, the present Nellore, Guntūr and Cuddapah districts were under the Pallavas during our period (225–610 A.D.) who had to fight hard against the Kadambas in the west and for some time with the Chōḷas in the south. The Bṛihatphalāyanas ruled the present Krishṇā District for some time after 225 A.D. when the Ikshvākus spread their rule from beyond the Ghats over the bulk of Āndhra. The fall of the Ikshvākus was followed by the rapid rise of the Kadambas and the expansion of the Vākātakas who set mutual limits to their empires in Eastern Hyderabad. The expedition of Samudragupta in the middle of the Fourth Century A.D. found Āndhra as well as Kaliṅga disorganised without a supreme potentate. By the end of the Third Century A.D., Ikshvāku rule in the Krishṇā and West Godāvarī districts was supplanted by that of the Śālaṅkāyanas whose tenure of power continued upto about 450 A.D. Then, the family of the Vishṇukuṇḍins, a protégé of the Vākāṭakas of the Central Provinces, superseded the Śālaṅkāyanas and ruled also over a little territory south of the Krishṇā for some time. Vākāṭaka-Vishṇukuṇḍin sway extended beyond the Godāvarī at the expense of the Kaliṅga kings even as far as Vizianagram. Subsequently the Gaṅgas of Kaliṅga stemmed the tide of Vishṇukuṇḍin invasion and proved a thorn on the side of the Vishṇukuṇḍins north of the Godāvarī. About the beginning of the Seventh Century a new force had arisen in Karnāṭa, viz., the Chāḷukyas. The Chāḷukyan tempest blew over the whole of the Deccan, uprooting some and crippling other old dynasties. A branch of the Chāḷukyas came to be established in the Āndhra country in the first decade of the Century and it flourished for four centuries till it was merged in the Chōḷa family.

The first book which attempted a history of Āndhra was Mr. Chilukuri Virabhadra Rao's *Āndhracharitra* in Telugu (Madras, 1910).

Dr. Jouveau-Dubreuil of Pondicherry has given a sketch of the dynasties of Āndhra in his *Ancient History of the Deccan*. His scholarly work on *The Pallavas* has brought in its train a number of publications, but the other dynasties of Āndhra have been comparatively untouched. In two respects, Part II of this book is an advance upon Dr. Dubreuil's work. While the learned writer gives a skeleton of facts, I have been able to supply the necessary flesh and blood and give a whole picture with a detailed account of the local habitats of the dynasties and their inter-relations. Again, during the last decade (after the publication of the *Ancient History of the Deccan*, 1920), wonderful archæological and epigraphical remains have been brought to light. Thus, the inscriptions of Nāgārjunakoṇḍa have opened a new world of facts and ideas and enabled me to write more than one chapter (see chaps. ii, iv and viii) on the Ikshvākus, whereas the French savant had to be content with twelve lines. The two Kanṭeru and the Pedda Vēgi copper-plates had not been discovered when Dr. Dubreuil wrote on the Śālaṅkāyanas. They have thrown new light on the history of the dynasty. They have been edited by the late Mr. K. V. Lakshmanarao and Mr. M. S. Sarma in the

Maharaja's College Magazine, October 1922, and in *Bharati*, vol. i. The facts from all the inscriptions concerning religion, administration and other problems have been fully utilized in the chapters dealing with the dynasties concerned as well as in the last two general chapters. In the chapter on the Vishṇukuṇḍins, again, new sources have come to light after 1920 in the shape of the two Īpūr copper-plates edited in vol. xvii of the *Epigraphia Indica*. The Āṇanda Gotra is a dynasty which does not figure in Dr. Dubreuil's book. I have written a few paragraphs on the same based upon their stone and copper-plate inscriptions.

Though much has been written on the Pallavas by Dr. S. K. Iyengar, Mr. P. T. S. Iyengar, Mr. Gopalan and others, certain facts connected with the dynasty are still obscure. Some new light is thrown in chapter vi on the origin of the Pallavas. In chapter ix, the relations among the Pallavas, the Chōḷas and the Kadambas, the genealogical tree and the question of two Pallava dynasties, are dealt with at length. I have not dealt with the problem of Trilochana Pallava here as my paper on this little known king has been already published by Mr. P. T. Srinivasa Iyengar in his *History of Tamil Culture*, pp. 383–88 (1929). In chapter xi which sketches briefly the inter-relation of Āndhra and Kaliṅga the beginning of the Gaṅga era is indicated. The chapter on commerce and colonisation reveals for the first time the widespread activities of the ancient Āndhras in those two fields. Administrative details gathered from the inscriptions form the subject-matter of the last chapter.

Finally, a few words on Dr. Dubreuil's learned Foreword.

(1) The Doctor is of opinion that the Ikshvākus replaced the Śātavāhanas *in the Telugu country*. While the *trend* of my opinion also is, more or less, the same as indicated in pages 6, 15, 38, 70, 78, 83, and 86 of my book, it may be noted that traces of the dynasty have been found only in Nāgārjunikoṇḍa, Jaggayyapēṭa and Amarāvatī.

(2) 'The Pallavas took the place of the Ikshvākus towards 275 A.D.' in the Amarāvatī region. I inclined towards a date later than the accepted 225 A.D. for the beginning of Pallava rule in my thesis on *The origin of Śaivism and its history in the Tamil land* (pp. 49–51). But, the absence of Ikshvāku remains in the Ceded Districts and Nellore emboldened me to fill with the Pallavas the void created by the disappearance of the Śātavāhanas from that region in 225 A.D.

(3) The Pallavas were displaced by the Ānanda Gotra in the country of Amarāvatī in the Fifth Century (about 400–450 A.D.). On pages 109 and 110 of my book may be read two footnotes assigning this new dynasty to the Fifth Century, more or less. But, I revised my opinion for two reasons: the Māngadur grant in Vengorashtra (about 450 A.D.) and the equation of Kandara's grandson and *Vegavatisanātha* which I took to mean Lord of Kanchi.

(4) The Vishṇukuṇḍins replaced the family of Ānanda in the Amarāvatī region in about 450–500 A.D. On pages 109 and 113 of my book I refer to the inscription at Velpūru, and on pages 38 and 112 of my book I raise a doubt if Amarāpura was the same as Amarāvatī. But, from these two pieces of evidence can we conclude that the Pallavas had no sway over the *present Guntur District* between 400 and 500 A.D.? It is more than what we can say at present.

In the chronological and genealogical tables at the end I have followed the dates and facts given in the body of the book.

While correcting the proofs of this Preface I noticed the publication of *Epigraphia Indica*, vol. xx, pt. i (January 1929) and *Annual Report of the Archæological Survey of India* (1927-8) which contain very useful information on the Ikshvākus and Nāgārjunakoṇḍa. In the former the inscriptions of Nāgārjunakoṇḍa are edited by the talented savant Dr. Vogel. He reads the third Ikshvāku as *Ehuvula* and not *Bahubala*. He raises the issue if Nāgārjunakoṇḍa was once the capital of Dhānyakaṭaka (see p. 51 below). He inclines to the view that Nāgārjuna lived in Nāgārjunakoṇḍa for some time (see p. 58 below). The inscription of Moda the Śaka at Nāgārjunakoṇḍa confirms my view of the foreign influences on Andhra history and culture (p. 68 below). Lastly, according to Dr. Vogel, 'Bodhisri does not appear to have been related to the royal family of the Ikhākus'.

The bibliography at the end contains the names of all the books and journals that I have consulted for writing this book.

Before closing this preface I may be permitted to put in a word in grateful acknowledgment of the great encouragement given to me by Dr. Sir S. Radakrishnan the present world-renowned Vice-Chancellor.

VIZIANAGRAM K. R. SUBRAMANIAN
December 8, 1931

ERRATA

Page.	*Line.*	*Read*	*For*
4	35	*Aitareya*	*Aitreya*
6	1	Bhaṭṭiprolu[1]	Bhaṭṭiprolu
6	19	Tamil culture	Tamils
6	30	*Early Āndhra history*	*Early History of Āndhradesa.*
7	17	107–128	102–128
11	8	Chejarla	Chējrāla
11	33	Sattanapalle (Śatavāhanapalle).	Vinukonda
21	1	interest	nterest
22	20	*Kalpa*	*Tantra*
28	21	Visākhapaṭnam	Vizāgapaṭnam
35	7	at Bairavakonda near	at
37	14	Śātavāhana	Āndhra
48	13	one storeyed	one-storeyed
49	25	motifs	motifis
60	31	*Kalpa*	*Tantra*
62	24	superstitious	superstitions
67	31	Śātavāhana	Āndhra
81	25	*Vishnu*, amsa IV, ch. 2, 3, 4 (slokas 72 and 111)	*Vishnu* IV, 2, 3.
85	25	Omit the sentence ' In all probability etc.'	
86	8	pupils	nuns
98	30	Vishṇugopa and others	Vishṇugopa
100		Footnote 1. This genealogical table is part of the body of the book and is followed in the book.	
105	34	Tamil culture	Tamils
107	17	nephew	cousin
112	18	Kumāravishṇu II	Kumāravishṇu III
122	12	Śatavāhana	Āndhra
124	42	Trilingi	Girjingi
131	9	Śātavāhanas	Āndhras

ABBREVIATIONS

A. B. I. A.	...	Annual Bibliography of Indian Archæology (Leyden).
Aham. ...	...	Ahanānūru.
A. B. O. R. I.	...	Annals of the Bhandarkar Oriental Research Institute (Poona).
A. H. of the Dec.	...	Ancient History of the Deccan by Dr. Dubreuil.
A. R. A. S. I.	...	Annual Report of the Archæological Survey of India.
A. S. W. I.	...	Archæological Survey of Western India (Report).
B. N. Ry.	...	Bengal-Nagpur Railway.
Bud.	...	Buddhist.
Bom. Gaz.	...	Bombay Gazetteer.
C. P.	...	Copper-plates.
E. C.	...	Epigraphia Carnatica.
E. H. of India.	...	Early History of India by Dr. V. A. Smith.
E. I.	...	Epigraphia Indica.
Fig.	...	Figure.
I. A.	...	Indian Antiquary.
Ins.	...	Inscription.
G. O.	...	Government Order.
J. B. B. R. A. S.	...	Journal of the Bombay Branch of the Royal Asiatic Society.
J. O. R.	...	Journal of Oriental Research (Madras).
J. I. H.	...	Journal of Indian History (Madras).
J. R. A. S.	...	Journal of the Royal Asiatic Society (London).
J. A. S. B.	...	Journal of the Asiatic Society of Bengal.
J. P. T. S.	...	Journal of the Pali Text Society.
J. B. O. R. S.	...	Journal of the Bihar and Orissa Research Society.
M. A. R.	...	Madras Archæological Report (Southern Circle).
M. E. R.	...	Madras Epigraphist's Report (Southern Circle).

M. S. M. Ry.	...	Madras and Southern Mahratta Railway.
Mys. Arch. Rep.	...	Mysore Archæological Report.
Puram.	...	Puranānūru.
Q. J. M. S.	...	Quarterly Journal of the Mythic Society, Bangalore.
Q. J. A. H. R. S.	...	Quarterly Journal of the Āndhra Historical Research Society (Rajahmundry).
S. I. I.	...	South Indian Inscriptions.
S. I. B.	...	South Indian Buddhist (Antiquities).
Yr.	...	Year.

CONTENTS

PART II

MAPS AND ILLUSTRATIONS

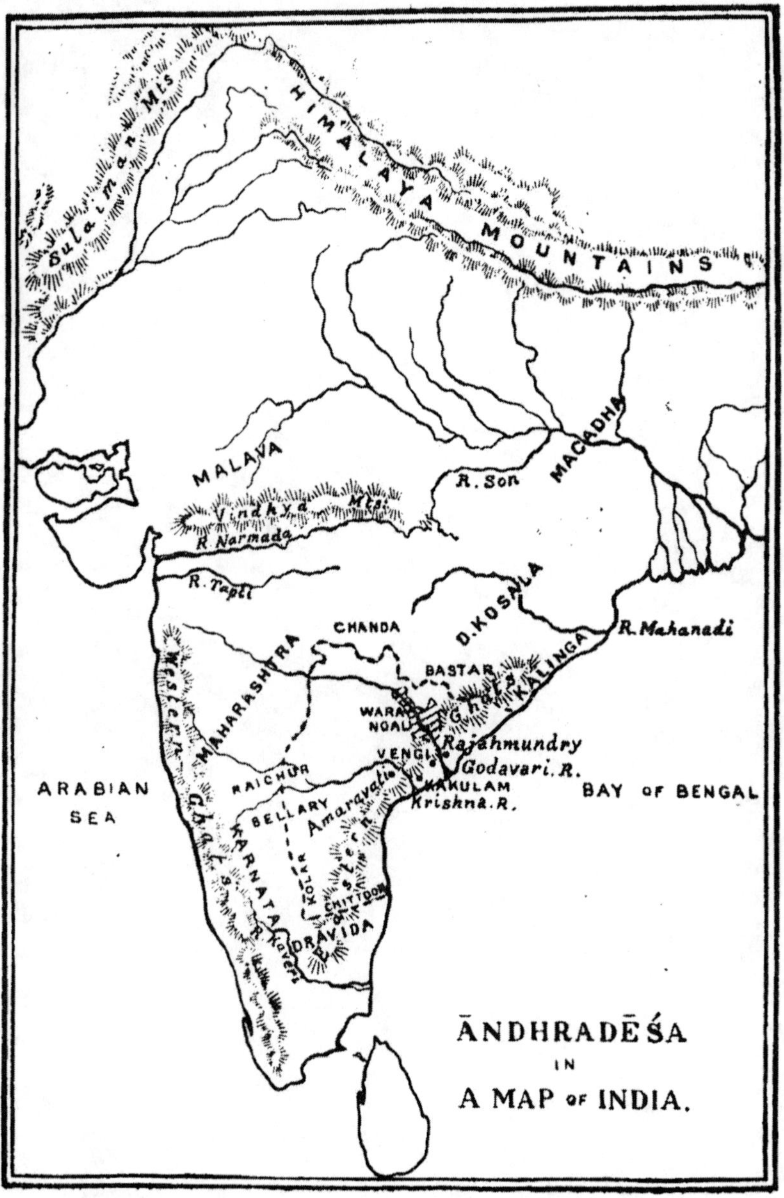

ĀNDHRADĒŚA IN A MAP OF INDIA.

PART I

BUDDHIST REMAINS IN ĀNDHRA

CHAPTER I

INTRODUCTORY

As early as 1912–3, Mr. Longhurst wrote that 'the Buddhist sites in the northern districts of the Presidency (of Madras) are of far more real archæological value than many of the great Hindu monuments of the South'.[1] A close study of the numerous ancient monuments of Āndhra reveals not only the antiquity of her civilization but also its exact nature, degree and affinities.

Āndhra Buddhism pre-Aśōkan

Much credence may not be given to the story that the Buddha himself visited Āndhra.[2] But, it cannot be doubted that Āndhra Buddhism was pre-Aśōkan. The Āndhras were already the followers of the Law in the time of the Emperor.[3] Neither he nor Dēvanāmpiya Tissa of Ceylon is said to have despatched a mission to Āndhra. Early Buddhist stories speak of the relic Stūpas of Majerika[4] which may be identified with the lower valley of the Krishna.[5] Early Buddhist literature[6] refers to the schools of *Andhaka* monks which were special to Āndhra and is confirmed on the point by the early inscriptions found in the

[1] *M. A. R.*, p. 4.

[2] Watters, *On Yuan Chwang II*, p. 209. The preaching Buddha is a very familiar figure in Āndhra art.

[3] *C. I. I.*, vol. i. The inscriptions of Asoka edited by Dr. Hultsch, Rockedict xiii. For Buddhist missions see V. A. Smith : *Asōka*, p. 166 and Geiger : *Mahāwamśa*.

[4] *J. A. S. B.*, vi, p. 856 ; xvii, Part II ; *J. R. A. S.* 1907, pp. 341–6 ; Cunningham, *Ancient Geography of India*, pp. 611-2. For the story of the tooth-relic, Turnour : *Mahāwamsa*, p. 241; *Daladavamsa* (in Pali) of a later date ; also *I. A.*, vol. xvi, p. 4, *J.R.A.S.* 1906, p. 665.

[5] Majer and Pātha Majer are two ancient places in Divi taluk, Krishna district. The country round seems to have been called Manjeradēsa. The Manjera is a tributary of the Godāvari but apparently Nāga Majerika of the Buddhist stories did not extend so far.

[6] *Points of controversy* or *Kathāvathu* (Oxford University Press) which is a part of *Abhidharma Pitaka*. *J.P.T.S.* 1889—*Kathāvathu atthakatha* ; 1888, pp. 57, 77, 96 ; 1904-5, p. 67. *J.R.A.S.* 1891, p. 409 ; 1892, p. 14 ; 1910, p. 413.

country.[1] However, the date of the beginning of Buddhism in Āndhra, the part played by the Nandas[2] and the early Mauryas[3] in the propagation of the Gospel, the causes for the phenomenal triumph of Buddhism compared with Brahminism and Jainism[4] are problems not only obscure and difficult to solve but beyond the scope of this book.

The age of Asōka

The earliest historical monuments of Āndhra are Buddhist. None of them is pre-Aśōkan. However, as Aśóka is known to have conquered only Kaliṅga, Āndhra must have been brought under Mauryan rule by Chandragupta or his son Bindusāra.[5] The connection of Aśōka with Āndhra is commemorated by his rock-edicts near Gooty.[6] Hiuen-tsang writes of Aśōkan stūpas south of the capitals of Kaliṅga and Kōsala and near the capitals of Āndhra and *Chuliye.*[7] Some of the stūpas of Āndhra must be counted among the thousands erected by Aśōka all over India.

[1] The *Chailyakas* are referred to in an Amarāvati inscription *E.I.X.* Ap. No. 1248 and 1250 ; the *Pūrvaśailas* in a Nāgārjunakonda inscription *M.E.R.* 1927, Ap. Nos. 214 and 219 of 1927 and in an inscription at Allūru, *M.E.R.* 1924, p. 97 ; and the *Avaraśailas* in a Nāgārjunakonda inscription *M.E.R.* 1927, Ap. Nos. 214 and 219 of 1927 ; and in a Peddavēgi inscription *M.E.R.* 1927, Ap. 219 of 1927 the *Avaraśailas* of Kamtakasēll (Ghaṇṭaśāla) are referred to. See *J.P.T.S.*, 1888, for two more peculiarly Āndhra schools—the *Rājagiriyas* and the *Siddhāthikas.*

[2] There are reminiscences of Nanda rule (the Nandas were not followers of Brahminism) as far south as Mysore in later inscriptions *E.C.* Bandanikke and Kupatur inscriptions.

[3] A Chandragupta is associated with Śri Śailam in the *Sthalapurāna* (*M.A.R.*, 1917-18, p. 20) and with Śravana Belgola in Mysore (*E.C., II*). Chandraguptapaṭnam near Śri Śailam was an ancient city. Bindusāra was a great conqueror according to Tāranātha (*I.A.* vol. iv, p. 363). There are allusions to Mōriyar invasions in *Puram*, p. 282 and in *Aham*, pp. 251, 281.

[4] Perhaps the cause is to be sought in the less austere, less exclusive and simpler nature of Buddhism which, in practice, absorbed much of the *Dasyu* cult. The references to the Āndhras in the *Aitrēya Brāhmana*, in the *Laws of Baudhāyana*, in the Mahābhārata (*vide* Aranya, Bhishma and Drōna parvas) and in the *Code of Manu* indicate that the Āndhras were not Āryan in religion.

[5] Perhaps Aśōka only subdued a mighty rebellion with great force.

[6] Aśōka is said to have gone on a special mission to the south according to the new edicts.

[7] Watters : vol. ii, pp. 198, 200, 209, 224. The pilgrim's capital of *Chuliye* was perhaps near Gooty (Gutti, after Gupta).

In the most ancient of the Amarāvati marbles may be seen the same spaciousness and vigour as characterize the sculptures of Bhilsa and Sānchi. In the most ancient of Āndhra inscriptions at Bhaṭṭiprōlu may be seen a southern variety of the Aśōkan Brāhmi alphabet,[1] the parent of the later Telugu script. Thus, in the reign of the illustrious Emperor, Āndhra culture came within the first close grips of northern sway, though, politically, the Āndhras 'doubtless enjoyed a considerable degree of autonomy under their own Rāja '.[2]

The Śātavāhanas, the earliest known Āndhra dynasty

After the death of Aśōka, (232 B.C.) the Āndhras assumed independence and their kings the Śātavāhanas began a career of expansion which was crowned by succession to the imperial throne of Magadha. The Purāṇas, speaking of the dynasties of Magadha, assign thirty Āndhrabhrityas or Āndhras for about 450 years after the fall of the Kanwas[3]. Since it has been found that the names of the kings of the Śātavāhana dynasty so far discovered in inscriptions are identical with some of the names supplied by the Purāṇas, it has been rightly inferred that the Śātavāhanas of the inscriptions and the Āndhras of the Purāṇic lists were the same. It is not possible on chronological or other grounds to assign for the Āndhra kings a period of four centuries and a half in the history of Magadha.[4] And the Śātavāhanas were essentially a dynasty of the Deccan according to tradition and other sources. If the Śātavāhanas were in origin a dynasty of the Āndhra or Telugu country or if the Paurāṇika based his statement about the Āndhra affinity of the Śatavāhanas on the fact that he found and knew them only as rulers of Āndhra, is a problem not easy to solve.[5] However, it may be noted that Āndhra was a well-organized and powerful state according to Megasthenes (end of the fourth century B.C.) and that the earliest kings of Āndhra according to unassailable inscriptional testimony were the Śātavāhanas, if we leave out of account the unidentified Kubēraka of

[1] *E.I.* vol. ii, p. 323. Buhler, *Indian Brahmi alphabet*, p. 24.

[2] V. A. Smith, *Early History of India* (*1924*), p. 218.

[3] Pargiter, *Dynasties of the Kali Age*, p. 72.

[4] R. G. Bhandarkar, *Ancient History of the Deccan*.

[5] *A.B.O.R.I.*, Poona, vol. i, p. 21, for the view of Dr. Sukthankar that the Śātavāhanas were not Āndhras.

Bhaṭṭiprōlu, perhaps a feudatory prince (third century B.C.). The Mackenzie manuscripts tell us of a Mukkanti Kāduveṭṭi or Trilōchana Pallava[2] (in one of them affiliated to Śālivāhana)[3] as the earliest king of the Telugu country. Some Buddhist stories have a nāga king Kāla (curiously enough resembling Kālabhartr Pallava) in Majerika, *i.e.*, somewhere at the mouth of the Krishna.[4] Purāṇic tradition speaks of the Ikshvākus as having ruled over large parts of the Deccan. There are also other traditions of Āndhra Vishṇu and his father Suchandra as the earliest rulers and the latter is mentioned as such in a late Buddhist work.[5] These conflicting evidences, however, do not prevent us for the present from affirming that the Śātavāhanas were of the Āndhra lineage and their hegemony extended from the earliest historical times over Āndhradēsa whence they expanded later into Mahārāshṭra[6] and Karnāṭa,[7] into Vidisa[8] and Magadha[9] and even as

[1] *E. I.*, vol. ii, p. 323.

[2] For full references to this semi-mythical figure, see my note 'Was Karikāla a contemporary of Trilōchana Pallava?' in *The history of the Tamils* by P. T. Srinivasa Iyengar, pp. 383–388 (Madras, 1929). Also, *Trilōchana Pallava and Karikāla Chōḷa* by Dr. Venkataramanayya (Madras, 1929).

[3] Wilson, *Catalogue*, vol. i, p. cxxiv; Taylor, *Catalogue*, vol. iii, p. 216. Rice, *Mysore ins.*, p. liii.

[4] Kālabhartr is found in the Vāyalūr inscription and in the Vélūrpālaiyam copper plates. For references to the grants see ch. ix. The Buddhist stories referred to raise the issue if the Āndhras or Telugus were nāgas which name occurs largely in inscriptions and in literature. For further light on the subject, see my thesis on *The origin of Saivism*, etc. (Supplement to the Journal of the Madras University, part ii, 1929) pp. 12–13 and my article on *Early history of Āndhradēsa* in the *Hindu* (*Illustrated Weekly*), May 18, 1930, p. 4.

[5] *Ārya Manjusri Mūla Kalpa*, vol. iii, p. 621, st. 1 (Triv. Skt. Series). For the tradition, see Campbell, *Telugu Grammar*, Int. p. ii, who quotes *Andhra Kaumadi*.

[6] Inscriptions of the founder of Śātavāhana independence, Śimuka, of his brother Kṛishṇa and of a successor of his, Śātakarṇi an *Asvamēdhin* and contemporary of Khāravela are found there. *A. S. W. I. R.* vol. v, pp. 59, 66.

[7] Śātavāhana coins and inscriptions containing the name Śātakarṇi have been found in Mysore and Kanara. *E.C.* vii, Part I.

[8] *E. I.* vol. ii, p. 87.

[9] Andhakavinda near Rājagriha and Andhavana near Sravaṣti occur in early Buddhist books. *Mahāvagga* (Trubner)

far as the South Peṇṇār in Dravida.[1] The very fact that the Śātāvāhanas were in the Northern Circars towards the end of their rule may indicate that they had discreetly retired home in the years of their decline. At any rate, no conclusive arguments have been put forward to upset the accepted theory.

Āndhra imperial power

Who among the Āndhra kings was responsible for the Kaṇwa tragedy? Did the Āndhra Śātavāhanas rule for some time from Pātaliputra? Or did the political centre of gravity shift to Paithan, leaving Northern India to its fate at the hands of the Śakas and the Kushānas? These questions cannot be satisfactorily answered. The association of the Sātakarṇis with the Ganges region in the Tamil *Silappadhikāram*[2] indicates that the Āndhra dynasty had a brief spell of supremacy over imperial Magaḍha.

A large part of the Deccan was under the Śātavāhanas from the time of their independence from Mauryan yoke till the reign of Gautamiputra Śātakarṇi, No. 23 in the Purāṇic list (102–128 A.D.).[3] He was the hero of the war of independence against the aggressive foreign hordes of Śakas, Pahlavas and Yavanas,[4] the restorer of the castes and of *Dharma* (which were jeopardized by the invaders) and the lord of the whole of Dakshiṇāpatha.[5] With the advent of Gautamiputra's son into power, there was a set-back to Śātavāhana dominion in the west[6] and the dynasty retreated slowly towards and established itself in the south and east where the inscriptions of Puḷumāyi Vāsishṭiputra,[7] Yajña Śri,[8] Śiva Śri,[9] Chandra Śri,[10] Vijaya[11] and Puḷumāyi IV[12] have

[1] Śātavāhana coins have been discovered as far as the South Peṇṇār. Rapson: Indian coins, p. 22.

[2] pp. 540–1 (Mah. V. S. Iyer's edition).

[3] This is the date given to him by V. A. Smith, pp. 221-2.

[4] The Śakas had already carved for themselves a principality round Nāsik and Nahapāna was one of the Śaka kings of Nāsik—*A. S. W. I. R.* vol. iv, p. 102. The Śaka inroads into the Deccan might have been caused by Kushānā expansion into North India even as far as Pātaliputra as evidenced by Chinese histories: *I. A.* vol. ix, p. 16; vol. xxxii. pp. 345 and 383.

[5] *E. I.* vol. viii, pp. 61, 67.

[6] The new foe of the Śātavāhanas was the Śaka dynasty of Mālwa founded by Chasṭana (78 A.D.).

[7] *E. I.* vol. x, Ap. No. 1248.

[8] *E. I.* vol. i, p. 95.

[9] *E. I.* vol. x, Ap. No. 1279.

[10] *E. I.* vol. xviii, p. 316.

[11] *M. A. R.* 1910-1, p. 14,

[12] *E. I.* vol. xiv, p. 153.

been found. The author of the *Matsya Purāṇa* depicts the closing scene of Āndhra rule as full of anarchy and sin brought about by *mlēchchas* and Yavanas. The last of the Śātavāhanas may be said to have ruled in the first quarter of the third century A.D.

The period of Śātavāhana rule in the Deccan (about 225 B.C.–225 A.D.) witnessed the growth of commercial and colonial intercourse and the development of Buddhism and Buddhist art. Nowhere can be seen to-day such a large number of ancient Buddhist foundations as in Āndhra. They are the relics of a culture which has gone to make up Āndhra civilization. All the earlier culture of the Deccan came to a definite shape under Buddhist stimulus out of which emerged the new Brahminical culture of the post-Śātavāhana period. The third century A.D. was thus the culmination of one epoch and the beginning of another in political and cultural history.

Telugu ancient and same as Āndhra

The Buddhists, wherever they went, used and improved the *vernaculars* or the languages spoken by the people for purposes of preaching and writing *vyākhyānas*. In what state Telugu was in the early centuries of the Christian era we do not know. But from certain references, it may be reasonably inferred that Telugu was *spoken* in the bulk of the area in which it is used to-day.[1] Telugu language and literature are certainly much older than the earliest Telugu inscription.[2] Doubts have been

[1] For the limits of Telugu land to-day; see Grierson: *Linguistic Survey of India* (*1927*), vol. i, part i, Introd. p. 91 and vol. iv, p. 577. Roughly, the Circars between Pulicat and Chicacole, Chittoor, the Ceded Districts *minus* a large portion of Bellary District, the eastern half of the Nizam's Dominion and a small bit of the Central Provinces comprise the Telugu-speaking area. The earliest traces of Mahārāshṭri and Kannada are found in the *Sapta-sati* of Hala (first century A.D.) and in the Oxyrhynchus papyrus (*Q. J. M. S.*, *1928*). A change of language in Āndhra is reported in northern Buddhist books (Watters, ii, p. 210). Ptolemy's Trilinga in Arakan and according to some, the Talaings of Burma may be said to have been derived from Telinga or Telugu.

[2] The first Telugu Grammar is the work of the famous Nannayya Bhaṭṭa (eleventh century A.D.). So, Telugu literature is older. Yuddhamalla's inscription in Bezwāḍa is in Telugu (*M. E. R. 1910*, p. 83). Telugu inscriptions and words may be found in the period before Yuddhamalla. Archaic Telugu inscriptions are found in Nellore and Cuddappah districts assignable

raised if the country of the Telugus was known as Āndhra from the earliest times. Āndhra was the name of the Telugu country from the third century A.D. according to inscriptional and literary evidences.[1] Even before that date, the Telugu country must have been otherwise known as Āndhra, as *Vadugu* (the Tamil name for Telugu) and Āndhra had become interchangeable by that time. If we do not identify the Āndhras of Megasthenes's account and of the inscriptions of Aśōka with the ancestors of the present-day Telugus and as the inhabitants of the present Telugu belt of land in Eastern Deccan, then they would be without a local habitation. Again, Buddhist literature of an early period locates the Āndhra country south of the Tēlivāhana and assigns to it special schools of monks popular only there. Some of these *Andhaka* schools are mentioned in inscriptions at

to the seventh century. Hiuen-Tsang remarks a change of language in Āndhra. Mahēndravarman I Pallava bears some Telugu *birudas*. There are stray Telugu words and forms in earlier inscriptions, e.g., the Chikkulla and the Peddavēgi grants. See chapters X and VIII for references. *Kathāsaritsāgara* (i, 36–49 ; 51) based on the ancient *Brihatkatha* speaks of *Dēsiya* as different from *Samskrita* and *Prākrita*. Colloquial Telugu forms are said to be found in Halā's *Sapta-sati* and in Vararuchi's *Prākrita Prakāsa*. There are strong traditions of the ancientness of Telugu. For this and for the definition of *Āndhra* and *Telugu*, see my article on *Early Āndhra History* in the Hindu (illustrated) *vide ante*. Also, Rājarāja Narēndra Pattābhisheka Sanchika (Telugu), Rājahmundry, 1922, for an article by Sōmasēkhara Sarma on Ancient Telugu, pp. 50–72.

[1] See P.T. Srinivasa Iyengar's article in *I.A.* vol. xlii, p. 276, for the view that Andhra came to be the name of the Telugu land only after the third century A.D. Andhra is the other name for the Telugu country according to the Mayidavōlu C. P. (*E.I.* vi, p. 84), Vātsyāyana's *Kāmasūtra*, Varāhamihira (*I.A.* xxii. p. 173), the Mahāwamsa (Geiger ch. 41), Buddhaghosha (who wrote *Āndhrāthakatha*), an inscription of the Anandagotra (*S.I.I.* v, 155 of 1899 ; vi, 155A of 1899), Hiuen-tsang and Daṇḍin (*Dasakumāracharitra* vii). Kumārila Bhaṭṭa (eighth century) speaks of *Āndhra-Dravida Bhasha I.A.* xlii, p. 200. The *Andhrapatha* of the Mayidavōlu C.P. (third century A.D.) is always spoken of as *Vadugavaḷi* in Tamil and there is no reason to think that *Vadugavaḷi* was newly coined after the third century A.D. since *Vaduga* as a name for the Telugu seems to be fairly older. (For *Vadugavaḷi*, see *E.I.* vol. iii, p. 76 ; *S.I.I.* vol. III, pp. 70, 90; *M.E.R.* 1904, p. 15; 1906–7 para 45 ; *I.A.* vol. xv, p. 175 ; Rice : *Mysore and Coorg* from ins. p. 17) Gautamiputra was Lord of Dakshinā patha (which extended upto Śri Sailam according to the later work *Ārya Manjusri Mūla Kalpa*) and Lord of Śrithana mountain (Śri Śailam) according to his son's ins. at Nāsik. The Periplus speaks of Maisolia as part of a kingdom extending far inland (80 A.D.).

Amarāvati, Nāgārjunakonda and other places and as such were beyond doubt, in the Telugu country. Lastly, if the Telugu country was not known as Āndhra in ancient times, how else was it known? Portions of the Telugu country were known as Majerika or Manjēradēsa and Māsāla[1] neither of which was the name of the whole of Āndhra extending from Tirupati to the Teli and from the sea as far west as a line drawn about the middle of the Nizam's dominion.[2] The recent discovery of the rock edicts of Āśoka near Gooty is one more proof that Āndhra or Telugu land was a well marked division of the Empire where he did not forget to immortalize himself. From these arguments, therefore, it follows that 'Āndhra' and 'Telugu' denoted the same territorial unit from the earliest times though there does not seem to be any etymological connection between the two words. The patronage of Prākrit literature by the Śātavāhanas was due to the religious and cultural influences of the age and the undeveloped state of Telugu from a literary standpoint.

Buddhism gave a great impetus to the advancement of Āndhra civilization in the earliest period of Āndhrā history and thus left rich legacies to the succeeding ages. To collect and study those legacies and to appraise their true value will be the task of the succeeding chapters of this part.

[1] Matsya, Ch. 22. Mahāvagga v. 13, 12. Masalia is found in the Greek accounts.

[2] For the change of language into *Vadugu* (lit. northern) beyond Vēngadam (Tirupati) see *Tamil varalāru* (in Tamil) by K. S. Srinivasa Pillai of Tanjore Pt. I (1922) p. 1 where he quotes Panampāranār, a contemporary of Tolkāppiyar. See also Aham 213 and 295. For the Tēli as a limit of Audhra, see the Jatakas trans. by Cowell, vol. i, p. 12.

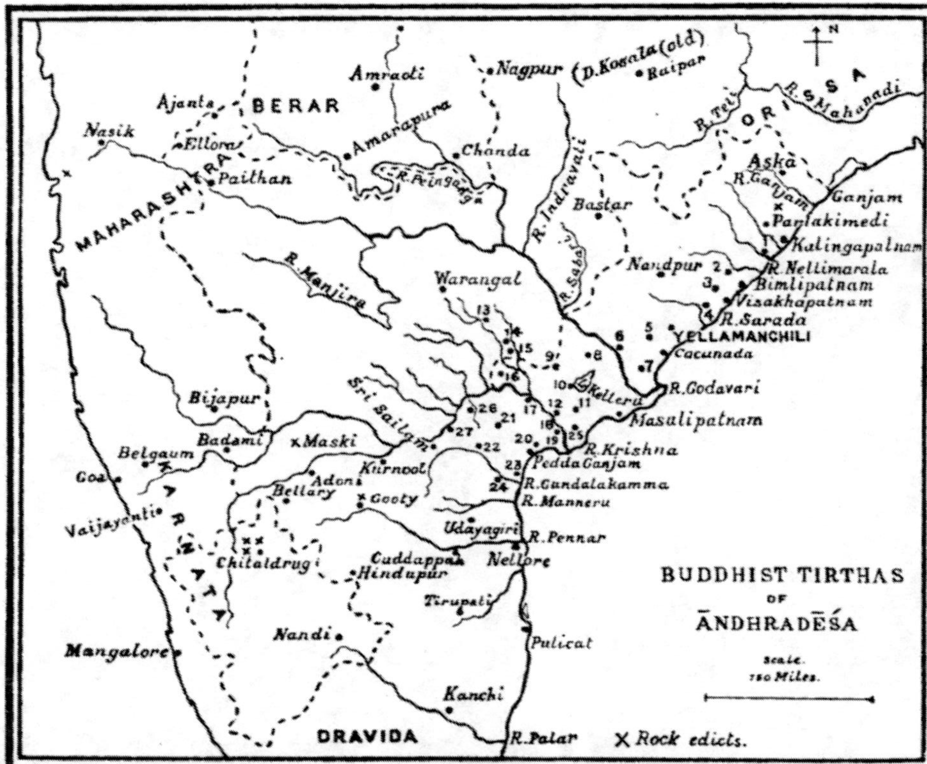

1. Chicacole.
2. Vizianagram.
3. Simhachalam.
4. Anakapalle.
5. Pithapuram.
6. Rajahmundry.
7. Ramachandrapur.
8. Tadipallegudem.
9. Guntapalle.
10. Ellore.
11. Gudivada.
12. Bezwada.
13. Kammamet.
14. Madira.
15. Yerrupalem.
16. Jaggayyapeta.
17. Amaravati.
18. Tenali.
19. Bhattiprolu.
20. Bapatla.
21. Narasaraopet.
22. Vinukonda.
23. Kanuparti.
24. Ongole.
25. Ghantasala.
26. Goli.
27. Nagarjunikonda.

CHAPTER II

THE MONUMENTS OF ĀNDHRA

Distribution

THROUGHOUT the Āndhra country, there are remains of Buddhist monuments. From Śālihundam in the north to Chinna Gañjām in the south and from Gooty in the west to Bhaṭṭiprōlu in the east, the soil of Āndhra was trodden by selfless monks and nuns from centuries before Christ. Rāmatīrtham, Sanghārāma, Kodavali, Arugolanu, Guntapalle, Jaggayyapēta, Rāmireḍḍipalle, Allūru, Bezwāda, Guḍivāḍa, Ghaṇṭaśālā, Nāgārjunakoṇda, Chējrāla, Garikapadu, Goli, Amarāvati, Peddamaddur, Pedda Gañjām and Kanuparti have yielded precious relics of a glorious civilization that flourished in Āndhra in the earliest period of her history.[1] The largest number of stūpas, chaityas

[1] Śālihundam, 6 miles W. of Kalingapatnam, Gañjām District.
Chinna Gañjām, M. S. M. Railway, Guntūr District.
Gooty, Anantapūr District, 5 miles from which Aśōkan edicts were found.
Bhaṭṭiprōlu, M. S. M. Ry, Guntūr District.
Ramatīrtham, 8 miles N. E. of Vizianagram, B. N. Ry.
Sanghārāma, near Anakapalle, M. S. M. Ry.
Kodavali, 9 miles N. W. of Pithāpuram, M. S. M. Ry.
Arugolanu, Tādipalligūdem Taluk, W. Godāvari District.
Guntapalle, 6 miles W. of Kāmavarapu Kōṭa, W. Godāvari District.
Jaggayyapēta, Nandigama Taluk, Krishṇa District.
Rāmireḍḍipalle, 6 miles from Madira, N. S. G. Ry. Also called Gummididurru.
Allūru, 5 miles from Yerrupālem, N. S. G. Ry.
Bezwāda, M. S. M. Ry., Krishṇa District.
Guḍivāḍa, M. S. M. Ry., Krishṇa District.
Ghaṇṭasālā, 13 miles W. of Masulipatnam, M. S. M. Ry.
Nāgārjunakoṇda, 1 mile from Pullāreddigūḍem and 15 miles from Mācherla, M. S. M. Ry., Guntur District. The site is on the right bank of the Krishna.
Chejrāla, Narasaraopet Taluk, Guntūr District.
Garikapādu, Vinukonda Taluk, Guntūr District.
Goli, 3 miles from Rentachintala, Gurzāla Taluk, Guntūr District.
Amarāvati, 18 miles from Guntūr.

and vihāras have been brought to light in the districts of Guṇṭūr and Kṛishṇa especially along the banks of the Kṛishṇa and her tributaries. While some ancient monuments have been destroyed by brick-quarriers, there are still unexcavated mounds awaiting the magic touch of the archæologist which, on being opened in due course, may add to the historical materials.[1]

Situation

The Buddhists generally chose for their monuments and residential quarters places which were endowed by nature with plentiful water-supply and with beautiful scenery and which were removed by some distance from the villages and crowded cities. Where the river or stream did not flow by the establishment, the Buddhists constructed big tanks and reservoirs traces of which may be found to-day in Bhaṭṭiprōlu and Jaggayyapēṭa. The courses of rivers have changed in historical times and it is, therefore, not unlikely that once the Kṛishṇa flowed nearer the establishments of Nāgārjunakoṇḍa, Bhaṭṭiprōlu and Ghaṇṭaśālā and that, similarly, the Muniyēru and the Pālēru were within a few minutes' walk from the monasteries of Rāmireḍḍipalle and Jaggayyapēta respectively. On the hills of Rāmatīrtham which is about four miles from the Nellimarala, a tank 65′ broad was dug, and the waters of the perennial springs there were collected in it. More interesting than the arrangement for water-supply was the system of drainage to which the monks of Rāmatīrtham paid equal attention. Traces of a canal from the Kṛishṇa (the important means of communication between the monasteries on or near the river and her tributaries) to the quarters of the monks are visible at Nāgārjunakoṇḍa. There is inscriptional evidence for the digging of wells and tanks on the hills hard

Peddamaddur, 4 miles S. E. of Amarāvati.

Pedda Gañjām, near Chinna Gañjām, Guntūr District.

Kanuparti, 6 miles from Pedda Gañjām.

N.B.—There is a paucity of Buddhist relics in Nellore and the Ceded Districts.

[1] *M. A. R.* 1889, p. 2, 19 ; 1892, 15 July p. 2 ; 1902, p. 18 ; 1903–4, p. 46 ; 1906-7, p. 4 ; 1907–8, p.8 ; *M. E. R.* 1923, p. 4 ; 1921-2, p. 6 for places containing mounds. *M. E. R.* 1925-6, p. 3, for vestiges at Velpūru, Guṇṭūr District ; *M. A. R.* 1888, 14 July p. 2, 14 for vestiges at Mōṭūpalle and Bāpaṭla, M. S. M. Ry.; 1910-11, pp. 66, 70, 71 for vestiges at Masulipatnam, M. S. M. Ry.

by for the benefit of the clergy residing there. To one who has seen the perpetual and delightful flow of waters (now made to irrigate rose and pineapple gardens) on the hills of Simhāchalam,[1] the description by Hiuen-tsang of the arrangements for water-supply in *Po lo mo lo kili* does not appear a myth. The monks knew how to derive the maximum benefit out of the natural advantages—unceasing springs in one place, ever-cool sea breeze in another and magnificently wild scenery in a third.

'The view from the hill (of Śālihundam on the south bank of the Vamśadhāra) is a very fine one and shows that the Buddhists had excellent taste in choosing a suitable site to set-off their peculiar type of monuments. When the stūpas were complete with their dome-shaped superstructures, tees and gilded umbrella finials, they must have presented a most imposing appearance on the summit of the hill and formed a conspicuous landmark for many miles in the surrounding country.'[2] Similar is the view from Sanghārāma, Simhāchalam, Rāmātirtham and many other places. The river with its roaring cataracts, the hills and forests with their wild magnificence and the isolation from the maddening crowds of the plains gave a special value to Nāgārjunakoṇda which offers even to-day the quietest spots for 'the simple living and high thinking' and for the communion with Nature that our ascetics desired to practise.

Stūpas

Stūpas, tōpes or dāgabas were the tombs erected by the Buddhists over the remains of the Buddha or any Buddhist sage, over sacred texts engraved on metal and over sacred spots. Sometimes, stūpas were built in honour of the Buddhas and the teachers. The word chaitya originally meant the same as the word stūpa, viz., a funeral mound, but, subsequently 'chaitya' came to signify a temple in which the stūpa or dāgaba occupied a prominent place in the apse.

The cult of the chaityas or stūpas was an ancient one. Not only *Siddhas* but also distinguished Rājas received the honour of chaityas being built over their remains. The Buddha exhorted

[1] B. N. Ry. *M. A. R.* (1908-9), p. 10. There are remains of a Buddhist stūpa on the Daralakonda Hill.

[2] *M. A. R.* 1919-20, pp. 34-38, for an account of the Buddhist remains of Śālihundam.

his followers not to worship him but to give his remains the honours of a *Chakravartin* (Emperor). Accordingly, stūpas were erected over his remains and in his memory, and homage was rendered to them. The symbols of Buddhism, the tree, the wheel, the *triśūla* [1] etc. were also reverenced. At a later stage, in the second century A.D., images of the Teacher came to be placed and worshipped in the stūpas, chaityas and vihāras. Invariably, there was a congregation of monks near every big stūpa and they lived on the alms of the faithful.

The age of the stūpas

Many of the stūpas of Āndhra are ancient. The stūpa of Bhaṭṭiprōlu has been assigned to the third century B.C. from the characters of the inscriptions on the relic casket which mostly resemble the Aśōkan script.[2] The stūpa (' *mahāchaitya* ') of Amarāvati has inscriptions in the Mauryan script and sculptures of an archaic style which date the age of the structure in the same century.[3] Some Mauryan letters of the second century B.C. were found on the base slabs of the stūpa (' *mahāchaitya* ') of Jaggayyapēṭa [4] whose ancientness is, therefore, as undoubted as that of the stūpas of Bhaṭṭiprōlu and Amarāvati. Some of the remains of Guntapalle may be located in the second century B.C. from a pāli inscription of a nun who constructed the steps leading to a monument.[5] Though unassailable inscriptional testimony is lacking as regards some other stūpas, they may also be placed in point of date in the same category as those named above, from archæological evidences. The sparse use of stone and absence of sculpture, the use of the dāgaba instead of the image in the apse of a chaitya and its nearness to the Tēli (compared with the Buddhist centres of the Krishṇa valley) beyond which the *Andhaka* monks lived according to the

[1] Perhaps an ancient symbol now made to represent the Buddha, the Dharma and the Sangha.

[2] For the stūpa and inscriptions of *Bhaṭṭiprōlu*, see Rea, *South Indian Buddhist antiquities* ; *M.A.R.* 1892, July 15, p. 2 ; *E. I.* vol. ii, p. 323. The earlier archæological reports were issued as G.O.S.

[3] *E. I.* vol. xv, p. 258 for the ins. of *Amarāvati.*

[4] Burgess : *Amarāvati* and *Jaggayyapēta*, p. 108.

[5] For the inscription and for the monuments of *Guntapalle*, see *M. A. R.* 1888, Ap. 30, pp. 11-12 ; 1889, Aug. 2, pp. 1-3 ; 1916-17, pp. 30-36. *A. R. A. S. I.* 1905-6, p. 166.

early Buddhist books—give Rāmatīrtham an early enough date as a Buddhist *tīrtha*.[1] The last argument of nearness to the Tēli holds good equally in the case of Saṅghārāma. Besides, the crude and primitive sculptures, the Aśōkan type of the monoliths and the absence of the usual rail and the chaitya window lead us to agree with Mr. Rea that the foundation of Saṅghārāma is shrouded in hoary antiquity.[2] From the nature of the structure and the remains, the stūpas of Guṇṭapalle, Guḍivāḍa [3] and Ghaṇṭaśālā [4] may be said to be as old. About the rest of the stūpas, no reliable evidence is available to trace their origin to the centuries before Christ.

Amarāvati has plenty of inscriptions in the Brahmi script of the second century A.D. and a few in the ornate Ikshvāku script of the next century. A few marbles which have survived the ruin of the Buddhist memorials of Chinna Gañjām [5] and Pedda Gañjām [6] bear inscriptions which locate their age in about the third century A.D. While Nāgārjunakoṇḍa [7] like Jaggayyapēta [8] has revealed Ikshvāku epigraphs 'in fine literary pāli', Gōli on the babbling brook the Gollēru bears the stamp of its age in a few Brahmi letters similar to those of the second period of Amarāvati.[9] Ghaṇṭaśālā has recently yielded a clue as to its antiquity in the marble slabs dug out of the *Koṭṭaidibba* which contain mutilated inscriptions assignable to the second century A.D.[10] Similar paleographic testimony is supplied by the

[1] For a second century inscription on a seal and for the Buddhist remains of *Rāmatīrtham*, see *M.A.R.* 1908-9, p. 10; 1909-10, p. 20; 1910-11, p. 13; *A.R.A.S.I.* 1910-11, pp. 78-87 for illustrations, etc.

[2] For the seals and coins and a pāli inscription at *Saṅghārāma* and its Buddhist remains, see *M.A.R.* 1908-9, pp. 1-10; 1910-11, p. 17. See *A.R.A.S.I.* 1907-8, p. 149 for illustrations.

[3] Rea, *S.I.B.* antiquities; *M.A.R.* 1892, July 15, p. 1 for *Guḍivāḍa*.

[4] Rea, *ante*; *M.A.R.* 1892, July 15, p. 2; 1919-20, p. 30 for *Ghaṇṭaśalā*.

[5] See *M.A.R.* 1888, July 14, pp. 8-10 for *Chinna Gañjām*.

[6] See *M.A.R.* 1888, July 14, pp. 2-11; 1889, Ap. 30, pp. 2-12 for *Pedda Gañjām*.

[7] *M.E.R.* 1926 and 1927, Ap. for *Nāgārjunakoṇḍa*.

[8] *E.I.*, vol. x, Ap. No. 1202 and 1203, for *Jaggayyapēṭa* inscriptions of the third century A.D.

[9] *The marbles of Gōli* (Bulletin of the Madras Museum) by T. N. Ramachandran.

[10] Some of the fragments of the marbles of *Ghaṇṭaśālā*, the author saw in the village and some more in the bungalow of the Zamindar of Sallapalli at Masūlipaṭnam.

antiquities of Rāmireḍḍipalli,[1] Allūru[2] and Saṅghārāma and by the Chaitya at Chējrāla.[3] The inscription of Śrī Chandra Śātavāhana at Kodavali fixes the date of the remains in or before the second century A.D.[4] Numismatic evidence is also forthcoming from some of the Buddhist sites, which helps us in a way in estimating the age of their relics. Thus, Śātavāhana coins were obtained in varying quantities from Amarāvati,[5] Ghaṇṭasālā,[6] Guḍivāda,[7] Rāmireḍḍipalle,[8] Saṅghārāma[9] and Rāmatīrtham.[10] In Guḍivāḍa as well in Bezwaḍa, Mr. Rea picked up a Roman coin.[11] One of the six clay seals of Rāmatīrtham bears the figure of a chaitya and the inscription '*Śailasaṅgha* of *Śrī Śiva Vijaya Rāja*' (Śātavāhana).

As late as the sixth century A.D. and even later, the Buddhist stūpas continued to exercise their influence over the Āndhras who visited the holy spots and showed their reverence to them in the shape of benefactions and votive offerings. A certain Siṁhavarman Pallava presented an image of the Buddha to the stūpa of Amarāvati (about the sixth century A.D.?)[12] In Jaggayyapēṭa[13] and, likewise, in Rāmireḍḍipalle[14] there is a marble slab with the image of the Buddha and an inscription below it in fifth century characters. In both the places are found a few inscriptions in later Chāḷukyan script also. The stone inscriptions of the Ānanda gōtra, a dynasty of about the sixth century A.D., are seen in the Chaitya of Chējrāla.[15] Coins and seals ranging from the fourth century to the ninth century A.D. carry the history of Saṅghārāma down to a very late period.[16] Śālihundam bears to-day the remains of a late age,

[1] For *Rāmireḍḍipalli*, see *M.E.R.* 1924, p. 3; 1927, Ap.

[2] For *Allūru*, see *M.E.R.* 1924, pp. 3, 97; 1906–7, p. 3.

[3] *M.A.R.* 1889, Ap. 30, pp. 12–18 for pāli inscriptions, etc., of *Chējrāla*.

[4] From *Timavaram* in Pithapur Zamin, Sir W. Elliot excavated four relic caskets. See *I.A.* vol. xii, p. 34; *M.A.R.* 1907–8, p. 3.

[5-7] Rea, *S.I.B.* antiquities; *M.A.R.* 1892, July 15, pp. 1–2.

[8] *M.E.R.* 1924, p. 3.

[9] *M.A.R.* 1908-9, p. 6.

[10] *M.A.R.* 1910–11, p. 14.

[11] *M.A.R.* 1888, Jan. 24, p. 4.

[12] *S.I.I.*, vol. i, p. 25.

[13] Burgess, *Amarāvati* and *Jaggayyapēṭa*, p. 111.

[14] *M.E.R.* 1924, p. 3.

[15] *M.E.R.* 1900, p. 5; *S.I.I.* vol. vi, Nos. 155 and 155A of 1899.

[16] *M.A.R.* 1908–9, p. 5; *M.E.R.* 1914, p. 5.

about the seventh century A.D., though it is probable that the roots of its greatness as a religious centre might be hidden in earlier centuries.

The style of the stūpas

The stūpas of Andhra were of the same style as the stūpa of Sānchi and of varying dimensions from the small stūpa of Gōli (8′ high and 60′ across) to the big stūpas of Bhaṭṭiprōlu (132′ in diameter) and Amarāvati (138′ in diameter and 100′ in height). On a circular or square base, a dome was raised and above the dome a square block containing the box of relics, if any. The *gala* was surmounted by a capital over which one or more umbrellas were placed. All round the stūpa there was a railing, leaving some space for circumambulation and marking off the sacred spot. Except at Amarāvati there was no noteworthy railing elsewhere in Āndhra. But in most of the stūpas of Southern Āndhra there were sculptured marbles all round the base. At the four cardinal points of the circular railing were gateways.

Most of the stūpas of Āndhra were solid masonry work. There are rock-cut stūpas at Sanghārāma and a stone-built stūpa at Guntapalle. In fact, Sanghārāma has groups of stūpas, each pinnacle being shaped into a stūpa.

The base of the stūpa of Ghaṇṭasāla was on radiating and concentric brickwalls. Similarly, the '*mahāchaitya*' of Nāgārjunakoṇḍa, a stūpa at *Frangnladinne* near Pedda Gañjām, and another at Śālihundam have a base or platform of the shape of the *chakra.* At Pedda Gañjām, another Buddhist symbol, the *swastika* was adopted in the place of the *chakra*.

To erect and balance a huge dome of brickwork as that at Bhaṭṭiprōlu or Amarāvati requires no small engineering skill. To convert a hill into innumerable stūpas as at Sanghārāma is no mean architectural feat. Considerable advance had been made in bricklaying twenty-two centuries ago as the bricks of Bhaṭṭiprōlu $1\frac{1}{2} \times 2'$ still retain their strength after having been exposed to wind and weather for such a long period.

Two kinds of chaitya slabs have been excavated at Amarāvati, one presenting in miniature the stūpa of the earliest epoch and the other the stūpa of the second century A.D. The stūpas of Āndhra were first bare structures surrounded by a wooden railing or fencing, stone railing being exceptional. The earliest to have a railing of a permanent material and with some sculptures here and there on it were the stūpas of Bhaṭṭiprōlu and Amarāvati. In the former were found remains of the enclosing rail, a marble pillar and a few sculptured marbles. Round the latter there was a railing of granite perhaps with a few archaic sculptures. There has come to light another instance of stone railing at Guntapalle in a stūpa of perhaps the second century B.C. The gateways of the Āndhra stūpas were not important as those of Sānchi, either from their size or from the sculptural standpoint. The *āyaka* pillars found at the four cardinal points and close to the stūpas are a peculiar feature of the stūpas of Āndhra and unknown to Sānchi. They are square at the base and octagonal above and perhaps once supported *manṭapas* or bore the emblems of the religion.

The Sculptures of the Stūpas

The sculptures of Āndhra fall into two classes: (1) archaic, affiliated in style to those of Bhilsa and Sānchi, and (2) of the second and third centuries A.D. betraying the assimilation of the 'Graeco-Roman' style of Gandhāra at its best.

The earlier sculptures are chiefly from Amarāvati and Jaggayyapēṭa. Little of a definite nature is known of the few marbles of Bhaṭṭiprōlu. The carving of a Rāja by his horse found at Garikapāḍu[1] is a fine specimen of art of the early Amarāvati school. Jaggayyapēṭa stands by itself with its flat reliefs, spaciousness and large, elongated figures, and is more closely related to the early paintings of Ajanta. The mound containing the biggest of a group of stūpas was 31½′ in diameter, the procession path 10½′ wide and the surrounding slabs 3′ 9″ above the floor. Inside the rail of slabs the stūpa was formed of earth and brick.[2] The slabs at the base have generally no sculptures while pilasters upon them are carved in the style of Piṭālkhora and early Amarāvati. The figures are larger than and not in high relief as, those of later Amarāvati. Their head-

[1] *M.A.R.* 1889, 30 Ap., p. 2. See *M.E.R.* 1908, p. 59 for a Brahmi inscription there. There must be some hidden remains at Garikapādu.

[2] Burgess, *Amarāvati* and *Jaggayyapēta*; *A.R.A.S.I.* 1905–6, p. 116 for illustrations of *Jaggayyapēta* remains.

Burgess, Pl. liv, fig. 2; lv., figs. 2 and 3 for typical sculptures from Jaggayyapeta.

B. 333.

Details of Carved Stone Beam (No. 1 Beam) Nagarjunikonda, Guntur Dt.

dress and ear-rings have more of the Ajanta type; and the figures lack the style and rapid movement of the later Amarāvati and Nāgārjunakoṇḍa sculptures. Nor is there the same profusion of figures at Jaggayyapēṭa. One of the marbles of Jaggayyapēṭa (now in the Madras Museum) is extremely interesting as an architectural model of great potentialities. A shrine or *puṇyaśāla* is carved on it with four pillars supporting it in front. The ascent to the shrine is by steps. Inside under a seat are the Śrīpāda over which is an umbrella with two hanging garlands. In each side-division stands a female, one of them holding a vessel of flowers. The building has a storey with an arched roof and chaitya windows. Over the roof are four ornamental finials.

The archaic sculptures of Amarāvati lack the elegance and finish of later-day work but are nevertheless bold and spirited. Among them are winged lions and other animals as in the cave of Piṭālkhora and on the slabs of Bhilsa.[1] The human and other figures are flat and possess more strength than proportion, and are on a larger scale. Their garments are as deftly delineated by the sculptor as they were woven by the skilful artisan. The turban, the heavy *kuṇḍalas*, the broad necklace, the *dhōti* round the waist with folds hanging were probably not mere conventional art but were really in vogue among the people of the times.[2] Figures of men or boys with short drawers driving the bulls, deer and elephants or holding them by the tail are nicely done. The abundant carvings of a later age in high relief and with sharper features will be dealt with in the next chapter. Suffice it to say here that the sculptures of later Amarāvati include not only the carvings on the rail round the stūpa but also those on the slabs fixed all round the base of the stūpa and on the slabs encasing the stūpa itself. In the sculptures of later Amarāvati, the image of the Buddha (which was unknown to Buddhist iconography before) plays a prominent part.

The school of Amarāvati art had its sway far and wide in Āndhra. Sculptures as sweet as those of later Amarāvati have been discovered in Chinna Gañjām, Pedda Gañjām and Kanuparti, in Gōli, in Nāgārjunakoṇḍa and in Rāmireḍḍipalle. Fragments of marbles have been found in Peddamaddur, Ghaṇṭaśāla,

[1] Burgess, pl. xxix-xxx.

[2] *Ibid*, pl. li.

Arugolanu and Kondrapolu[1] which prove the existence of sculptures there in the past.

Two marbles, one with finely carved semi-circular lotus leaf patterns and the other with a nice seven-hooded nāga on one side and a dāgaba, lotuses and rows of *triśūlas* and lions on the other, are reported to have been excavated from the *Kollidibba* at Chinna Gañjām. A mile north of Pedda Gañjām is *Franguladinne* ' the mound of the Franks ' where a marble with the Buddha and a number of dwarfs beneath his seat and some sculptured lions were dug out. This mound together with the *Bogandānidibba* and the *Śākaladānidibba* reveal the extent of the Buddhist city of Pedda Gañjām. The marbles of Pedda Gañjām treat of the usual Buddhist themes and present to us the same motifs.[2] From the *Dipāladibba* of Kanuparti[3] containing many other mounds, marble piers have been removed and built into the local temples. Of the marbles, one has a coiled nāga, a moulded capital and a *triśūla*.

Some of the marbles of Gōli are still on the spot built up into a small fane which has, within, a big and beautifully sculptured seven-hooded nāga (belonging to the stūpa) in light green marble twisting itself in intricate coils. At the root of the central hood of the nāga is a platform with a small stūpa. On the stūpa the dwarfs and the *āyaka* pillars have been shown. Below the stūpa is a *kalaśa*. The stūpa in the hood looks exactly like a *linga*. The rest of the sculptures are now in the Madras Museum. Some of the *Jātakas* and incidents in the life of the Buddha are depicted in them. The Buddha has the usual halo and flowing robes and devotees salute him by falling flat on the ground or by raising the joined palms to their heads.

Nowhere have such extensive Buddhist remains been brought to light as at Nāgārjunakoṇḍa.[4] They are of more than provincial

[1] *M.A.R.* 1893, July 14, p. 2. There were also some stone sculptures. It is interesting to note that marble sculptures are rarely found beyond the present W. Godavari district.

[2] *M.A.R.* 1889, 30 Ap. pp. 9-12.

[3] *M.A.R.* 1888, July 14, pp. 11-13.

[4] *M.E.R.* 1926 and 1927 ; *A.B.I.A.*, Leyden 1926 and 1927 ; *A.R.A.S.I.* 1925-6, p. 141. Mr. Longhurst has earned an immortal name by his excavations here. There are three reliefs from this place in the Musee Guimet, Paris. Dr. Dubreuil was the first to spot out the recently excavated remains in Guntur District.

B. 370.
CARVED PILLAR No. 2, DETAIL OF ANOTHER SOLDIER FIGURE, NAGARJUNIKONDA, GUNTUR DT.

nterest when we take into account either the style of the art or the nature of the Gospel preached from the heights of Parvata or the extent of its sway overland and overseas. The stūpas of Nāgārjunakoṇda had neither the ornamental gateways of Sānchi nor the elaborately carved rail of Amarāvati. They had probably a rail of wood on short brick or stone walls. The sculptures in bold relief in light green marble, so far discovered, were found round the base of a stūpa on a hill at the eastern end of the present site of ruins. The chaitya slabs and the alternating compartments of scenes from Buddhist stories are similar to those of the so-called 'inner rail' of Amarāvati in style and finish. There was a sculptured coping all round. On the whole, some of the friezes are more beautiful, more vigorous and, obviously, more fresh than those of the latter stūpa.

Besides the usual scenes from the *Jātakas* 'the jungle book of the Indian story tellers' in panels fringed with the human pair and other familiar motifs, there are a number of scenes which cannot be identified and which portray, in all likelihood, local life, story and history. The latter are usually scenes where kings and queens were engaged in various activities. A bearded Scythian warrior in trousers and tunic with long sleeves holding a spear in hand, some nude figures, some Bacchanalian scenes with drinking horns, the dress of the Buddha and some other figures reveal the debt of the Āndhra workmen to the 'Graeco-Roman' style which must have travelled to the Kṛishṇa by land and by sea. The rest of the sculptured scenes are the usual Buddhist themes petrified. The panels usually depict the Seven Steps, Renunciation, and Preaching from the life of the Buddha. The figures of the Buddha are bald in some panels (Nāgārjuna ?), while they have curly hair and possess great beauty in others. The folds of his dress are well depicted in all the compartments. The most curious panel is that containing Hanumān carrying three figures on his back. The sculptures were popular picture books giving delight and instruction without a language, *cadjan* or teacher. There are the usual dwarf, *makara* and roll ornaments. Among animals, elephants are sculptured with great skill. Attractive and spirited figures, and scenes permeated with an air of realism are a familiar feature of the marbles. They have elegance, movement and expression. Man and nature are well delineated, and grace, motion and anatomy are all there. In the technique and finish of untranslatable charm, the classical influence is clearly traceable. The marbles were finished with a fine coating of white stucco as at Amarāvati and perhaps painted also likewise.

The big stūpa on the hill of Rāmireḍḍipalle (Gummiḍiḍurru)[1] has all round its base 34 reliefs in the same grey marble of Amarāvati and Jaggayyapēṭa sculptures. The sculptures are excellent and well preserved and are of the Amarāvati school. Some of the chaitya slabs have a seated Buddha in the centre, while, in others his symbols take his place. The Buddha has curly hair, a halo and full robes and is sometimes in the preaching pose. In one panel, the central figure has a turban and bangles like the kings of a later date. The lotus and vase ornaments are used in profusion.

The Relic-caskets

From most of the stūpas of Āndhra, relic-caskets have been obtained though we cannot be sure if the relics were of the Buddha or of some lesser teacher. From the inscriptions on the relic-casket of Bhaṭṭiprōlu and on the *āyaka* pillars of the '*mahāchaitya*' at Nāgārjunakoṇḍa, it is learnt that both the memorials enshrined the relics of the Buddha. *Ārya Manjusri Mūla Tantra*,[2] a late Buddhist work, notes that the stūpa of Amarāvati was erected over a relic of the Enlightened One. The great care that was taken to preserve the sacred relics is seen in the number of caskets one put in the other, beginning with a big stone box and ending with a small, beautifully manufactured casket or phial of some precious metal which actually encased the object of veneration. Beryl and crystal caskets from Bhaṭṭiprōlu, and silver and gold caskets of beautiful workmanship from Nāgārjunakoṇḍa are an index to the high level of excellence the art of the goldsmith had reached. If further proof were needed, there is a gold necklace of a nice pattern found inside the stūpa of Rāmireḍḍipalle.

'What you prize most, you offer to God' is well illustrated by the memorial offerings found together with the smallest of the caskets actually covering the relic. Pearls, precious stones, gold flowers, jewels, beads, *trisūlas* and twenty-four small coins

[1] Besides the references given before, *see* the *Times of India* (Illustrated Weekly), Bombay, March 25, 1928, p. 15.

[2] Vol. I, p. 88.

B. 384.

Great Stupa (showing Buddha Relics after Cleaning), Nagarjunikonda, Guntur Dt.

(with the *triśūla* and the sacred *pada* encircled by a *nāga* engraved on them) were found in Bhaṭṭiprōlu. The most curious object found there was a book formed of a long strip of thin metal folded together with Aśōkan characters pricked on it evidently with a metal point. Here is a miniature of the *cadjans* which contained the Law and were carried by the clergy to refresh, if need be, their retentive memories. Near the southern gate of the Amarāvati stūpa, Mr. Rea discovered a big *chunam* ball which contained a pot, inside which was a casket of pure gold in the form of a dāgaba (3¾" high and 1½" in diameter) with an umbrella on the top.[1] The dāgaba contained six small gold flowers and a piece of bone. The ivory articles and the seal in *lapis lazuli* (with the lion and a Pali inscription inside it), taken together with the above evidences speak volumes of the state of the art of the jeweller and engraver in those palmy days. While the inscriptions cut on stone in Bhaṭṭiprōlu are flawless, the inscription on such a hard substance as crystal reveals marvellous skill.

The images of the Buddha

Images of the Buddha of stone, limestone, marble and bronze have been discovered in plenty in the districts of Guntūr and Krishṇa and in small numbers in the other districts. When Hinayāna had given place to Mahāyāna, images of the Buddha were set up at the cardinal points of the stūpa, in small chapels adjoining it and in the chaityas where hitherto the dāgaba had occupied the sanctum of the apse. Big stone images of the Buddha were found in Śālihundam, Gunṭapalle and Allūru,[2] and limestone images in Gunṭapalle. A stone image of the Buddha with the graceful flowing robes of the Amarāvati style graced one of the chaityas at Rāmatirtham. Marble images in the round which are defaced and mutilated on account of neglect have been discovered in Amarāvati, Bezwāda,[3] Nāgārjunakoṇda and Pedda Gañjām. Mr. Rea records the discovery at Vidhyādharapuram in Bezwāda two marble statues of the Buddha and two big hands of white marble of a statue of the Buddha. At the same place, Dr. Dubreuil brought to light two heads of the

[1] *M.A.R.* 1909–10, p. 32.
[2] *M.A.R.* 1906-7, p. 3. The image is now in the museum at Bezwāda.
[3] Sewell: Lists, vol. i, p. 47; *M.A.R.* 1888, Jan. 24, pp. 2, 4.

Buddha and a trunk of a Buddha image dressed in toga.[1] The figures have Roman features and are extremely good-looking. The muscles of the face are well shown and the eyes are without pupils. The images in the round at Nāgārjunakoṇḍa are massive and they occupied the sanctums in the chaityas. Large statues of the Buddha, with curled locks and flowing robes must have stood on the *Bhogandānidibba* (in Pedda Gañjām), if we may judge from the fragments left of them, and the half-a-dozen images from the 'mound of the Franks'.[2] There were also images of brick and mortar and shaped in plaster as the one at Śālihundam. Life-size images of gold are reported by Hiuen-tsang to have existed in Parvata, one of the Āndhra *tīrthas*, but for obvious reasons, none of them has seen the light of day.

At Buddhāni,[3] Buddhist images of copper 1′ to 2′ in height on pedestals were discovered. They are of the fifth century A.D. They are perfectly and delicately modelled and their robe is smooth and tight. At Amarāvati also,[4] some images were found, the biggest of which 1′ 4¾″ high represents the Buddha as a *guru* addressing his disciples. They are said to belong to an earlier date than the images of Buddhāni. In this new species of art too, Āndhra was equally skilled. It would appear that these bronze Buddhas of Āndhra travelled across the seas to preach in Further India.

Chaityas

Every big stūpa had a chaitya and a vihāra adjoining it. The bare walls and foundations alone of some chaityas with the dagaba in the apse are seen to-day at Nāgārjunakoṇḍa. Guṇṭapalle, a veritable treasure-house of Buddhist buildings, and Saṅghārāma, presenting a picturesque multitude of Buddhist structures, have preserved for us some of the most ancient of the chaityas of Āndhra.

A circular rock-cut Buddhist temple at Guṇṭapalle is assigned by the archæologist to the second century B.C. It has a vaulted roof domed and ribbed like an umbrella in imitation of a wooden building. The façade of the shrine is of the horse-shoe type in

[1] The Pallavas (Pondicherry), p. 10.

[2] Franguladinne or 'mound of the Franks' is one mile north of Pedda Ganjam.

[3] 18 miles from Rēpalle, M. S. M. Ry., *J.R.A.S.* 1895, p. 617; *I.A.* vol. i, p. 153.

[4] *M.A.R.* 1907-8, p. 2.

B. 168.
ROCK-CUT CHAITYA, FRONT VIEW, GUNTAPALLE, KISTNA DT.

which are represented the ends of rafters and affords an illustration of the truth that the stone-mason's art was developed out of the carpenter's. The chaitya contains a monolithic model of a stūpa. In comparing the chaitya to the Lomas Rishi rock-cut shrine at Barabar and the Sudāma shrine, Mr. Longhurst writes thus: 'A section through the building shows that in outward appearance, the roof of such structural temples took the form of a hemispherical dome, apparently covered with thatch, with a horse-shoe gabled porch in front of the shrine. The latter was the usual form of entrance and roof construction of all Buddhist buildings in early times, whether temples, monasteries, palaces or dwellings, and appears to be merely a development of the primitive barrel-vaulted or wagon-headed hut, similar to those erected by the Todas of the Nilgiris, at the present day, a style which culminated in the handsome Buddhist chaityas at Ajanta, Elura and elsewhere.'

There is a two-storeyed rock-cut temple with some archaic sculptures on the eastern hill at Sanghārāma. Above the entrance to the chaitya is a small, cross-legged, contemplating Buddha, while, a life-size nude Buddha stands on one side. The chamber is 30′ × 30′ × 8′ supported by sixteen pillars 2′ square with a little sculpture on each. A monolithic stūpa 4′ high is in the centre with a procession path all round. In the upper storey is a smaller shrine with figures of the Buddha cut on side panels. Over the entrance again is a niche with a seated Buddha. Beyond it is a rectangular chamber with an inner shrine on the back-wall of which is carved a seated Buddha with a cobra hood over it. Though some of the features of this chaitya are different from those of the usual apsidal ended one, it may be held on other grounds that it belongs to the early period of Mahāyāna.

There are examples of brick chaityas at Guntapalle, Chējrāla and Śālihundam. Remains of similar chaityas with stone dāgabas at the apse are to hand from Rāmatirtham and with the image in the place of the dāgaba from Vidhyādharapuram[1] in Bezwāda. The brick chaitya at Guntapalle is assignable to the second century A.D. from the resemblance of the stone sculptures to those of Amarāvati. It is 53′ 7″ × 14′ 5″ inside and apsidal ended. The doorway is spanned by a semi-circular brick-arch.

[1] *M.A.R.* 1888, 30 Ap. and 24 Jan., pp. 2–4.

There is a niche on each side of the gate which contained an image of the Buddha made of limestone. The roof was of brick and plaster and decorated with earthenware finials.

The apsidal ended barrel-vaulted chaitya at Chējrāla[1] is a rare structure 22′ 10″ × 8′ 9″ × 22′ inside and built of large bricks with walls 4′ thick. The front is a horse-shoe shaped gable in which as well as in general plan and construction it resembles the large chaitya at Guṇṭapalle. The pāli inscriptions, the Buddhist marble columns with the lotus medallions, the style of the temple, the absence of a drainage hole in the sanctum and the adaptation of a Buddhist *Jātaka* for its *sthalapurāna* have made the archæologist conclude that originally the Kapotēsvara temple at Chējrāla was a Buddhist chaitya. The dipping of the roof and the increased width of the entrance give the building considerable acoustic properties. And the Buddhists are said to have paid considerable attention to lighting and to acoustics in the construction of their chaityas and halls.

Terra-cotta etc.

The history of *terra-cotta* figures is a fascinating theme by itself. *Terra-cotta* and stucco were extensively used for decorating the chaityas. Among the interesting remains at some of the Buddhist centres are *terra-cotta kammals* and flowers, *terra-cotta kalasas* and umbrellas, *terra-cotta* toys of animal figures and images of men and animals in plaster. Other curious vestiges of the social life of the times unearthed by the archæologist are jewels, ivory articles, a spindle, seals, iron instruments of various kinds, articles of bronze, vessels of wood and earthenware (the latter of several patterns) which were used largely for domestic purposes and polishing, hammer and grinding stones.[2]

Vihāras

Not even a single specimen of the residential quarters of the monks has come down to us though it is undoubted that there were several monasteries in Āndhra in the halcyon days of

[1] *M.A.R.* 1889, Ap. 30, pp. 12-18, 1917-18, pp. 33-36. The measurements given in the book are generally taken from Government reports. There must be hidden remains of a stupa, etc., hard by.

[2] *M.A.R.* 1910-11, p. 15 ; 1908-9, p. 5.

Buddhism.[1] The Chinese pilgrims give us a description of a many-storeyed vihāra which may be identified with the vihara that once dominated the extensive establishment of Nāgārjunakoṇda. Hiuen-tsang describes a great *saṅghārāma* (not far from Vengila) which had high halls, storeyed-towers and beautifully ornamented balconies.[2] In front of this convent were two stone stūpas, one several hundred feet high. The monks and nuns had an organization of their own and allotted duties to perform for the advancement of their religion and community. Each big monastery had a well-equipped library for the benefit of its inmates and was a fountain of learning. The monasteries have all gone to untraceable ruin on account of age and the perishable materials used in their construction. The originals of the monasteries were the large natural caves which continued to be tenanted even after the erection of splendid vihāras.[3]

It is curious indeed that no traces are found of monasteries near the best known and the most ancient of the stūpas of Bhaṭṭiprōlu and Amarāvati. But, from the inscriptions of Bhaṭṭiprōlu may be gathered that the clergy there were divided into committees and thus had a local habitation. An inscription of Simhavarman at Amarāvati makes us understand that he listened to a discourse there. And Tāranātha writes that the great monastery near Lhāsa with 7,700 monks and a university with six colleges was built after the model of a monastery at Dhānyakaṭaka, the Monte Casino of the Deccan in the early centuries.[4]

An inscription at Allūru records a gift of lands to a *nigaya* or school of the *Pūrvaśailas* which resided there at the time but no trace remains to-day of a vihāra close by. Ruins of a large vihāra are found at Arugolanu, once a Buddhist city of vast size. Similar remains of many vihāras exist to-day at Nāgārjunakoṇda where the cells of the monks can be seen. The bare pillars with hooks in them once supported *maṇṭapas* or halls of assembly. South-east of the site of the stūpa of Jaggayyapēṭa are the lower

[1] According to Hiuen-tsang there were forty monasteries in working order in Andhra and Dhānyakaṭaka.

[2] Probably this *saṅghārāma* was that of Guntapalle.

[3] *E.g.*, the caves of Aripālem near Anakapalle were inhabited by monks. *M.E.R.* 1925-6, p. 3.

[4] *I.A.* vol. iv, p. 363.

parts of pillars of a *maṇṭapa*. On the hill of Guntapalle, again, are clear remnants of an ancient and large vihāra, small rock-cut vihāras and a large pillared hall. The large rock-cut cells of the monastery still remain. 'The façade of the monastery had one main entrance in the centre flanked by two little windows and two entrances into the side wings. Both doorways and windows are decorated with little horse-shoe shaped gables of the usual early Buddhist type, with simulated wooden fanlights or screens, above the semi-circular door and window frames.' Lastly, Rāmatirtham and Sanghārāma have rows of cells with small niches in the walls for keeping lamps and in the former are rows of massive stone piers indicating the existence there of a large hall in the past.

Influences of Buddhism

All the early remains of Āndhra are Buddhist and the Buddhist remains are so plentiful that Āndhradēsa must have been intensely devoted to the religion once and for long. Most of the Buddhist foundations continued to flourish for a time after the third century A.D. The Brahminical revival in the Deccan had begun as early as the time of Fahian. But, as late as the time of Hiuen-tsang, there were 10 monasteries with 500 monks in Kaliṅga (South Gañjam and Vizāgapaṭnam districts), 20 monasteries with 3,000 monks in Āndhra [1] and 20 monasteries with 1,000 monks in Dhānyakaṭaka. In the last kingdom were also a large number of deserted monasteries. In the Ceded districts, the Buddhist monasteries were in ruins and the Brahminical and Jaina religions were popular.[2] Thus, the sway of Buddhism over the Āndhras between about 300 B.C. and 300 A.D. and its continued influence for another four hundred years meant that the warp and woof of Āndhra culture was largely Buddhist.

Āndhra architecture, sculpture and painting began and developed under Buddhist auspices. Writing,[3] literature, education (every monastery was a school) and learning had a similar origin and history. The Telugu language has had a stimulus in the course of its evolution from various other languages that

[1] Āndhra was half of Kalinga in size according to Hiuen-tsang.

[2] Watters : Vol. ii, pp. 198, 209, 214, 224.

[3] The early inscriptions of Bhaṭṭiprōlu (third century B.C.) prove the high level of culture then.

came into contact with it like Pāli, Sanskrit, Kannada, Mahārāshtri, Tamil and perhaps even Greek. Of these, the earliest to mould the language into proper form was the Buddhist Pāli. The Buddhist assemblies (*sanghas*) regulated by discipline and decorum, their notions of equality, racial, social and sexual, their stern morals, their intellectual pursuits, their clean, simple and communal life, and, above all, their spirit of missionary enterprise which made them enter into the hearts of the people and cultivate the popular tongue and which led them on as preachers of the gospel far beyond the seas transcending all racial and geographical boundaries—these form the very bone and marrow of Āndhra civilization. Lasting impressions were left by the mendicants on the princes and the people and a salutary atmosphere of *Dharma* was created. Fahian says of North Indian monasteries (which was true of the South Indian also) that chambers, beds, coverlets, food, drink and clothes were provided for the inmates without stint or reserve which is eloquent of the spirit of charity then prevalent. Unmoved by honour or reproach, revered by the people and respected by kings for their character and learning, these seekers after Truth were visited in their seclusion and self-imposed poverty and honoured with grants and offerings wherever they went. The extensive humanity of the age is contained in the phrase 'for the welfare of all living things' used to denote the purpose of a grant in Nāgārjunakoṇḍa.

Things which had stirred our ancestors' minds and imagination to their depths, words which had swayed generations, temples and Gods which had sat close to their hearts and homes for centuries, is it possible they have lost their vitality for ever because the temples are in ruins, the images mutilated and the sacred writings effaced? On the other hand, is it not likely that the broad idealism of to-day, that cosmopolitanism and freedom characterising Andhra Society and art and the peculiar make and themes of Āndhra art and literature bear the marks of their Buddhist origin? The rock of which Andhra culture was hewn, the pit out of which Āndhra culture was dug was Buddhist.

Decline of Buddhism

The causes for the disappearance of Buddhism from Āndhra need not be specially sought, for, it was a feature throughout India. Buddhism was absorbed by Brahminism on the popular as well as the intellectual side. There was little difference between Mahāyāna worship and the worship of the revived Brahminism. Both were the resultant of the movement of *Bhakti* which was a reaction against Vēdic exclusiveness, Jaina asceticism and Buddhist moralism. Asvaghosha's *Buddha Charita* sounded the note of the new movement in religion. Salvation except with the yellow robes was denied by Hinayāna. Mahāyana was more liberal and altruistic. Mahāyāna was more picturesque and popular.

The introduction of Gods and Goddesses and *Bodhisattvas* or saints similar to the Hindu deities and the development of *Vajrayāna tantrism* attended by mystic rites accelerated the decline already started by the laxity in discipline and morals and the lack of fervour in the monks and nuns. *Mādhyamika Śūnyavāda* which stressed on the non-existence and illusion of everything led to the *Yōgāchāra* which affirms the reality of inward thoughts. Mystic *tantras* arise mostly out of *Yōgāchāra* and they degenerate into *śaktic* rites. It is therefore significant that, at any rate, in Āndhra every Buddhist mound is popularly known as *Lanjadibba* and *Bhogandanidibba* (the mound of the prostitute).[1]

In this connection, mention must be made of the traces of the *śakti* cult found at Sālihundam. The life-size figure of Mārici in stone in the *ālidha* (angry) pose is fine with her upper part nude (except for ornaments) and the lower clad in thin cloth with a girdle round the loins. She has three faces and six arms and her head-dress has a halo behind. She carries the bow and arrow. At her feet are two *Dhyāni* Buddhas. She is the *śakti* of Amitābha and the Goddess of Dawn. There is another nicely carved Marici with the same features. There is a four-armed stone image of Tāra in *padmāsana* pose. She is the *śakti* of Avalōkitēsvara and still one of the most popular deities. There is another two-armed Tara with two female worshippers.

These images represent the growth of 'a mystical sex symbolism' like the *tantric sakti* worship. To each *Bodhisattva* was assigned a female counterpart and male and female deities came to usurp 'the religion of no deities.' Chicacole, Śrikākulam,[2] was

[1] Some derive the Telugu *Sāni* (dancing girl) from *Swāmini* (nun). The other phrase *Rākshasa gudilu* is rare but easily understood as a name given by the Brahminical opponents.

[2] There is another Śrikākulam at the mouth of the Krishna which was an early capital according to tradition.

perhaps the Śrikankāli of the Buddhist *śaktas.* Dhānyakaṭaka too became *Vajrayānist* and perhaps thus acquired the name Dhāranikōṭa, the place of *Dhāraṇis.* From an examination of certain sculptures, statues and paintings in Mukhalingam,[1] it may be inferred that a debased kind of Buddhist *śaktaism* of the Vajrayāna with its blood-thirsty deities and immoral worship must have prevailed there. Thus, degeneracy set in fast and reduced the number and popularity of the Buddhists. From the spacious times of the stūpa of Bhaṭṭiprōlu to the lesser days of the remains of Śālihundam, Buddhism had passed through various stages. And, though all the people were never Buddhists as Buddhism allowed no laity, the influence of the monks and nuns was potent to do good or evil. Latterly, their influence was evil rather than good.

The stūpas which were attended, reverenced and patronized by the people were exchanged for Śiva and Vishnu. But for popular and royal regard for the religion, thousands of monks and nuns could not have flourished. Besides the loss of patronage—we do not meet with Buddhist grants after the third century, A.D. generally—there must have been persecution and destruction of Buddhist buildings and libraries to some extent. Otherwise, we cannot explain the entire absence of Buddhist literature in Āndhra.[2]

The religion that started with condemnation of rituals ended by becoming as ritualistic as Brahminism. The ignorer of God began to worship many Gods and their female counterparts. The creed of pure morality came to be lodged in brothels miscalled monasteries. Any association of men and women in mystic rituals which countenance drink takes but little time to develop into a den of immorality. The canker, once it gets in eludes nipping and spreads slyly along over the whole organism. The disciples of Him who preached in the open air and taught in the groves were entombed in monasteries (which became the distinguishing feature of Buddhism) with their knowledge encased in shelves of palm-leaves. Ideas ceased to grow, scholastic learning alone won laurels and there was no longer

[1] *M.E.R.* 1919, p. 8.

[2] But there is no certain evidence of persecution except in later traditions. For some traditions, see Venkataramanayya N: *Trilochana Pallava, etc.*, p. 37. Also *Krishna District Manual*, p. 268.

the spirit of change and progress to counteract the growing decay. In a word, there were more scholars than prophets or perfected men. The old faith had degenerated and had to be rejuvenated. Nāgārjuna, like another Buddha, rose to the greatest heights of intellectual and philosophic eminence. But, the decay that had set in continued. The people bound for millenniums to their spirits and superstitions were not moved further into new spheres of life and thought, and concessions were made to their weakness and partiality for a God, a personal Being who lives and loves, the rock and refuge of the people. The Buddha became another God to them. But, Nāgārjuna was not to blame. No good thing can continue for ever, it degenerates and the cycle begins again. Pure morality is no religion for the masses when it is inadequate even for the elect. The code of discipline—abstinence and morals—though not so austere as that for the Brahmin or Jaina *Sanyāsis* was far too stringent for the bulk of the large number of monks. Hiuen-tsang notes quarrels among the monks of Dhānyakaṭaka as the cause of their ruin and the king, taking advantage of it, closed some monasteries. Similarly, growth of indiscipline must have brought down many other establishments. Higher notions of self-knowledge and self-improvement without external aid do not make a lasting appeal to the people who linger still in a labyrinth of deities and superstitions. Equality of the sexes and their free mixing in the vihāras were great ideals but were disastrous in result on account of the ultimate domination of the sex instinct.

Buddhism went the way it began. It was a reform upon Brahminism and was absorbed by it when it reformed itself and opened its wide portals of *Bhakti* to all. Its principles and doctrines lie embedded in the *Upanishads* and in the systems of Hindu philosophy. *Karma* is the Hindus' doctrine; so are *ahimsa* and *sanyāsa*. Neither Gautama nor Aśōka preached hatred of the *varṇas* or of the Brahmins. In fact, Aśōka went the other way and exhorted reverence to be shown to the Brahmins and to the social order. We are not sure if the followers of the Buddha who were not monks discarded the village deities and *vedic* ceremonies altogether; but he condemned them, purified religion, introduced abstinence and gave a conscious ideal. Only the Vēdas and sacrifices the Buddha disliked. The Buddhist path was paved with noble truths and not strewn with the bleeding remains of victims. Ethics was the foundation of the religion and its best justification. The Brahmins were hit hard by the new religion which became popular among the *non-Dwijas* who were taught in their own language the doctrines of mercy, right conduct and pure life. The Brahminical religion of sacrifices and *sanyāsa* was open only to a few and their sacred language too was only for the elect, but in the post-Buddhist age, the *Bhakti* cult was cosmopolitan and found expression in popular tongues.

Usurpation of Buddhist Centres

The Jains and the Brahmins converted the Buddhists' buildings sometimes into temples for their gods and profited by their example in raising new structures. This fact coupled with the paucity of early Brahminical and Jaina remains in Āndhra shows that in point of popularity Brahminism and Jainism were negligent factors as compared with Buddhism in the earliest epoch of Āndhra history. Jainism was very popular in Karnāṭa and Dravida but never so in Āndhra. The successive usurpation of Buddhist Rāmatirtham by the Jains and the Hindus, the existence of a famous Hindu shrine at Buddhist Simhāchalam, the conversion of Sanghārāma and Guntapalle into *Linga Kshētras*, the presence of shrines dedicated to Amarēśvara, Kapotēśvara and Śri Śailēsvara in three famous Buddhist centres and the excavation of *lingas* and *pāṇivaṭṭams* in Buddhist Peddakanchērla[1] and Jain Dhānavulapāḍu[2] respectively—these speak for themselves of the origin of the Hindu revival on the decline of Buddhism. That there were Brahminical temples in Āndhra from the third century A.D.[3] can be proved from inscriptions;

[1] Vinukonḍa taluk, Gunṭūr district, *M.A.R.* 1894, July 10, p. 1. I am told that there are stupalike things in the *Lakshmi peetam* found in many Telugu households and they are called *Budlu* (Buddhalu ?). The idol at Simhāchalam has a linga shape and no proper explanation is given for it.

[2] Jammalamaḍugu taluk, Cuddapah district, *M.A.R.* 1903-4, p. 27. As for Jaina remains in Andhradeśa see Dr. B. Seshagiri Rao's *S. I. Jainism* (Vizianagram). Also the *District Gazetteers*. A number of Jaina images are reported to exist in a number of places in Godavari District and Jaina remains in the Ceded Districts. Drākshārāma is believed by some to have been once a Buddhist *ārāma*. There are a few Jaina traces in the temple. The structure is a noteworthy one in the country which possesses only a few beautiful Hindu temples. There is the influence of the Chalukyan style. The place is in Ramachandrapuram taluk, East Godavari District.

[3] The earliest known temple is that of Vishṇu at Dālūra (third century A.D.). The name 'Śiva' and the word 'Vigraha' occur in the earliest inscriptions at Bhaṭṭiprōlu.

and the scores of *Dēva* temples noted by Hiuen-Tsang as having existed in his time could not have sprung in a day. But, of their style, little is known and the presumption is that it was not different from the style of the earliest Hindu temples extant in and round Bezwāda which was a copy of the Buddhist style exhibited in the rock-cut and structural buildings of Gunṭapalle.

Survival of Buddhist Art

There was no chasm between 'Buddhist', and later 'Hindu' Art as the workmen and their books and models were the same. Save for the differences in the themes and some motifs, and variations following the development of art and the nature of the religion, no marked changes are noticeable at the start, one naturally evolving into the other. The easy occupation of Buddhist chaityas and caves by the Hindus explains the absence of any disparity between the two styles. All the earlier art was absorbed by the Buddhists and all the later art evolved from theirs.

In and round Bezwāda may be seen to-day a large number of rock-cut cave temples at Mogulrājapuram, Sitānagaram and Unḍavalli. They are all mostly simple in plan and construction. They represent a continuation of the Buddhist art of scooping out cells adapted for the Hindu gods. While the circles of the dead developed into the stūpas on the plan of the circular hut, the square stūpas of the Āryans served as the ground plan for the cells of the typical Hindu temple. A number of small shrines exist by the side of the three-storeyed rock-cut temple of Unḍavalli, square uni-cellular sanctums which were the nuclei of later big temples. The big temple of Unḍavalli itself is of the style of a Buddhist vihāra. The difference in the ground plan between the Buddhist and later Hindu temples notwithstanding, the dark sanctum (with the idol instead of the relic) and the semi-circular dome or the *vimana* (hollow unlike the solid stūpa) in the latter betray their Buddhist origin and conception.

It is well known that the rock-cut cave temples in and round Bezwāda[1] are the earliest surviving Hindu shrines of Āndhra,

[1] For Bezwāda, see *M.A.R.* 1910-11, p. 20; 1919-20, p. 26; 1888, 30, Ap. 2.

For Mogulrājapuram, *M.A.R.* 1888, 30 Ap.; 1919-20, pp. 27-9.

For Unḍavalli, *M.A.R.* 1888, July 14, p. 3; *A.R.A.S.I.*, 1919-20.

For Sitānagaram, *M.A.R.* 1888, July 14, pp. 4-5.

nothing being known of structural Hindu edifices till a very late date. These have been rightly attributed to the Pallavas and the Vishṇukuṇḍins, the former carrying the style into the Tamil country. The *Dvārapālas* and the pillars with lotus, vase and lion ornaments remind us of the Buddhist sculptures of Amarāvati.

One stage removed from these early Hindu temples is the group of beautiful rock-cut temples at Udayagiri in Nellore District [1] belonging to the sixth and seventh centuries. More developed than the group of Udayagiri is that of Mahābalipuram both belonging to what is called the Pallava style.[2] It is a commonplace that the Seven Pagodas of Mahābalipuram represent the various styles of temple-building known at the time. A clear analysis of the styles of the Pagodas will set at rest any doubts concerning their Buddhist parentage. The Dharmarāja Ratha is a storeyed vihāra; the Draupadi Ratha is a *manṭapa* with a roof slightly different from that familiar in Amarāvati sculpture; the Nakula-Sahādēva Ratha has the exterior of a chaitya hall on a small scale; and the Bhima Ratha is like the chaitya of Chējrāla. Only the Ganēśa Ratha having a *gōpura* with a barrel-vaulted roof at the apex presents some difficulty. The *gōpura* is the dominating feature of the Dravidian temple by day and by night, as the stūpa overshadows every other building in a Buddhist *tīrtha*; but it does not stand over the sanctum in later Hindu architecture but is in the compound wall of the temple. The symmetrical arrangement of miniature *vimānas* and *gōpuras* and groups of figures on the *gōpura* is similar to a like arrangement of miniature stūpas and groups of sculptures in famous stūpas. But, as already pointed out, the plan of the later Hindu temple was square or rectangular as different from the circular or apsidal plan of the Buddhist. While the stūpa of Amarāvati was a huge semi-circular structure, the *gōpura* of a South Indian temple is a huge pyramidal structure based on the style of the storeyed vihāra. In the Ganēśa Ratha, the *gōpura* looks like a series of laboriously mounted oblong platforms in diminishing size crowned by the barrel-vaulted roof, the dome-shaped stūpa being lost sight of and only the platform on which it stood being

[1] *M.A.R.* 1920-1, p. 29.

[2] The Pallava is the only early Āndhra dynasty whose association with Āndhra can be traced continuously for not less than five centuries.

developed. The modern *gōpura* is but a development of the principle of building in the chaitya at Chējrāla with the gate on the long side and without an apse. It may also be remembered that there were vihāras of a pyramidal shape with as many as five storeys as the one noted by Fahian in Dakshīna. In details like the procession path, chaitya windows, finials, pillars with capitals before the main shrine, groups of smaller fanes, sculptural motifs, votive offerings, inscribing the gifts, festivals, etc. the later Hindu temple follows the Buddhist style. Elements of Buddhist iconography have entered into the Hindu, not to speak of the softening influences of Buddhism over the other religions.[1]

Some more remains

The ruins of some of the ancient cities have not yet been systematically explored and surveyed. There are relics of an ancient city at Chandraguptapaṭnam[2] near Śri Śailam and at Dantavaktrakōṭa in Chīcacole taluk. Dharaṇikōṭa near Amarāvati has extensive mounds. As at Dantavaktrakōṭa and Dharaṇikōṭa, ancient coins are picked up from time to time at Kaliṅgapatnam also[3] which contains mounds worthy of excavation. Above all, there are the extensive remains of Dendaluru and Pedda Vēgi and Chiṇna Vēgi[4] which belong mostly to the epochs of the Śālankāyanas and the Vishṇukuṅḍins. It is curious that nowhere (including the vast acres of relics in Vengi) have ancient civil buildings been preserved. There are traditions of palatial civil buildings and here and there vestiges of them occur as at Nāgārjunakoṇda, but they are insufficient to give us even an inkling into their size or style.

[1] Siva as a *guru*, the *linga* under the *nāga* and Vishṇu *sayana* are, to some extent, counterparts of the preaching Buddha, the Buddha under the hoods of Elapatra and the *mahāpārinirvaṇa*.

[2] *M.A.R.* 1917–18, p. 20.

[3] *J.B.O.R.S.*, 1930.

[4] *M.A.R.* 1888, 30 Ap., pp. 9, 13–14 ; 1902, p. 19. Six miles from Ellore, M. S. M. Ry. Dendalūru is about 12 miles from Ellore.

CHAPTER III

THE MARBLES OF AMARĀVATI

OF the Buddhist centres of Āndhra, Amarāvati is the most widely known. It is about 18 miles from Guntūr and about the same distance from Bezwāda. Built on the right bank of the broad and navigable Krishna (connecting by water year in and year out all the religious centres on both banks of the river) Amarāvati held a position of supreme strategic importance also. Without the disadvantages and dangers of a situation on the coast of Coromandel, it had the benefit of communication with the sea.[1] It stood as the gateway of commerce along the Krishna which served to fertilize its fields, to disseminate its culture and to distribute its goods.

A mile to the west of Amarāvati are the ruins of Dharanikōṭa, an important political centre of the Śātavāhanas where numerous Āndhra coins have been picked up. The location of a Pallava viceroyalty at Dhānyakaṭaka in the third century A.D.[2] and the mention of Dhānyakaṭaka as a separate kingdom by Hiuen-Tsang all point to its great political importance.

Amarāvati recalls to our mind the selfless labours of Colonel Mackenzie but for whose discovery all the marbles would have been burnt into lime and but for whose spirited and withal exact drawings the picture of the stūpa will be incomplete. Elliot, Sewell,[3] Burgess[4] and Rea[5] have successively worked at the spot and on this noble theme. Fergusson's *Tree and Serpent Worship* is a monumental work though marred by a few erroneous opinions expressed in it and it treats of the Amarāvati marbles in the British Museum and the drawings of Mackenzie. The

[1] Amarāvati is 62 miles from the mouth of the Krishna.

[2] *E.I.* vi, p. 84.

[3] Report on the excavation of the Amarāvati stūpa in 1877.

[4] The Buddhist stūpas of Amarāvati and Jaggayyapēta.

[5] South Indian Buddhist antiquities ; *M.A.R.* 1888, Sept. 11, 1889, Ap. 30, *G.O.* 383, p. 2 ; 1905-6, p. 2 ; 1906-7, p. 2 ; 1907-8, p. 2 ; 1909-10, p. 32. For illustrations of Amarāvati, besides the above, see *A.R.A.S.I.*, 1905-6, p. 50 ; 1908-9, p. 88.

magnum opus of Burgess, his book on Amarāvati is still the picture-Bible on that chapter of Āndhra history.[1]

The stūpa, with its roots far down into the age of the Mauryas, stood firm and entire and received benefactions as late as the twelfth century.[2] Hiuen-Tsang, the devoted pilgrim that he was, goes into raptures over the magnificent but largely deserted convents, galleries and pavilions of Dhānyakaṭaka.[3] The inscription of Puḷumāyi Vāsishṭiputra carries the age of the '*Mahāchaitya*' of the *Chaityakas* to the second century A.D., while the inscriptions in the Mauryan script[4] would put back its age by another four hundred years. While Dhānyakaṭaka figures in an inscription of the Ānandagōtra line of kings who seem to have taken Āndhra after a fight with the lord of the *Beṇṇa* (Krishna), it is doubtful if the Amarapura of the Vishnukuṇḍin inscription refers to this ancient city of Āndhra. The inscriptions in Ikshvāku script and the earliest references to the Vākāṭakas at Amarāvati are full of significance though it is not known if the Vākāṭakas were indigenous to Āndhra.[5]

The exact date of the foundation of the stūpa is as obscure as that of many another stūpa in Āndhra. The original mound was of the same type as the stūpas of Sāñchi and Bhaṭṭiprōlu and of the same century. The capital discovery of large quantities of marble in Āndhra is a landmark in the history of Āndhra art.[6] Broadly speaking, the sculptures fall into two classes, one akin to the art of Bhilsa and Sāñchi and the other displaying the assimilation of the Gandhāran style which elevated at a stroke the tone of Āndhra art and made it a joy for ever. Additions were made and renovations effected till the third century A.D. since we have some inscriptions in the ornate Ikshvāku script

[1] The Amarāvati marbles are now shared among the museums of London, Calcutta and Madras. There are a few in the National College, Masulipaṭnam (are they from Ghanṭaśāla ?) and in the Bezwāda museum. For the history of the excavations, see Sewell : Lists I, p. 63.

[2] *E.I.* iii, 91 ; vi. 155 ; x. 44. Also 269 and 270 of 1897, M.E.R.

[3] Watters : ii, 214 ; Beal : ii, p. 221.

[4] *E.I.* xv, p. 258 Pulumāyi has made a grant at Nāsik to the monks of Dhānyakaṭaka, E.I. viii, p. 67.

[5] For Amarāvati inscriptions, see *E.I.* xv, p. 258.

[6] Light cream colored marble is still dug out in Mallavaram and other places in Palnād. Finely colored Cuddappah building stone is obtained in Nandigāma taluk and limestone is found in plenty in Śattenappalle taluk.

which have required as much skill as the most pleasing of designs there. But, the bulk of the embellishments were made in the second century after Christ in the script of which period many of the epigraphs are engraved.

All that wealth could bestow, all that power could command, all that art could embellish, Dhānyakaṭaka was beautified with, as the foremost city of the 'Lord of Dakshināpatha'. If religion could be expressed in stone, the picture gallery of Amarāvati would answer. That religion can permeate and ennoble the meanest cobbler, the inscriptions of Amarāvati would testify.[1] The imperceptible shading of one art into another and the melting of all in a universal harmony may be experienced by a concentration on the best relics of Amarāvati and Nāgārjunakonda. Here is a monument decorated not merely by royal patronage and the munificent purses of the nobles but by the people at large, the merchants, the goldsmiths, the poor mendicant ascetics, the humble and devoted pupils whose love is chiselled there forever. It speaks volumes of the pious zeal and refined tastes of the commonalty and the acme of perfection reached by the decorative arts. The whole world of floral designs and the varied, animated and crowded scenes of men and animals convey the minute care, the *Himālayan* patience and the manual skill of the Āndhra artists of 2,000 years ago whose lavishness of detail is equalled only by the exuberance of their fancy. These masterminds have so effaced themselves in their work and are so lacking in the later day egotism that we do not know the name of even one of them.

By putting together the fragmentary evidences supplied by the excavations and the miniature stūpas on the slabs at Amarāvati, the '*mahāchaitya*' which had gone to ruin long before Colonel Mackenzie, has been reconstructed by historic imagination aided by the science of archæology. On what is now a mere site with not a trace of the central stūpa and railing[2] reared its head a mighty monument 138′ in diameter and about 100′ in height. With the sculptured marbles painted in colors, covering and surrounding the stūpa, this finest memorial to Buddhism in the world must have presented a pleasing appearance for miles around and exercised a sobering influence on the

[1] *E.I.* x, Ap. No. 1273.

[2] There are now the remains of a small stūpa with marble slabs at the southern entrance of the big stūpa.

minds of men. By day and by night, the majesty of the religion of self-control was brought home to the citizens. It was the *Dipāladinne* (mound of lights) in fact as well as in figure of speech. The busy capital near at hand with its palaces, bazars and all the ancient splendor of India stood in striking contrast to the calm dignity and the soothing repose of this enchanting mausoleum, the very seventh heaven of symbolical expression. Hard by this monument of the '*Bhagavat*' must have stood many a smaller tomb to the hierarchy of lesser teachers and monasteries and *manṭapas*, traces of which are not, however, extant. For, no big stūpa worth the name stood without a chaitya and vihāra.

A devotee who desired to pay his respects to the great stūpa at Amarāvati in the second century A.D. entered by one of the four gates near which were some small chapels and dāgabas. The gates were at the four cardinal points of the circular enclosure known as the Outer Rail. Apparently, the gates were unimportant and not of the Sāñchi type.

The Outer Rail

The Outer Rail was formed of upright slabs about 10′ high above the level of the paved procession path. These uprights were connected by three cross-bars which were fitted into the mortices in them. Above and supported by the uprights was a coping frieze, 2′ 9″ in height. On the external face of this compound rail were found sculptures of a uniform and general type. On the pillars were sculptured a disc in the centre with half discs above and below.[1] The discs were characterized by beautiful leaves and creepers in concentric bands. At the two ends of the pillars, above and below the half disc were bands depicting animals and flowers. Between the discs were sculptures of the dāgaba, the Buddha, the *nāga*, the tree, etc. attended by devotees in the upper space and by dancing dwarfs in the lower. The cross-bars[2] connecting any two pillars were full of discs with leaf-patterns. The coping of the rail had a long wavy roll of flowers carried by human figures here and there and bearing one or other of the Buddhist symbols.[3] Though the outer sculptures of the Outer Rail are conventional,

[1] Burgess, pl. vii, fig. 2. [2] *Ibid.*, pl. xvii, fig. 2 ; xviii, fig. 1.
[3] *Ibid.*, pl. xx, fig. 1.

the marvellous and rhythmical varieties of floral patterns and designs, the sinuous rolls and the humorous dwarfs reveal no small skill. The work in stone was evidently copied from earlier work in wood and metals—softer materials than stone—admitting any amount of dexterous work by the carpenter and goldsmith.

On the inner side of the Outer Rail, *i.e.*, to the left of the circumambulating devotee were sculptures not only pleasing to the eye, but instructive to the mind. The uprights bore on the inner side again a disc in the centre and semi-discs above and below, the latter decorated in the same manner with the frieze of animals and flowers at the ends. The central disc and the bands above and below it were sculptured with scenes from the *Jātakas*, episodes from the life of Gautama the Buddha, and varied pictures of domestic and religious life with vivid local coloring now and then.[1] Writes Dr. Burgess, 'it is only in the paintings of Ajanta and Bāgh that we find anything comparable to the rich variety and excellence of art displayed in these sculptures'.[2] The whole popular lore of the Buddhists was depicted on them, an art copied on a grand scale in Borobudur in Java at a later time. While the contrast in this respect between Sāñchi and Amarāvati is striking as the sculptures in the former were on the gateways alone, the evolution of the art into greater skill and freshness and more profusion, luxuriance, elegance and animation (permeated by the new spirit more akin to Mathura and Gandhāra than to Sāñchi), cannot also fail to attract our notice. The subject-matter is the same, conventions about figuring particular scenes in a particular manner, *e.g.*, as to dress, ornaments, etc., had grown in Buddhist art, but still the realism, individuality, expression and freedom of figures and objects at Amarāvati and Nāgārjunakonda are of arresting interest. In a sense, the art had developed a delicate nicety from the pristine vigor of Sāñchi but it has all the charm of a mellow evening. 'Continuous representation, linear treatment and the relative independence of the single figures' are its chief characteristics. The cross-bars which connect the pillars were filled on the inner side also with discs in concentric rings of leaf design. The central disc alone is a panel of figure sculptures of various types and combinations.[3] The inner side of the coping

[1] Burgess, pl. vii, fig. 1. [2] *Ibid.*, p. 26. [3] *Ibid.*, pl. xvii, figs. 1, 4.

above the Outer Rail is also filled with figure sculptures of various scenes from life.[1] Thus, the inner face of the Outer Rail is a contrast to the outer as the former alone meets the eye of the devotees.

The Inner Rail

To the right of the devotee was what used to be called the 'Inner Rail' composed of slabs carved with miniature chaityas alternating with pillars bearing the *chakra*. It was close to the stūpa and the slabs were fixed in it. The richest and the most elaborate carving exemplifying the zenith of Āndhra genius in stone could be seen in the 'Inner Rail' so appropriately assigned to a later date than the Outer Rail and plausibly connected with the art of Nāgārjunakonda and the great Saint. The circumference of this railing 6′ high has been computed to have been about 521′.[2]

Enclosed by the chaitya slabs was the stūpa about 435′ in circumference at the base. It was covered with sculptures upto the capital in tiers. The tee and the umbrella at the summit crowned the whole edifice which was periodically lighted and festooned.

The chaitya slabs of the 'Inner Rail' were of a uniform type.[3] The chaitya on the slab 5′ 8″ high and 5′ 10″ broad stood between two *chakra* pillars with a frieze of sculpture above. It has an outer rail with cross-bars between the pillars with a plinth carved with the wavy roll. The gate is shown with pillars decorated with lions at the base and capital, and on two other sides a view of the gates is given. By the gate are seen devotees with offerings. At each side of the gate stands a dwarf with a tray on his head to receive the offerings of the faithful, and by his side is a flower vase. The stūpa itself is divided into various panels. In the centre is the throne with one or other of the Buddhist symbols[4] attended by devotees with or without *nāga*

[1] Burgess, pl. xx, fig. 2.

[2] The measurements of the various parts of the stūpa are taken from the book of Burgess.

[3] *Ibid.*, pl. xxxix, figs. 1, 2.

[4] The relic-casket, the horse (Kanthaka), the lotus vase, the empty throne, the footprints, the Bodhi tree, the *triśūla*, the flaming pillar, the dāgaba, the *chakra*, the nāga, etc. The flaming *triśūla* is 'the counterpart of Agnilinga' (Fergusson). The author has seen people in South Kanara with peculiar caps suggestive of the nāga men and women in Amarāvati sculptures.

hoods. In some of the slabs is the polycephalous snake. In some others is the Buddha himself amidst his audience or under the hoods of Elapatra with a halo round his head or with the horse by his side or with the elephant kneeling to him. He sits cross-legged and is always found preaching to a crowd of listeners. His hair is worked up in the Indian fashion and not gathered in a knot as in Gandhāra. His eyes are open and his face is smiling. His hand is in the *dharmachakra* or *abayamudra* pose. The drapery has well-marked folds and is held by the left hand. The dress covers both shoulders in some figures while generally the right is bare. On a stray chaitya slab may be seen two medallions of sacred sculptures in the place of the Buddha.

The base of the stūpa on the slab can be seen adorned with slabs carved with Buddhist symbols and having a coping. Above the front slab rise the *āyaka* pillars, octagonal shafts with square carved capitals decorated with the wheel and the dāgaba. In the middle of the dome is a broad belt of very rich sculpture from the Buddhist stories. Still higher up are square and round medallions of sculptures. At the top of the dome is the square box and the latter is crowned by umbrellas. Towards this, the *dēvas*, *yakshas* and *nāgas* are flying.

The Chakra Pillar

The chakra pillars[1] have at the base a throne with cushions and *śripāda* attended by two persons with fly whisks and worshipped by another two. The shaft is beautifully divided into sections ornamented with busts of men and animals. Above are three lions over which is the rayed wheel. On each side of the shaft are five figures riding on different animals. Above the top most of the group is a female dancing excitedly and above her a *yaksha*. Towards the wheels, heavenly beings are seen flying.

Over the whole, *i.e.*, the *chakra* pillars and the chaitya slab between them, runs the frieze[2] ornament with animals below and a broad band above with the Buddhist symbols attended by devotees and with scenes from the life of the Buddha. Between these are inscriptions in second century characters.

Besides the above-described type were chaitya slabs with little sculpture. The former was the miniature of the

[1] Burgess, pl. xliv, fig. 1. [2] *Ibid.*, pl. xlii, fig. 4 and pl. xlviii, fig. 4.

'*mahāchaitya*' of Amarāvati, as it was in the second century A. D. While, the latter was representative of the monument as it was before that period.[1]

Images of the Buddha

The images of the Buddha discovered at Amarāvati belong to Mahāyāna which countenanced the worship of the Buddha and the *Bodhisattvas* who gave *nirvāna* to the faithful. The images must have been added to the stūpa and placed in the chapels at the gateways and in the chaityas. They are of varied types and in the Gandhāran style. They had generally the *usinisa*, a definite cranial protuberance, and ample robes, and the head was covered by small, short curls.

The biggest image is 5'5" high but its hands and feet are broken off. It is of the conventional type with the ample robe thrown over the left shoulder and arm and descending upto the ankles and displays greater skill than its kind in Ajanta. Even the big and flabby images of Amarāvati[2] and Nāgārjunakonda are stern and dignified to look at. There are smaller images as badly defaced and of the same type. The left hand is on the lap and the corner of the robe, on the wrist. The halo over the head and the covering of both the shoulders are evidently copied from Gandhāra. There are also images of the Buddha in stucco and bronze which exhibit considerable skill in art, the bronzes[3] being of the standing and preaching type.

There are other statues in the round which might be figures of kings. One of these exhibits great care and accurate skill. A necklace with seven strings with a square clasp round it, the belt holding the cloth in position and even the very threads of the cloth are represented in detail.

Animals and Men in the Sculptures

The animals at Amarāvati are characterized by the same naturalness as at Sāñchi and possess more of freshness. The lions sculptured on the pillars in the chaitya slabs (which are miniature Asokan *lāts*), the elephants, tigers, horses and birds

[1] Some specimens of the second type have the many-headed cobra twisting round the stūpa signifying the great devotion of the nāgas to the Buddha.

[2] *A.R.A.S.I.*, 1905-6, pl. li. Burgess, pl. li.

[3] *Ibid.*, 1908-9, pl. xxviii.

are well done. Human figures of various cuts and proportions, foreign and native, are drawn with determination, curiosity, attention or pathos as the case may be, from the squat and pot-bellied servants to the beautiful kings and queens. In one panel, the muscles of the strong man are well indicated,[1] while, in another[2] the beauty of woman is shown with considerable skill. At one place, a fighting scene is drawn very spiritedly with weapons raised,[3] and troops on foot, horse and elephant advancing. A pathetic scene is vividly represented at another place.[4] The scenes of ecstatic dance[5] and musical treat[6] are full of life and realism in which may be found a rich variety of musical instruments. All the strains of music that delighted their ears, all the poetry that bubbled out of their lips and instruments, the very rhythm of the dance itself—are conveyed to us without an explaining label or inscription. In accurate floral decoration of a hundred varieties, vase ornaments and the rich animal sculptured panels, the artist has shown wonderful imagination and sense of symmetry. The best representation of man (a feature of Greek art) is combined here with the best representation of animals, leaves and flowers. There is movement in the animal, human and other studies, and figures are not of a dull, flat or uniform type, but have individuality, variety and realism.

Social Life

The social life depicted in these sculptures is not exclusively Āndhra and they present us with varieties of dress, jewels and furniture. Roughly it may be said that the wearing of an upper garment was exceptional for men as well as women. Slim women sparsely dressed or clad in thin muslins reveal their coy and furtive graces, and girls, romping and merry, move about singing and dancing with their characteristic nonchalance. Ample and full robes, robes twisted round the waist with loose hanging folds, robes covering only a few inches above and below the waist, blouses, tunics and drawers which required tailoring (which was perhaps new and foreign), turbans of various elevations according to rank—a few studded with medallions—all these are represented

[1] Burgess, pl. xi, fig. 4.
[2] *Ibid.*, pl. xii, fig. 1.
[3] Fergusson, pl. lxi, fig. 1; Burgess, p. 38.
[4] Burgess, pl. vi, fig. 2.
[5] Burgess, pl. xvii, fig. 1; pl. xxv, fig. 2.
[6] *Ibid.*, p. 35, fig. 7.

here.[1] Heavy ear-rings, bracelets and necklaces are worn by both sexes, while no woman is without the tinkling bangles and anklets so profusely worn even to-day by Āndhra ladies. There does not seem to be any evidence of nose-rings or of bodices. The kings wore turbans with jewels and medallions, and plenty of ornaments and were attended with the *chatra* and the *chāmara*. Brahmins generally wore their cloth in the present day *kacham* fashion and covered the upper part of the body. The hair was worn in a variety of ways but the prevalent fashion seems to be not to shave the head. There are instances of women working up their hair in plaits and into knots bedecked with bands and jewels.

. Men and women mixed freely and equality between the sexes was the rule. Women are seated before men and wives before their husbands in the domestic scenes. The husband with his two wives seated on either thigh is a happy exemplar of domestic harmony,[2] and scenes of music or learned discourse or dance in which women occupy the same place as men are highly characteristic of the religion which allowed women freedom to become nuns, to make gifts and to seek *nirvāna*. However, the Buddha permitted only floral paintings in the monasteries and temples and not figures of men and women. He was at first distrustful of the principle of sex equality. But, Buddhism had to adapt itself to the currents of feeling then in existence among the masses. Equality between the sexes, the freedom of the fair sex, a deep appreciation of sexual beauty and an unconventional social life conveyed to us by the art of Ajanta and Amarāvati seem thus to be removed from the austere ideals of the Buddha and the Āryan missionaries. In fact, a deep study of the fair sex is a marked feature of the artist of Amarāvati which would do credit to Vātsyāyana himself.

The chairs, stools, footstools, cots[3], thrones with cushions, plates, goblets and flasks and the *kāvadi* to carry loads reveal to us in full the domestic life of the age. The peacock and the dog

[1] Burgess, pl. xxxii, fig. 1. Vessantara Jātaka, the princess, is seen wearing a petticoat, bare above the waist and carrying a *kāvadi* like a cooly.

[2] Burgess, pl. xxxii, fig. 1. Between the discs is the Vessantara Jātaka in which the King is seated with two wives.

[3] Cots are mentioned in the Mayidavōlu plates (third century A.D.) Bullock-carts with solid wheels (as in our temple car) figure in ancient sculptures and may be seen even today in remote villages.

fed from a dish were some of the pets of the household. Among the means of transport familiar to the Amarāvati sculptor may be mentioned, besides the chariots, the horses and elephants used by the few, the boat and the country bullock-cart.

Influences of Amarāvati Sculptures

Even if the above pictures did not portray local life exclusively, what impressions they produced on the Āndhra people and what influences they exercised on the life of the age is more than what we can determine at present. It is well-known that Buddhism carried with it, wherever it went, a civilizing, softening, ennobling and educative influence and left lasting impressions in literature and philosophy, in marvellous artistic and engineering feats, in stupendous stūpas and vihāras, in big tanks and well-arranged parks and squares. Its religion was pure morality and its God, man perfected (the Buddha). Not he, as he was but man, but his symbol was to be worshipped. How far such a transcendental system was followed by the people steeped in superstitions and fears is a question difficult to answer. To the people who believed in all, Buddhism gave a new hope and vision. To the philosophers who disbelieved in all, it gave a new system of thought and inquiry. To the Kings who patronized all, it furnished peace-loving and moral subjects. That Buddhism had the wholesome effect of freeing individuality from bonds which weighed down its enterprise is a point beyond dispute. The wide travels of the Buddha depicted in stone had a liberalizing tendency, the north and the south came under the same cultural spell, life became full and culture spread to foreign lands. It is impossible to believe that the beautiful expression of the Amarāvati marbles did not stimulate men into poetry or stir them into dramatic action. Apart from the peculiar pleasure and pride we feel in possessing these works of art and calling them our own, there is also their inherent value according to any scheme of cultural values. In the words of Mr. Sewell, these gems of ancient Indian art are priceless for the wealth of the information they contain on all that makes the past history of a nation valuable or interesting to the student, the antiquary or the statesman.

Architectural Styles

Architecture as an art was as much indebted to the Buddhists as sculpture. The sculptures of Amarāvati are the models of a large variety of the then existing architectural styles which the later Āndhra art developed. There are the circular and rectangular huts suggestive of the countryside and religious buildings on those models.[1] There are small chapels with domical, curvilinear and rectilinear roofs.[2] The origin of these types is no doubt to be found in the elastic bamboos bent in towards the centre. Later lithic work copied the original work in wood. There are civil buildings in the Amarāvati sculptures with railed verandahs, arched gateways and arch decorations in the main part.[3] They are storeyed, balconeyed and finished at the top with terraces. Pillars[4] like the Asokan *lats*, pillars with arched tops, octagonal based, circular banded and square capitalled pillars are seen in plenty. In one-storeyed building there are five *ṣṭupi*-like ornaments or finials in a row on the roof and from the two chaitya arched windows peep out human heads.[5] In another is the barrel-vaulted roof as that found in the ox-cart or the palanquin[6] depicted in some scenes. Beautiful *maṇṭapas* are found in some other panels. Altars with the *pada*[7] which have been found at Amarāvati, and altars with other symbols like the flaming *triśūla* (so peculiar to Āndhra) were originally temples for worship and they served as models for later religious architecture. At Kārle so deservedly famous for its fine pre-Gandhāran sculptures and at Guntapalle, a veritable storehouse of Āndhra buildings, is seen at its best the arched chaitya gateway, while at Chējrāla is found the developed barrel-vaulted roof.

Foreign Influences on Indian Art

Indian art is, according to some, a grand mosaic in which Persian, Greek and other elements shed their lustre. The so-called bell-shaped capital, the honey-suckle ornament (which is but an Indian motif in fact) and even the use of stone for

[1] Burgess, pl. xii, fig. 3 ; xxi, fig. 2 ; xxv, fig. 2 ; xxvi, fig. 2 ; xxvii, fig. 1 ; xlix, fig. 2.

[2] *Ibid.*, pl. xlv, fig. 3 ; xxi, fig. 2 ; xxxviii, fig. 4.

[3] *Ibid.*, pl. xviii, fig. 2 ; xlii, fig. 7.

[4] *Ibid.*, page 93, fig. 28 ; pl. v, fig. 2 ; pl. xxi, fig. 2 ; pl. xxv, fig. 2 ; pl. xxvi, fig. 1. For small *lāts* of the Asokan type, see the chaitya slabs. The buildings were mostly of wood or brick.

[5] *Ibid.*, pl. xviii, fig. 2 ; pl. xi, fig. 2 for a smaller building.

[6] *Ibid.*, pl. xi, fig. 1 ; pl. xxvi, fig. 2 ; pl. xxvii, figs. 1 and 6.

[7] *Ibid.*, page 31, illus. ; pl. xvii, fig. 4.

building are traced to Persia, while, the winged animals, mythical plants and monsters (abounding in Indian fables) came from Assyria. The image of the Buddha with the folds of clothing and a face like Apollo's and a halo like Athene's was first cut in the workshop in Gandhāra under Graeco-Roman influences. In the classical style, the delineation of the muscles of the body and the modelling of the body are particularly noteworthy. The acanthus ornaments of Amarāvati are Greek according to some but it is so only in name as they possess the same vitality and beauty of form as the Indian lotus.

But, the conception of Indian art as a seed sprouting into rich foliage and flowers stimulated in growth by foreign influences now and then will be more real and historical. Long before Asoka, there were *lāts* ornamented with the lotus, miscalled the bell. To acquire the mature skill in stone displayed in the Sāñchi gateways and the earliest of the Amarāvati sculptures must have taken centuries. However, in dress, in a few motifs and scenes and in a certain polish of style, the classical influence is perceivable and it must have travelled to Āndhra by land as well as by sea.[1] The dominant impulse was undoubtedly Indian.

Some Opinions

'The Amarāvati sculptures,' says Dr. Marshall, 'indeed appear to be as truly Indian in style as those of Bhārhut and Ellora. They follow as a natural sequence on Mauryan art, when that art was finding expression in more conventionalized forms. They have inherited certain motifis and types which filtered in from the north-west, but these elements have been completely absorbed and assimilated without materially influencing the indigenous character of these sculptures'.

The sculptures of Amarāvati are as remarkable a product of Āndhra genius as some of the paintings of Ajanta whose originality no one has doubted. As Havell[2] has pointed out, 'the bas-reliefs of Amarāvati (forming the decoration of the railing and of the marble casing of the stūpa itself) should properly be studied in connection with the fresco-paintings of Ajanta. They

[1] According to V. A. Smith (see his History of Fine Art), the art of Amarāvati was indebted to the art of Alexandria of the age of the Antonines, p. 150.

[2] A handbook of Indian Art, p. 38.

must have resembled the latter very closely when the color and gilding with which they were finished were intact; the technical treatment also is usually much more pictorial than plastic.' The most ancient paintings in Ajanta which has 'art with life in it' and 'scenes taken from Nature's book' in Caves IX and X are closely related to the Sāñchi sculptures and may be ascribed to the period and patronage of the Āndhra kings.[1] The treatment of Amarāvati is original and local according to Fergusson[2] who would however trace its origin to the Hellenic style. By concluding that 'the best reliefs of Amarāvati are also the best Indian sculptures', Grunwedel[3] emphasizes the decided predominance of the Indian element.

In comparing the Gandhāran art with that of Amarāvati, Rothenstein[4] wonders 'how one can prefer the somewhat clumsy and provincial Gandhāran carvings to the dignified, supple and exquisitely carved figures and the lotus and animal designs which ornamented the temples at Mathura, Sārnāth or Amarāvati'. Codrington [5] believes that 'however foreign the art of Gandhāra may be, its inspiration is admittedly Indian. Its iconography also is Indian in origin and derived from Indian sources. . . . It must, however, be acknowledged that the classical element in Gandhāran art, hybrid as it is, and decadent from the beginning can never have been the dominant factor'.

As regards the Graeco-Roman origin of the Buddha image, Dr. A. Coomaraswāmy concludes thus: 'The only possible conclusion is that the Buddha figure must have been produced simultaneously, probably in the middle of or near the beginning of the first century A.D. in Gandhāra and in Mathura in response to a demand created by the internal development of Buddhism which was common ground in both areas, in each case by local craftsmen, working in the local tradition.[6] In fact, long before the first Buddha image was made in the Gandhāran workshop, Indian masons had made images with the *usinisa*, curly hair and long ear-lobes as at Bodh Gaya. The *lakshanas* of a *Mahāpurusha*

[1] A.R.A.S.I. 1903–4, p. 130.
[2] Tree and Serpent Worship, p. 157.
[3] Buddhist Art in India, p. 157.
[4] Codrington, Ancient India, Introd., p. 4.
[5] *Ibid.*, p. 51.
[6] History of Indian and Indonesian Art, p. 60.

were well-known long before the first century A.D. The pose of the Gandhāran Buddha as a *guru* or *yōgi* is entirely Indian. The history of image-making can be traced back to the age of Mōhenjo-Dāro and *terracotta* figures have an unbroken record from the earliest times.[1]

Hiuen-Tsang's Dhānyakaṭaka

A controversy has raged over the location of Hiuen-Tsang's capital of Dhānyakaṭaka where he lived for some time, learnt *Abhidharma* from Subhūti and Sūrya and taught Mahāyāna.[2] Fergusson, Sewell, Burgess, Watters and V. A. Smith,[3] identify the capital with Bezwāda. Says Watters 'it is hard to understand how anyone could propose to identify a large monastery among hills and streams and having spacious chambers and great corridors with a building which is merely a remarkable *tope* situated on a plain.' But, it must be confessed that Hiuen-Tsang's account is too meagre for any positive identification. He locates a monastery of the *Pūrvaśailas* east of the capital and another of the *Avaraśailas* west of it on a hill. A former king erected them, made a path by the river (connecting them) and built halls with broad corridors of rock. They had all the artistic elegance of a great mansion and all the beauty of natural scenery. They were resorted to by saints and by 1,000 brethren every year for the rainy season. For a hundred years, in the time of the pilgrim, they had been *deserted* and desolate. In a hill cave south of the capital lived Bhāvavivēka.

From the above account, it does not follow that the two monasteries were very near the capital. There are no extensive Buddhist remains at Bezwāda to justify our identification of the capital with it. A local Pallava inscription at Amarāvati calls the place Dhānyaghaṭa. There are evidences in the extensive mounds of Dharaṇikōṭa and in Buddhist books of the existence at one time of big institutions there. If we are to judge from the extent of the establishment which accommodated hundreds of monks every year, Vijayapuri (Nāgārjunakonda) would be more suitable than Vijayavāda (Bezwāda). Let us, however, await

[1] For some prototypes of the Buddha image, see *Cambridge History of India*, vol. i, plate xix.

[2] Watters : II, pp. 217-18. Beal : *Life*, p. 137.

[3] *Ibid.*, Appendix.

further excavations at Nāgārjunakonda which promises to be a wonder-house of art-treasures of unequalled beauty and of inscriptions of inestimable value. Neither Amarāvati nor Bezwāda could have been deserted and desolate in the seventh century, while Nāgārjunakonda, an ancient capital of the kingdom of Dhānyakaṭaka (which was so called after the town of the same name), was perhaps desolate at the period. Mr. Rea and Dr. Cunningham were against the identification of Hiuen-Tsang's capital of Dhānyakaṭaka with Bezwāda. The former argued that the establishment of Amarāvati might have extended as far as the hills of Peddamaddur[1] four miles to the south-east where remains of a stūpa and vihāras and of a few marbles are found. That Amarāvati was known as Dhānyakaṭaka and lent the name to the kingdom itself (Dhānyakaṭaka) is certain. But it does not necessarily follow that Dhānyakaṭaka-Amarāvati was the capital of the kingdom in the time of Hiuen-Tsang.

The age of Amarāvati was the age of fine marble sculptures in Āndhra. There were a very large number of skilled marble masons and sculptors in the country who attained a certain individuality in the art and thus came to form the 'Amarāvati school of art.'

[1] *M.A.R.* 1889, Ap. 30, p. 2. G. O. No. 383. Public.

CHAPTER IV

NĀGĀRJUNA BODHISATTVA, THE KING OF MONKS

If individuality is the keynote of the art-gallery of Ajanta, the chaitya of Kārle and the 'house beautiful' of Amarāvati, it reached its perfection in Nāgārjuna Bodhisattva, patriarch and philosopher. If the Āndhra imperial hegemony was lost in obscurity, the Āndhras made ample amends by conquering the heart of Āryavarta through their brightest gem, more lustrous than their *Kohinoor* and *Golconda*,[1] the sage of Parvata, a versatile genius and a wonder of the world. Legends have grown so thickly over this illustrious personality that it is difficult to get a true picture of him and his activities. But he stands clearly associated with the new phase of the Buddhist religion, the Mahāyāna, as its systematizer, expounder and propagator, if not its originator. The author of *Mādhyamika* and *Śūnyavāda*, Nāgārjuna was 'one of the four suns that illuminated the Buddhist world.'[2]

Nāgārjuna was a South Indian Brahmin who turned Buddhist like many other Buddhist savants. The exact country of his birth is unknown, though it is said to be Vidarbha (Berar) in one account.[3] According to Hiuen-Tsang, the prince of Chinese pilgrims, Nāgārjuna first lived in a monastery near the capital of Dakshina Kosala which seems to have once extended its sway as far as the Krishna. Next, the sage lived in *Po lo mo lo kili* which has been correctly interpreted as Parvata, the name that is applied to Nāgārjunakonda by an inscription discovered there recently. Parvata was above 300 *li* from the capital of Dakshina Kosala according to the same authority of the seventh century

[1] Krishna District Manual for the tradition about the two diamonds, p. 247.

[2] Watters: I, p. 245.

[3] For legends and traditions of Nāgārjuna, see Walleser: The life of Nāgārjuna from Tibetan and Chinese sources (Reprinted from Asia Major); *J.A.S.B.*, vol. li, pt. i, p. 115.

A.D.[1] So, Nāgārjuna, a subject of the Śātavāhana king, as we shall see presently, lived mostly in Āndhra and was a naturalized, if not a born, Āndhra.

Legends would make us believe that Nāgārjuna was ordained in boyhood to avert a death at seven which had been foretold. But, we have reasons to think that he mastered Brahminical learning which he had at his command before he donned the yellow robe. He is said to have attained *siddhi* by the favour of Tāra at Kāñchi according to one version and by the grace of Chandika at Nālanda according to another. Be that as it may, he soon earned a high reputation for scholarship and could compose poetry as well as he could discourse on philosophy.

His journey to the *nāga* world led to his discovery there of the complete *Prajnāpāramita* which was lost on the continent. The *nāgalōka* at the bottom of the sea might be Ceylon which afforded ample field to later scholars like Buddhaghosa and Buddhadatta. Nāgārjuna learnt the *Vaipulya* and other *sūtras* there and brought also a casket of relics over which he erected a stūpa. The stūpa referred to may be identified with the '*mahāchaitya*' at Nāgārjunakonda to which the Ikshvāku royal house devoted so much attention. On his return from the voyage which brought him great fame, he converted his king and 10,000 Brahmins. For one hundred years after his death, temples were erected to his memory and he was worshipped in them.

His Omniscience

There is no branch of knowledge with which Nāgārjuna is not associated. He claimed omniscience, and an interesting story is told by Hiuen-Tsang relating to his knowledge of everything in connection with the introduction of Āryadēva to the aged philosopher.[2] With his remarkable scholarship, transcendental wisdom and all-embracing *karuna*, he was a true Bodhisattva. As a *siddha purusha*, he could make himself invisible. As a constant friend of Nature, he knew the course and influence of the stars and the virtues and ways of every plant and herb. In fact, in the latter field of medicine, Nāgārjuna is a name to conjure with. No medical treatise would fail to invoke his

[1] Watters : II, p. 201. [2] Watters : II, p. 200.

blessings.[1] He himself revised *Susruta* and is said to have written *Kaksha puta tantra* and *Ārogyamanjari*. His eye prescription was well known in China; his cure for poisons is deservedly praised by Bāna ; and his recipes for several diseases were inscribed on public pillars, as a great Emperor had similarly made known the Law of the Buddha 400 years before him. Above all, he discovered the elixir of life, the loadstar of many ancient researchers and their grave. Knowing the secret of life, Nāgārjuna prolonged his life indefinitely as well as his king's. The story goes that he gave up his life with which was bound his king's at the earnest entreaty of the surviving heir to the throne.[2]

The *Rasaratnākara* of Nāgārjuna has a reference to his abode in Parvata and deals, among other things, with his experiments in the killing of mercury, diamond, etc., which entitle him to rank as the father of Indian Chemistry. The epoch seems to have been one of unusual and restless inquiry as Nāgārjuna himself speaks of another scientist Sākanda whose experiments were famous.[3] Nāgārjuna was the inventor of the processes of distillation and calcination and an authority on minerals. He was the first to describe the process of roasting iron and to prepare black sulphide of mercury. So, his monastery on Parvata as a college of science must have witnessed many an experiment in Botany, Metallurgy and Chemistry and the able professor must have gathered round him a number of students to assist him in the discovery of truth. No ancient seer in the world has been free from the lure of alchemy, the almost killing quest for the philosopher's stone which would relieve the poor and shower manna to the many. Our illustrious sage was no exception to the rule. And the wonderful part of the story as told by Hiuen-Tsang is that he succeeded in his efforts and converted rocks

[1] P. C. Ray : History of Indian Chemistry, vol. i, p. xcii (Williams and Norgate). Also Journal and Text of the Buddhist Text Society of India, vol. iii, p. 15 (1897).

[2] According to Tāranātha, the Tibetan historian (about 1608 A.D.), the royal contemporary of Nāgārjuna lived 150 years and perhaps the sage lived double the proverbial span of life as he has passed down to posterity as one of our long-lived sages. See I.A. iv, p. 363. Also Takakusu : Itsing's records of the Buddhist religion, p. 35.

[3] P. C. Ray, vol. ii, p. 6 and *Sanscrit Texts* at the end of his book, p. 12.

into gold to provide his king with the large funds required for building the splendid vihāra on Parvata.

His Works

Nāgārjuna was essentially a philosopher. But philosophy then was synonymous with knowledge and every Buddhist or non-Buddhist monk was something of a naturalist and doctor. Nāgārjuna's cure for spiritual ills was original. It was *Śūnya !*

Only twenty-four out of his many works have come down to us, thanks to the Chinese but for whom our Buddhist literature would have utterly perished.[1] *Prajnāpāramita sāstra,*[2] *Prajnā-mūla-sāstra tika,*[3] *Prajnāpradipa-sāstra kārika,*[4] *Mūla-madhyamika sāstra, Sūnyasaptādhi, Madhyāntanugama sāstra,*[5] *Dasabhūmi vibhāsa sāstra,*[6] *Dvādasa Nikāya sāstra,*[7] *Vivāda samāna sāstra,*[8] *Pramāna vihētana, Upāya Kausalya hrdaya sāstra, Vigraha Vyāvartini Kārika*—are some of his books which represent his capacities as a philosopher, logician and debater. His prodigious and encyclopædic scholarship is impressed on every work of his.

'The world has a conditional existence, neither absolutely real nor absolutely unreal. . . . As a fact, no object has a nature or self-existence. Thus, the world is an aggregate of relations in virtue of which it revolves like a water-wheel. . . .' Again, 'origination and cessation, coming and going, etc. the fundamental conceptions of relation are really unreal and give rise to our prejudices. There nestles in them the principle of unrest and misery, and as people cling to them their life is an everlasting prey to the pendulous feeling of exultation and mortification.' 'Where there is conditionality, there is no truth. So, to attain truth, conditionality must be completely cast aside. Then, you reach truth or void'. '*Śūnyāta* is *nirvāna* an unconditional condition in which all contradictions

[1] I. A. xvi, p. 169. Only 20 according to Watters II, p. 204.

[2] Nanjio's catalogue of Chinese Tripitaka No. 1169, an encyclopaedia of Mahāyāna.

[3] Giles: History of Chinese Literature, p. 119.

[4] Nanjio: No. 1185. [5] *Ibid.*, No. 1246. [6] *Ibid.*, 1180. [7] *Ibid.*, No. 1186.

[8] *Ibid.*, No. 1251. Tāranātha mentions two more works *yukti sastika* and *vaidulya*. See Watters, II. see also S. C Vidyabushan: History of Indian Logic (Calcutta University).

are reconciled '.[1] Some of these precious pearls of thought were taken up by another gigantic though not versatile intellect, *Śri* Śankara.

In theory a nihilist and atheist, in practice he is said to have introduced worship and devotion.[2] If his theory of illusion led logically to the *māya* of Śankara, his practice of Mahāyāna led on to the Hindu *Bhakti* cult. 'The figure of Nāgārjuna, so prominent in the history of the rise of Mahāyānism, shows a double character. It is, on the one side, the name of an influential person, the first eminent leader of a school imbued with Hinduism and the methods of Indian scholastic philosophy. On the other hand, Nāgārjuna is simply a comprehensive name of the activity of Mahāyānism in the first phase of its onward course.'[3]

One more work of Nāgārjuna may be mentioned here, his *Suhrillēkha*[4] (all his works he wrote in Sanskrit) to his king which was committed to memory by the young and old in India in the time of Itsing (seventh century A.D.). The letter is of interest for the advice 'to practise the threefold wisdom that we may clearly understand the noble eightfold path and the four truths to realize the twofold attainment of perfection. Like Avalokitēsvara, we should not make any distinction between friends and enemies. We shall then live hereafter in the *Sukhāvati* for ever, through the power of the Buddha Amitābha whereby one can also exercise the superior power of salvation over the world'.[5]

The Hill of Nāgārjuna

From the description of Nāgārjuna's life and works, let us turn to the question if this king of monks lived in Nāgārjunakonda and lent his name to the sacred hill.[6] It may be noted

[1] S. C. Vidyabushan : *ante*.

[2] The great Nāgārjuna is to be distinguished from his lesser namesakes the *Vajrayānist* and the alchemist, the latter mentioned by Alberuni. That the great sage himself was a *tantrist* is not to be doubted. See Alberuni : *India* (trans.), p. 189.

[3] Kern : Manual of Buddhism, p. 123.

[4] Nanjio : Nos 1440, 1441 ; I. A. xvi, p. 169 ; *J.P.T.S.* 1883 and 1886.

[5] Takakusu : Itsing, pp. 158–62.

[6] There is a local tradition that Nāgārjuna was a king, but it appears to be as baseless as a similar reference to him in the *Rāja taramgini* Trans. by Stein ii, p. 19.

that the site of the recent excavations is called Vijayapuri in Parvata in an inscription found there. This Buddhist Parvata is but fifty miles, as the crow flies, from the Hindu Parvata or Śri Śailam and there is a tradition that the former is one of the gates of Śri Śailam. Both the Hindu and Buddhist Parvatas must have been sacred from ancient times. There are no extant Buddhist traces in Śri Parvata of the Hindus in Kurnool district though a town of no small importance must have stood near it. So, the Parvata with which Nāgārjuna is associated in Chinese and Tibetan literatures must be the Buddhist Parvata or Nāgārjunakonda and not its namesake of Kurnool district.

Fahian, the first well-known pilgrim who came to India from China has left us only a few lines about Dakshina. He speaks of a *Po lo yu*, i.e., Parava or Parvata, a monastery on an isolated rock, of a pyramidal shape, with five storeys each ornamented with the figures of an animal and with 1,500 cells in all. It was well supplied with water by a wonderful arrangement and windows were cut in the rock to let in air and light. It was a *sanghārāma* of the former Buddha Kāśyapa. It must be said at once that no remains have yet been found on the rock of Nāgārjuna which stands apart and prominently. But, it may be surmised that Parvata was corrupted into *paravata* which means a pigeon.[1] The situation of Fahian's *Po lo yu* fits in with that of Nāgārjunakonda.

Hiuen-Tsang's *Po lo mo lo kili*, meaning black peak or black bee, is the same as Fahian's *Po lo yu*. Both descriptions agree more or less, but the account of the later pilgrim is more reliable as he visited Dhānyakaṭaka to which kingdom belonged Nāgārjunakonda. 'The solitary peak of the mountain towers above the rest. . . . The King Sadvaha, for the sake of Nāgārjuna, tunnelled the rock and built a *sanghārāma*. In the midst of long galleries with eaves for walking under and high towers, the storeyed building reaches to the height of five stages, each stage with four halls with vihāras enclosed. In each vihāra was a statue of Buddha cast in gold, of the size of life, wrought with consummate art and singularly adorned.' The arrangements for water and light are similar to those described by Fahian. 'In the topmost hall, Nāgārjuna deposited the scriptures of Sākyamuni

[1] Giles: The travels of Fahsien, pp. 62–3.
Beal: Bud. records of the W. World (Trubner), vol. i.

Buddha and the writings of the *Pusas*. In the lowest hall were the laymen attached to the monastery and the stores and the three intermediate halls were the lodgings of the brethren.' *Po lo mo lo kili* is Parvata if it is taken as equivalent to black peak or black bee. For, Parvata is but an offshoot of the Nallamalais (lit. black mountain in Telugu) and Parvata might have been mistranslated as the hill of Pārvati whose other name is Bhramari.[1]

The Date of Nāgārjuna

Various arguments may be put forward to fix the age of Nāgārjuna in the second century A.D. Perhaps he lived on for a decade or two in the third century also. Chinese and Tibetan accounts[2] differ as to the date of Nāgārjuna, but there seems to be a general agreement as to his contemporaneity with Kanishka. In the list of patriarchs,[3] Nāgārjuna is the next but one after Asvaghosha who was for some time at the court of the great Kushān monarch, and Vasubandhu the contemporary of Samudragupta and his son was sixth from Nāgārjuna. In fact, Kanishka, Asvaghosa and other contemporary names figure in the works of Nāgārjuna.[4] According to the *Mahāwamsa* of Ceylon, Āryadēva the disciple of Nāgārjuna was a contemporary of Vohara Tissa and Abhaya, kings of the island in the third century A.D.[5] There is an inscription in the stūpa of Jaggayyapēta in fifth century characters of Reverend Nāgārjuna's disciple's disciple.[6] The inscriptions of Nāgārjunakonda contain the names of some eminent *Bhikshus* like Bhadanta Ānanda, Dharma Nandi, Chandramukha and Nāga. Nāgārjuna seems to have had two well-known disciples other than Āryadēva, named Nanda and Nāga[7] and it is not improbable that they took an active part in beautifying the spot made holy by their *guru* and induced the royal family to render all the necessary help. It is very strange that in all

[1] The name of the Goddess of Śri Śailam to-day. See Watters : II, p. 201 for an account of *Po lo mo lo kili*.

[2] Itsing, p. 181 ; *I. A.* xvi, p. 353 ; Rājataramgini I, st. 173 and 177.

[3] *I. A.* ix, pp. 148, 315.

[4] S. C. Vidyabushana : *ante*.

[5] Geiger, ch. 36.

[6] Burgess, p. 111. Jayaprabha, the disciple of Nāgārjuna, is mentioned here.

[7] Itsing *I. A.* xvi, p. 170 ; Walleser, p. 21.

the inscriptions hitherto discovered, there is no mention of Nāgārjuna who was also known as Nāgāhvaya (called Nāga).[1] There is no likelihood of the occurrence of the great *muni's* name as merely Nāga without distinguishing and distinguished epithets.

The inscriptions of Nāgārjunakonda are in the beautiful flowery Ikshvāku script of the third century A.D. and the sculptures of the same style as the casing stabs of Amarāvati belong to the same epoch more or less. In fact, Tāranātha mentions that Nāgārjuna erected 'the inner rail' at Amarāvati which enshrined some relics of the Buddha.[2] Since the chaitya slabs of Amarāvati and those of Nāgārjunakonda are almost of the same style, it may be conjectured that the latter were carved early in the third century A.D. after the decease of the saint. According to one account, his *Prajna Mūla Sastra* was translated into Chinese by Hsu Kan between 196 and 221 A.D.[3] We know for certain, however, that his life and some works were rendered into Chinese by Kumārajiva about 401 A.D.

The Contemporary Kings

There are conflicting traditions recorded by Tāranātha and others regarding the royal contemporary or contemporaries of Nāgārjuna. Neither Upēndra (Vishnu) the Nāgarāja, who helped the sage in his search for the lost book on transcendental wisdom, nor Munja of Orissa, who took orders and erected some vihāras at the instance of Nāgārjuna, can be considered historical.[4] The other alleged contemporaries are Bhōja of Vidharba who also embraced Buddhism, Nimai Chandra of Aparānta removed by three generations before Chandragupta I (Gupta) and Śankara of South India who was vanquished together with thousands of Brahmins.[5]

[1] Manjusri Mūla Kalpa, III, pp. 616–7.

[2] According to Manjusri Mūla Tantra I, p. 88 and some Buddhist stories.

[3] Giles : History of Chinese Literature, pp. 119–20.

[4] In regard to the latter, a reference to the kingdom as that of Ikshuvardhana in traditions may afford a clue to the contemporaneity of an Ikshvāku.

[5] While Bhōja was a general name for the Kings of Berar, Śankara is said to be mistranslation of the original Tibetan name for Śātavāhana (P. C. Ray II, p. xxii.) In Sandanes of Broach mentioned by the *Periplus* may be traced a member of the Chandra family. J.R.A.S, 1918, p. 110.

Śātvāhana or Śālivāhana was the family name of the kings of Āndhra between about 225 B.C. and 225 A.D. after which date the Śātavāhanas disappear from the canvas of history. There is some one Śātavāhana who cannot now be properly identified round whom a good crop of legends and literary traditions have grown up and they have not left out Nāgārjuna unenmeshed. Besides, in *Rasaratnākara*, Nāgārjuna and Śālivāhana, and Ratnaghosha and Māndavya are brought together.[1] Hiuen-Tsang mentions Śātavāhana as the king and patron of Nāgārjuna and his dominion must have comprised Dakshina Kosala proper and Āndhra proper as monasteries were built by him for the sage in both. Itsing calls the King Śāntaka of the Śātavāhana family[2] Nāgārjuna's *Suhrillēkha* mentions a name Jantaka or Jetaka or Sindhuka King of Shingṭu (India) and styled Śātavāhana.[3] These names do not carry us any further than that a certain Śātavāhana (Sindhuka occurs in the list of Āndhra Kings in the *Vāyu Purāṇa*) was the contemporary of Nāgārjuna. The Śātavāhana, according to all testimony, was powerful and ruled over the Central Provinces and Āndhra. There was no such powerful Śātavāhana after the second century A.D.

The Ikshvākus very probably expanded south on the decline of the Śātavāhanas and were till then subordinate to them. The surname of the Ikshvākus and the name Chāntamūla bear a resemblance to those of the Śātavāhanas also called Śānta or Śāntivahanas or merely Śata. Still, there is not even a scrap of sound evidence to equate the sage of Parvata and Mahārāja Vāsishṭiputra Chāntamūla the first Ikshvāku and patron and performer of Brahminical rites.[4]

The Age of the Saint

The age of Nāgārjuna was an age of general and all-round culture, a period of expression with the tongue and the style, the chisel and the brush. Nāgārjunakonda stands to-day as the best monument of that epoch. Parvata, from the heights of which flowed Mahāyāna and Mādhyamika, has brought Āndhra a reputation which will endure as long as a single stone is left of

[1] P. C. Ray—*ante*.
[2] Takakusu, pp. 158-62.
[3] Beal: Life of Hiuen-Tsang (Trubner) Introd., pp. 20-21.
[4] Chāntamūla is Skt. Śāntamūla.

that sacred mount. All the art, all the philosophy and literature of the Buddhist epoch and what is more, the emotional instincts, the critical acumen and power of expression underlying them all are a priceless legacy which has entered into the intellectual make-up of the scholars and people of Āndhra. And to this legacy has richly contributed Nāgārjuna Bodhisattva, the Aristotle of Buddhist lore, the Christ of Mādhyamika, and the St. Paul of Mahāyāna, a magical name baffling the most brainy in sheer intellectual power and moral force.

Nāgārjuna's Successors

Āryadēva, the Buddhist zealot, Bhāvavivēka the skilful dialectician and Dignāga who lived for some time near Vengi were some distinguished names who shed lustre on Āndhradēsa after the time of Nāgārjuna. In her favourable climate were composed many works of rare ability.

The most prominent of Nāgārjuna's disciples was Āryādēva also known as Dēva, Kānadēva and Nīlanētra the fifteenth patriarch. Religious zeal and fiery eloquence brought about the untimely end of this South Indian savant at the hands of an assassin. A sound scholar, a widely travelled man, and a writer of distinguished ability, he scored many a triumph over the *tirthikas* in Chuliye, in Kosala, in Pātaliputra and elsewhere and occupied a high place in Nālanda. In his *Śatasāstra*, he refutes Sānkhya and Vaisēshika. In his *Chitta Visuddhi Prakarana*, he ridicules the Brahmins' superstitions regard for the Ganges. He is said to have been fond of preaching the *Andhakavinda Suttanta*.[1]

Itsing places Bhāvavivēka earlier than Dignāga and Dharmapāla. Whereas, he is held as a contemporary of Dharmapāla by Hiuen-Tsang. He was a follower of Nāgārjuna and lived in a cave south-west of the capital of Dhānyakaṭaka. He is the author of a number of learned and subtle works, *Mahāyāna-pearl-in hand śāstra*, *Prajna-lampśāstra*, *Sānkhya Tarkajvāla*, etc. He was a skilful dialectician who 'externally displaying the Sānkhya garb, internally propagated the learning of Nāgārjuna.' He was perhaps an Āndhra.[2]

A contemporary of Kāḷidāsa and disciple of Vasubandhu, Dignāga of Kāñchi became a distinguished *Yogāchāri* and

[1] Watters: I and II.

[2] Watters: II.

largely lived in Āndhra. He travelled through Mahārāshṭra and Orissa controverting the *tīrthikas*, converted a minister of the King of Orissa and founded sixteen mahāvihāras. He was the founder of pure logic, which he distinctly differentiated from religion and philosophy. The *Pramāna Samuccaya* 'one of the grandest literary monuments' was composed on a solitary hill with a stone stūpa near Vengi, capital of Āndhra. It was the earliest work on modern pure *nyāya* which developed *pramāna* or evidence of knowledge. According to Beal, Dignāga had to controvert Īsvara Krishna, author of the Sānkhya Kārika in Āndhra. This star of the first magnitude in Logic was author of 100 treatises according to Itsing. Some of his works were rendered into Chinese by Paramārtha in the sixth century A.D. He died in a forest in Orissa. According to Hiuen-Tsang, Dignāga or Jina was an Āndhra.[1]

Dharmakīrti was the pupil of another South Indian luminary Dharmapāla of Kāñchi. Undaunted by social ostracism, Dharmakīrti propagated Buddhism, defeated Kumārila Bhaṭṭa the champion of sacrificial religion, controverted the Jains and tried to bring back Kaliṅga into the Buddhist fold. But, his missionary efforts were unavailing as, according to Hiuen-Tsang, Buddhism had reached its nadir in Kaliṅga.

Several monks apparently of great distinction are found in inscriptions at Amarāvati, Nāgārjunakonda, Jaggayyapēṭa and Rāmireddipalle, but nothing more is known of them than their names.

[1] Beal, vol. ii. Watters, vol. ii. Itsing by Takakusu. S. C. Vidhyabushan—*ante*. I.A. IV, p. 363.

PART II

THE HISTORY OF ĀNDHRA BETWEEN 225 AND 610 A.D.

CHAPTER V

INTRODUCTORY

Puḷumāyi IV was the last of the Śātavāhana kings. His rule must have ended about 225 A.D. allowing about four centuries and a half for the Āndhra dynasty after the death of Aśōka. During the bulk of this period, the Śātavāhanas were essentially a Deccan power under whose aegis there was progress in all fields of activity. Signs of decline had already been in evidence a hundred years before the final exit of the Śātavāhanas from the stage of rule. Trouble was brewing in the north-west frontier of their dominion. The Śakaṣ, Pahlavas and Yavanas were making headway when Gautamīputra Śātakarṇi became alive to the danger and stemmed the tide of the foreign invasions. How far into the Deccan their inroads had been made already, we are unable to know. But certain it is that the foreign hordes had come to stay. They continued to show attention to the Śātavāhana empire which they coveted. Puḷumāyi, son of Gautamīputra, tried to conciliate them through the good offices of the daughter of Rudradāman [1]; but, their innate predatory habits and cupidity were roused into activity by the weakness of the Āndhra kings. Guided by discretion, valour failing, the successors of Yajña Sri confined themselves to their Āndhra homeland. Peace, however, was not vouchsafed to them. The expansion of the Ikshvākus from Dakshina Kosala and the assertion of the Pallavas south of the Krishna were the two events that inaugurated the new century. The Śātavāhana empire was dismembered; the last of the royal line flits out of existence from the Bellary region, thanks to the Pallava; and the aggressive Ikshvāku gave short shrift to the remnants of Śātavāhana power elsewhere.[2]

[1] This is Dr. Smith's view. But Dr. Dubreuil holds a different view. P. 44, *Ancient History of the Deccan*.

[2] There are some Āndhra coins in the Central Provinces of some scions of the old stock. *J.R.A.S.* 1903, 304; V. A. Smith: Catalogue of coins in the British Museum, p. 208.

The Foreign Element

Coincident with the break-up of the Śātavāhana power were the fall of the Kushānas and the rise of the Sassanids of Persia. What relationship these events bore to one another is unknown. But, it is likely that the rise of the Sassanids announced by a flourish of their war trumpets even far beyond their frontiers[1] might have extinguished Kushāna hegemony and applied some pressure to the Śakas and others to push further into India. Whatever the ultimate cause was, there was disintegration and darkness in India when the Āndhras of the Purāṇas ceased to rule. A number of foreign dynasties are said to have ruled in the post-Śātavāhana period, like the Gardabhins, the Śakas, the Yavanas, the Tusaras, the Murundas and the Maunas. After these came the Kilakila Yavanas[2] and Vindhyaśakti (250 A.D. ?). The reminiscences of Yavana rule in Orissa and Āndhra,[3] references to Yavana benefactions in early Deccan inscriptions and to Yavana traders in early Greek and Tamil books, the relationship between the Pahlavas and the later Pallavas and the mention of Gandhāra and Yavana as familiar kingdoms and of marriage relations between the Ikshvākus and the Śakas in inscriptions at Nāgārjunakonda[4]—these confirm that the foreign element in the Deccan population was not inconsiderable, that the foreigners who were hitherto neighbours of the Śātavāhana empire spread over it and that the new dynasties had foreign mixture in them though they adopted Hindu habits and manners, *gotras* and ancestry in entirety.

The Assertion of Śātavāhana Feudatories

Among the native dynasties of the post-Śātavāhana period, the *Matsya Purāṇa* mentions a branch of the Āndhras known as the Śri Parvatiya Āndhras of whom there were seven ruling for

[1] Journal and Text of the Buddhist Text Society of India, November, 1893, vol. i, Part iii, p. 18. Translation from *Sumpahi Choi Jung* which contains reminiscences of a Persian invasion of India repulsed by a king of Magadha, Dharma Chandra, who belonged to a generation after Huvishka.

[2] Pargiter : Dynasties, p. 72. The Vishnu Puraṇa calls Vindhyasakti himself a Kilakila Yavana.

[3] Wilson : Catalogue of Mackenzie MSS., Introd., p. cxxiv ; Hunter : Orissa, vol. i, p. 206 ; Vaidya : Mediaeval Hindu India, vol. i, p. 351.

[4] *A.B.I.A.*, Leyden, 1927, p. 11.

52 years. They had begun to rule even while the main Āndhra dynasty had not died out. The Ābhiras, another of the Śātavāhana feudatories ruled for 67 years after the extinction of their masters' rule.[1] From inscriptions we learn that, in South Deccan, the nāga officials and princelings like Skandanāga [2] asserted their independence and soon gave way to the Pallava who, according to later tradition, obtained a kingdom by a nāga marriage. The Pallava, when he first appears in history, is seated at Kāñchi with an extensive empire extending to Bellary on the one side and Amarāvati on the other. Beyond the Krishna, the Telugu country was ruled by the Bṛihatphalāyanas along the coast up to the Gōdāvari and the Ikshvākus in the rest.

Worldly dominion is not eternal, it changes hands according to certain physical and moral laws. The fortunes of the Pallavas, the Bṛihatphalāyanas and the Ikshvākus were shifting. A revival in the power of the Chōḷas of the south made its force felt on the ruler of Kāñchi; the repercussions of the waves of the newly risen Kadamba dynasty made the Pallava halt in his march towards hegemony, acknowledge the Kadamba as a brother king and share with him a part of his territory; [3] and, above all, the invasion of Samudragupta temporarily paralyzed the Pallava by encouraging his enemies. The Pallava bowed to the inevitable and retreated for a while into his homeland of Nellore and Guntur to return to Kāñchi with added vigour. Save for this short interregnum, the Pallavas ruled from Kāñchi the bulk of Āndhra south of the Krishna uninterruptedly till the Chāḷukyas drove them to hide behind the walls of their capital. No doubt, they had to put up a hard fight all the while on the Kadamba—Vākāṭaka war zone to their west and on their northern frontier with the newly risen dynasties, the Śālankāyanas and their successors the Vishṇukuṇḍins.

The Śālankāyanas inherited the Ikshvāku and the Bṛihatphalāyana kingdoms between the lower courses of the Krishna and the Gōdāvari. About the middle of the fifth century A.D. the Vishṇukuṇḍins displaced the Śālankāyanas with the help they

[1] *E. I.*, viii, p. 88, for an inscription of Mādhariputra Isvarsēna, Abhira.

[2] *E. I.*, xiv, p. 153. For inscriptions of the Chūtus, see *E. I.*, vii, p. 51; x, Ap. No. 1021, 1195.

[3] *E. I.*, viii, p. 24, Tāḷaguṇḍa inscription.

secured from the Vākāṭakas of the Central Provinces.[1] The last of the Vishnukuṇḍins accepted defeat at the hands of Puḷakēśin II and gave up his crown to the valiant Chāḷukya.

Beyond the Gōdāvari, the veil of impenetrable darkness that prevailed about the history of the region is lifted by the expedition of Samudragupta. No trace is available there to-day of Ikshvāku or Vākāṭaka rule though it is not possible to believe that both left the country out of their ambitious schemes. For sometime after 350 A.D., figure certain kings like Chandravarman of an unknown dynasty. The Gaṅgas of Kaliṅga get into the limelight about the middle of the sixth century, found an era, try to beat back the aggressive Vishṇukuṇḍins who had carried their banner of victory as far as Rāmatirtham and produce a series of powerful sovereigns who maintain their independence intact till they stoop to the Chāḷukya and let the deluge pass over. But, the Chāḷukyan hegemony had come to stay. With a natural boundary on the east and with their own kinsmen on the west, the Chāḷukyas of the Telugu country apprehended troubles from the Pallavas on the south and the Kaliṅga kings on the north. From the seventh century onward, we read of Pallava-Chāḷukya wars in the place of Pallava-Kadamba conflicts and of Chāḷukya-Kaliṅga rivalry instead of Vishṇukuṇḍin-Kaliṅga encounters.

Sad as is the story of the wars, one cherishable object had been achieved. The whole of Āndhra came under one rule. After the fall of the Śātavāhana, the country was partitioned among three or more dynasties. The beginnings of Telugu literature, the completion of the Brahminical revival and the increased economic activity resulting from a strong, unified administration were the greatest blessings of the long Chāḷukyan rule.

These, in fine, are the landmarks in the history of Āndhra between 225 and 610 A.D. dealt with in the following chapters. The account is imperfect here and there for want of more reliable evidences like a picture drawn by an artist with scanty data, but, so far as it goes, it has not violated the standard of Clio.

[1] The Vākāṭakas expanded into Andhra in the wake of Ikshvāku fall, set back the tide of Kadamba progress and proved a thorn on the sides of the Śālaṅkāyanas and the dynasty of Kaliṅga.

CHAPTER VI

THE EARLY PALLAVAS (ABOUT 225–340 A.D.)

The Pallavas, a mixed stock

MUCH has been written on the origin of the Pallavas. But, it is still true to say that 'no complete answer can be given at present'.[1] The Pallavas appear as a ruling dynasty in the south and south-east of the Śātavāhana empire immediately after the last Śātavāhana king, Puḷumāyi IV. Their earliest inscriptions are like the Nāsik inscriptions of Gautamiputra Śātakarni;[2] and their early coins[3] are similar to those of the Śātavāhanas whose rule is said, on numismatic evidence, to have extended upto the Pālār. It is, therefore, likely that the Pallava dynasty started its career as a feudatory of the Śātavāhana.

The Pallavas were first a Telugu and not a Tamil power. Telugu traditions know a certain Trilōchana Pallava as the earliest Telugu King and they are confirmed by later inscriptions. The first Chaḷukya King is said to have been met, repulsed and killed by the same Trilochana near Mudivemu (Cuddappah district). Reference has already been made to a Buddhist story making Kāla, the Nāgarāja (resembling Kālabhartr an early Pallava name) king of the region at the mouth of the Krishna. We have also the evidence of the *Mahāwamsa* which makes mention of a large number of monks attending a consecration ceremony performed by Duttagāmini from *Pallava Bogga* (100 B.C.). *Pallava Bogga* may be identified with the kingdom of Kāla in Āndhra which had close and early maritime and cultural relations with Ceylon and which was an ancient and popular home of Buddhism.[4] The earliest inscriptions of the Pallavas were found in the districts of Bellary, Guntur and Nellore and all the inscriptions of the dynasty till the rise of

[1] V. A. Smith, *Early History of India*, 1924 ed., p. 490.

[2] *E. I.*, vol. vi, p. 84; vol. i, p. 2; vol. viii, p. 143.

[3] They are doubtfully assigned to the Pallavas, see Rapson, *Coins of the Andhras, Kshatrapas, etc.* pp. 20–1, 82; Also Rapson: Indian Coins, p. 128.

[4] Geiger, Ch. xxix for *Pallava Bogga*. For Trilōchana, see Chapter IX below. For the story of Kāla, see *J. R. A. S.* 1907, p. 341

Simhavishnu were found in the districts of Guntur and Nellore. It is established on inscriptional testimony that the Telugu country south of the Krishna formed the bulk of the Pallava kingdom till the last quarter of the sixth century A.D. The omission of the Pallava from the lists of the Tamil dynasties in tradition[1] and early literature and the mention of Trilōchana Pallava as a foe of the Chōḷa in the Karikāla traditions and in the Chendalūr copperplates (fifth century A.D.) lend weight to the argument that the Pallava was an intruder into the Tamil country.

According to the Vēlūrpālaiyam copperplates (ninth century A.D.) which may be taken to contain reliable traditions of the origin of Pallava power, Virakūrcha obtained a kingdom by a nāga marriage. In fact, the early relations between the Nāga and the Pallava had become so well established by the time that the myth of the birth of Pallava himself to Asvathāman and a nāga princess had grown. So, at any rate, in the ninth century, it was acknowledged that the Pallava was not a nāga as he had to marry into a nāga family to elevate himself to the kingly position. On certain evidences, it has been argued elsewhere[2] that the Telugu country, at least the southern part of it, was nāga.[3]

The earliest Tamil literature that throws any light on the region associated with the Pallava locates a certain Tiraiyan the elder[4] in the modern Gūdūr taluk of the Nellore district with a kingdom extending to Tirupati (or Vēngadam) if not even beyond it. This Tiraiyan is called the elder to distinguish him from another Tiraiyan the younger[5] whose capital was Kāñchi. The younger Tiraiyan is traced to the solar dynasty (of Ayōdhya) and late Tamil commentators identify him as the illegitimate son of a Chōḷa king and a nāga princess.[6]

1 The Mackenzie MSS. According to traditions and the *Periyapuranam*, Karikāla introduced civilization into Kāñchi. So, the Pallava came to Kāñchi only after the Chōla.

2 The Origin of Śaivism, etc., pp. 10, 16.

3 Whether nāga denoted a race, cult or culture is not clear.

4 Aham, 85; 340.

5 *Pattuppāṭṭu-Perumbāṇārruppadai*, 29–30, 454. He and Karikāla are sung by the same poet.

6 In his full name Tondamān Ilam Tiraiyan, the last part Tiraiyan refers to the tribe to which he belonged, the tribal name originating in *tirai* (wave, or sea *sāgara*) which the prince of Kāñchi must have taken after

The Pallavas are the earliest to be associated by inscriptions with the region extending round Kāñchi. The Tiraiyar are one of the earliest to be associated by literature with the same region. If the Tiraiyar were nāgas, as it is likely since the prince of Kāñchi seems to have obtained the name Tiraiyan from his nāga mother, then the Pallavas who were not nāgas originally, came to be mixed up with them. This amalgamation of the two is borne out by a very late Tamil account which classifies the Pallava Tiraiyar as a section of the Tiraiyar.[1] It is partly on account of their mixed caste that the Pallavas were known later as *Kayavar*, *Nisar* (low caste), etc. much in the same way as the early Sanskritists classified the foreign hordes under *mlecchas*.[2]

Another tribe that is located in and beyond the region of Kāñchi by Early Tamil literature is the *Aruvālar* whose chiefs are said to have belonged to the *Oviya naga* family.[3] Neither their exact habitat nor their relation, if any, to the *Bassaronagos* of Ptolemy is known.[4] Be that as it may, the second hint that is thrown out by Tamil literature only emphasises the nāga affinity of the dynasties that ruled in the northernmost part of Tamiḷaham and beyond it. And that the Pallavas were not nāgas may be presumed from the two distinct references to nāga marriage in the Vēlūrpālaiyam plates.

The original home of the Pallavas has to be looked for outside the first Pallava kingdom in Āndhra as the lower valley of the Krishna was occupied by tribes of the Nāga stock and as the Pallava had no Nāga affinities at first. And, there will be no straining of evidence if we identify them with the Pahlavas, an ancient people who appear together with the Śakas and the Yavanas in early Sanskrit literature like the

his mother's tribe and not after his father's as the Chōḷas are not called Tiraiyar anywhere. The second part of the full name *Ilam* (young, skanda?) is used apparently in contradistinction with *Perum* (elder, Bṛihat) which was borne by the Tiraiyan of Pavittiri. And the designation Toṇḍamān, similar to Malayamān and Adigamān has a territorial significance, denoting the land of *toṇḍai* creepers.

[1] Kanakasabai Pillai. The Tamils, 1800 years ago.

[2] Gopalan: The Pallavas, Introd.

[3] *Pattuppāṭṭu-Sirupanārruppadai*, lines 111–126.

[4] M'Crindle, Ptolemy ed. by Majumdar, pp. 65, 185.

Purāṇas and the *Epics*[1] and in some early inscriptions of Vāsishṭiputra Puḷumāyi[2] and Rudradāman.[3] Dr. Jouveau-Dubreuil has traced, as far as available evidences permit, the evolution of the word and the migration of the people, Pahlava.[4] Suffice it to note here that these foreign hordes seem to have penetrated into the Deccan even before Gautamīputra as he found confusion in the social order and restored the system of castes. They seem to have come afresh to destroy the Śātavāhana empire ultimately. Evidences of Yavana rule, of marriage relations between the Śakas on the one side and the Śātavāhanas and the Ikshvākus on the other, and of a huge cataclysm, social and political, brought about by foreigners according to the *Matsya Purāna* have been pointed out in a previous chapter. The Śakas and the Yavanas have merged in our society like the later Yue-chi and the Huns and so have the Pahlavas. But, in regard to the latter, the name is still retained.[5] When the Pahlavas made inroads into Āndhra and mixed with the local tribes is enveloped in darkness.

Dr. S. K. Iyengar who has expounded the indigenous theory of the origin of the Pallavas relies upon the later equation of the Pallavas with the Toṇḍaiyar, the Kāḍavar and the Kāduveṭṭis,[6] the last titles being acquired by the clearing of forests. It is remarkable, however, that early Tamil literature inhabits the later Pallava region of history with tribes which bear no obvious relations to the Pallavas. Another interesting argument of Mr. Iyengar is the reference to two distinct Pallava kingdoms by Rājaśēkhara of about the tenth century, one in the south and the other in the north-west. But, it will be readily granted

[1] See Venkayya's article in *A.R.A.S.I.*, 1906–7, p. 221.

[2] Nāsik ins. E. I. viii, pp. 5, 9.

[3] *E.I.*, viii, p. 37. Girnar ins.; Suviśākha Pahlava was Rudradāman's minister.

[4] The Pallavas.
Ancient History of the Deccan, p. 55.

[5] Some of the Persian and Assyrian motifs in early Amarāvati sculptures may serve to remind us of early Pahlava associations with the Telugu country.

[6] *J.I.H.* ii, Pt. i.
Some contributions of S. India to Indian culture.
Gopalan: The Pallavas: Introduction.
See also—Foulkes: The Pallavas, M. Srinivasaiyengar: Tamil Studies.

that the Pallavas of the south had changed beyond recognition of their original affinities in the course of centuries of stay in and of amalgamation with the Āndhra and Tamil peoples.[1]

Again, Mr. Rasanāyagam[2] has ingeniously worked out the Chōḷa-nāga origin of the Pallavas, basing his thesis on early Tamil literature. His theory would be plausible enough if a single reference to their Chōḷa relationship had been left in the Pallava inscriptions. Nor is there any the slightest resemblance between the mythical ancestries of the Chōḷas and the Pallavas (though the Chōḷas and the Tiraiyar seem to be connected in a way in this respect). Both the scholars have, however, unravelled one-half of the Pallava mystery.

The only safe conclusion on the evidences available to us is 'it is possible that the Pallavas were not one distinct tribe or class, but a mixed population, composed partly of foreigners and partly of South Indian tribes or castes, differing in race from the Tamils, and taking their name from the title of an intruding foreign *dynasty*,[3] which obtained control over them and welded them into an aggressive political power'.[4] As the Pallava-dynasty could not have risen to such a prominent and powerful position (which it occupied in about 225 A.D.) in a short space of

[1] Dr. Iyengar quotes Tirumaṅgai's 'The Pallava, who is the ruler of the Toṇḍaiyar' to prove his identification of the Pallavas with the Toṇḍaiyar. P. xi Introd. Gopalan: The Pallavas. For one thing, there is not even a single reference to the Pallavas as a tribe in the inscriptions of the Telugu country whereas the 'Toṇḍaiyar' denotes a tribe or tribes of the land Toṇḍai. Secondly, a ruler of a tribe or tribes need not be of the same tribe. Thirdly, the reference of the Āḻvār probably distinguishes the Pallava from the Toṇḍaiyar. Curiously, on pp. xvii and xxiv, *ibid*, the Doctor speaks of the coming of the Pallavas into Tondaimandalam from the south-eastern marches of the Satavahana territory (what those 'marches' were is not defined) whereas he was, just six pages above, identifying the Pallavas and the Tondaiyar. Since Tondai and Tondaiman are mentioned in the so-called Sangam literature, shall we say that the Pallava was in the Tamil country in the so-called Sangam age *i. e.* early centuries A.D.? Again, the Pallavas as a people have to be distinguished from the Pallavas as a dynasty. Did the Pallava tribe or family come into Tondai from the 'marches'?

[2] *I.A.*, vol. lii, p. 75.

[3] Italics ours.

[4] V. A. Smith, 1924 ed., pp. 466, 482.

time, it is probable that it occupied a high place in the Śātavāhana court, governed a part of their empire as vassals and in time stepped into their shoes in South Deccan having, in the meanwhile, strengthened its position by marriage and other means.

Genealogy and Events

All our information about the Early Pallavas is derived chiefly from the Mayidavolu,[1] Hirahadagalli[2] and Kandukuru copper-plates[3] from the districts of Guntur, Bellary and Nellore. Since they are paleographically of the same age, it is possible that the kings in them refer to the same person. Thus, the following genealogy may be constructed.[4]

Sivaskanda's father About A.D. 225.
|
Mahārāja Śivaskandavarman *or*
Vijaya Skandavarman
|
Yuvarāja Buddhavarman
married Chārudēvi
|
Buddh(yan)kura

Since the father of Śivaskandavarman, the first Pallava king definitely known to history, could have become independent ruler of the region round Adōni in Bellary district only after Puḷumāyi of the Myakadōni inscription (about 225 A.D.), his

[1] *E.I.*, vol. vi, p. 84 ; *M.E.R* 1900, p. 4.

[2] *E.I.*, vol. i, p. 2.

[3] *E.I.*, vol. viii, p. 143.

[4] The table of kings of the earliest period on p. 33 of Mr. Gopalan's book contains some obvious mistakes : (*a*) There is no reason why he should omit Buddhavarman and put in Buddhyankura as the son of Skandavarman since he admits Buddhavarman as a ruler on p. 34 ; and on p. 48 he distinguishes Sivaskanda from Vijayaskanda. (Vijaya is a prefix indifferently applied to kings and capitals). (*b*) It is not explained how a Vīravarman is placed before Vishṇugōpa (340 A.D.) on p. 33 and how the same Vīra, apparently, is placed after Vishṇugōpa on p. 59. (*c*) On p. 39 again there is some confusion *re* : Buddhavarman-Buddhyankura. See p. 165 of his book for the contents of the British Museum or Kandukūru C. P. On p. 35 he says that the *decisive* consideration for identifying Sivaskanda with Vijayaskanda is paleographical similarity between their plates. On p. 39 paleographical considerations lead him to place Vijayaskanda between 275 and 340 A.D. after Sivaskanda.

accession to sovereign power may be dated towards the beginning of the second quarter of the third century A.D.[1]

The first Pallava king bequeathed to his son an extensive empire and a definite economic and religious policy as Śivaskanda does not appear to have struck a blow to build the empire and as he continued the patronage of Brahminism. Śivaskanda's father gave a great impetus to the revival of Brahminism (which was dormant on account of Buddhism) by his *yajñas* and grants of lands and crores of gold pieces to Brahmins. His distribution of one lakh of ox-ploughs must have been in pursuit of a definite scheme of forest reclamation and spread of agriculture in his kingdom. From his capital city of Kāñchi, Skanda's father ruled as far as Bellary on the one side (as Skanda has enlarged his grant there) and the Krishna on the other where there was a Pallava viceroyalty according to the Mayidavōlu copperplates.[2]

[1] Gopalan fixes the passing of Tonḍamandalam into the hands of the Pallavas from the Chōḷa feudatories about the closing years of the third century A.D., p. 36. On p. 35, he assigns Bappadeva to A.D. 215 and Skanda, his son, to about 240 A.D. If Tonḍai was not conquered by Skanda at least, who conquered it? We know so little about Skanda's successors but we know for certain that Kāñchi was his father's capital. The ruler of Kāñchi must always be presumed to be the ruler of the surrounding region. On p. 59 Gopalan assigns Śivaskanda to 220 A.D. and Vishṇugōpa, apparently, separated from him by a generation to 340 A.D.

[2] Is it possible that Vīrakūrcha was the father of Śivaskanda? Mahārāja Virakōrchavarman was a pious and victorious warrior according to the fragmentary inscription at Darsi (*E.I.* vol. i, p. 397) dated in the reign of his great grandson. Its alphabet is archaic and must be assigned prior to Ōṁgōḍu II, C.P. If in the time of the donor of the Darsi fragment the alphabet was archaic, then his great grandfather Vīrakōrcha must be assigned to a more ancient period. This Virakōrcha cannot be identified with Vīravarman of the copperplates (*I.A.*, vol. v, p. 154) as the Darsi fragment could not have been engraved in archaic alphabet in the time of Vīravarman's great grandson whom we know to be Siṁhavarman, donor of Ōṁgōḍu II, C.P. So, it is more reasonable to identify this Vīrakōrcha with the Vīrakūrcha of the Vēlūrpāḷaiyam plates (*S.I.I.*, vol. ii, pt. v) who 'acquired a kingdom simultaneously with the hand of a nāga princess' and thus founded the greatness of the Pallavas. If Vīrakūrcha, father of Śkandasishya, was the first independent Pallava King, we may not be wrong in identifying him with Bappa or father of Skandavarman Maharaja. According to the Vēlūrpāḷaiyam plates, Vīrakūrcha is removed from Kālabhartr by a generation or so. Is it likely that the Śātavāhana hegemony

Mahārāja Śivaskandavarman succeeded his father during whose reign he had played his part as Yuvarāja. He styles himself Dharma Mahārāja, agnishṭōmin, vājapēyin and aśvamēdhin. He was thus a more powerful sovereign than his father but there is no certainty that his empire was bigger than his father's. At the time of his rule, about the middle of the third century A.D., the Bṛihatphalāyanas ruled what was later known as the kingdom of Vengi and the Ikshvākus were perhaps in possession of the Āndhra country stretching from about Śri Śailam northward and extending indefinitely into Dakshina Kōsala and along the coast north of the Gōdāvari. How far south of the Krishna and for how long a period Ikshvāku sway extended is a matter for speculation though it cannot be doubted that Amarāvati with some epigraphs in Ikshvāku script was once and for a short time part of the Ikshvāku empire. How far south of Kāñchi Pallava sway extended we are unable to say but it is known from later sources [1] that there was to be a Chōḷa revival against which the Pallava could hardly contend. If Pallava power in the time of Śivaskanda covered a considerable part of Karnāṭa outside Bellary is not known, though we are told later that the Kadamba with the alliance of Brihat Bāna fought from the forests of Śri Śailam and wrested a part of his kingdom from the unwilling hands of a successor of Śivaskanda.[2]

There are two achievements attributed to a Skandasishya whom we cannot positively identify with Mahārāja Śivaskandavarman. One is the capture of the *ghatika* (university town ?) of

in Guntūr and Nellore districts was already undermined before Vīrakūrcha as it was done in some other parts of Āndhra by the Ikshvākus?

It is very strange that Gopālan locates Vīrakūrcha two generations before Yuvāmahāraja Vishṇugōpa (p. 33). He is identified with Vīravarman (same as the Vīravarman of his table on p. 33?) But see pp. 51 and 59. On p. 59 he locates Vīrakūrcha (Vīravarman) two generations after Vishṇugopa. On p. 54 Vīrakūrcha ascended the throne in 358 A.D. as his son Skandasishya (donor of Ōṁgōḍu C.P. i) was a contemporary of Satyasena, Kshatrapa. So, two generations of kings have ruled between 340 A.D. and 358 A.D., granting that Vishṇugōpa ceased to rule in 340 A.D. On p. 61, Gōpālan suggests that Vīrakūrcha alias Vīravarman is mentioned in the Darsi fragment. Then, the (archaic) fragment belonged to the age of Siṁhavarman, donor of three copper-plates. Strangest of all, is the alleged marriage between Chūta Pallava and a nāga princess referred to by Gōpālan on p. 61.

[1] Velūrpāḷaiyam C. P. *S.I.I.* ii, pt. v.

[2] Ṭālaguṇḍa ins. *E.I.* viii, p. 24.

a Śatyasēna [1] and the other is the construction of the *orukal* (single stone) *mantapa* at Tirukkaḷukunram (Chingleput district).[2] In the language of the inscriptions as well as in the administrative organization of Śivaskanda's reign may be noticed distinct northern influences which came in the train of the northern religions.

Nothing is known about the successors of Śivaskanda. The copperplate grant of Chārudēvi dated in the reign of Vijayaskandavarman, her father-in-law, records a grant to a temple of Nārāyana whose cult was already old in the Nellore district.

The next Pallava that we hear of is Vishṇugopa of Kāñchi (340 A.D.) who is said to have been defeated, among others, by the illustrious northern Emperor Samudragupta.[3] The Pallava was still at Kāñchi between the time of Śivaskanda and the time of Vishṇugōpa. But, what happened after Vishṇugōpa to the Pallava hold on Kāñchi we are merely left to conjecture. By this time, far-reaching political changes had taken place. The Ikshvākus were a small power, and their whereabouts unknown; the Śālankāyanas had usurped the kingdom of the Bṛihatphalāyanas and extended their rule upto the Ghats; the Kadambas were just rising under the fervour of a Brahmin Kshatriya; and from the Chōḷa country came a new wave of expansion which engulfed Kāñchi and its lord. The unsettlement caused by Samudragupta's expedition, the fury of the aggressive Kadamba and the Chōḷa deluge, gave endless trouble to the Pallava Vishṇugōpa or his successor. He had no other alternative than a flight to his Telugu homeland as the only other direction where he could have sought refuge was the deep sea to the east.

The Pallava was only biding his time. Kumāravishṇu mentioned as having lived sometime after Skandasishya, captured Kāñchi. And Buddhavarman, son of Kumāravishṇu, was a

[1] Vēlūrpāḷaiyam *C. P. J. I. H.*, vol. ii, pt. i, p. 39 for Dr. S. K. Iyengar's identification of Satyasena.

[2] *E. I.*, vol. iii, p. 279.

[3] While Dr. V. A. Smith dates Samudra's Southern expedition in 350 A.D. Dr. Dubreuil assigns the great event to 340 A.D. Strategic reasons must have directed the king's attention first to the north but Dr. Dubreuil follows Harisēna who composed the Allahabad ins. and dates the southern expedition earlier.

veritable submarine fire to the ocean of Chōḷa forces.[1] The Chōḷa fire was quenched and Kāñchi once more became the Pallava metropolis and continued to be so for five centuries. The Kadambas could not be so easily disposed of and many a hard battle had to be fought by the Pallava and by the Vākāṭāka to keep them within limits. Once, they overran the whole Tamil country and the Pallava bowed to the storm and let it blow over. The interesting story of the Pallava-Kadamba duel and of the doings of the successors of Vishṇugōpa of Kāñchi (about 340 A.D.) will be dealt with in a separate chapter.

[1] Vēlūrpāḷaiyam C. P. Dr. S. K. Iyengar takes the 'Chōḷa forces' to refer to the Kalabhras of Chōḷa. p. xxiii. Introd. Gopalan: The Pallavas. *See* p. xxiv for his view that there was no Chōḷa interregnum at Kāñchi before Kumāravishṇu. But, in the case of the first, the word 'Chōḷa' need not be strained to refer to a Kalamba of Chōḷa who may not be a Kaḷabhra and may turn out to be a Kadamba or of some native stock of Tanjore district. The logical inference from the Vēlūrpāḷaiyam plates can be none other than that the Chōḷa was in Kāñchi and Kumāravishṇu and his son drove him out. Gopalan after expressing agreement with his Professor's opinion suggests that Kumāravishṇu might have captured Kāñchi from a cousin of his or from the Kadamba thus tacitly coming round to the views that there were two branches of the Pallava and that there was an interregnum at Kāñchi before Kumāravishṇu. For Kalabhra-Kalamba and for Pandit Raghavaiyengar's view of the native Kalamba, see P. T. Srinivasaiyengar: History of Tamil Culture (Madras).

CHAPTER VII

THE IKSHVĀKUS (ABOUT 225–340 A.D.)

THE name Ikshvāku carries back our memories to the glorious Solar dynasty of Śri Rāmachandra. According to the *Purānas*, of the 100 sons of Ikshvāku, 48 ruled Dakshina. The foundation of Asmaka and Muḷaka (on the Upper Gōdāvari)[1] is ascribed by the *Purānas* to the Ikshvākus. While Lava ruled Uttara Kosala from Śravasti and became the founder of the dynasty of the well-known Prasenjit, Kuśa founded the city of Kusasthali[2] at the foot of the Vindhyas, married a nāga princess and held sway over Dakshina Kōsala (the kingdom proper corresponding to the modern Chattisgarh division of the Central Provinces). The last of Kuśa's descendants known to the Purāṇa was Brihadbala, but, we have reasons to think that the dynasty did not end with the beginning of *Kali* as the Purāṇas would make us understand. The recent discovery of valuable epigraphs at Nāgārjunakoṇda has given the lie direct to the tradition that Ikshvāku rule became extinct in centuries before Christ. Perhaps, even Bahubala, the last of the kings known from the said inscriptions was not the last of the Ikshvākus.[3]

Ikshvāku relationship was coveted

The high prestige that the Ikshvākus enjoyed in the Deccan may be gauged from the desire of many of the South Indian dynasties to associate themselves with them in one way or other. The Chōḷas and the Gaṅgas[4] claimed descent from them. The

[1] Muḷaka is north of Asmaka. Or, it may be the later Muḷiki nādu of inscriptions, round Śri Śailam. *Vāyu*, 88, 177–8, 198, 207. *Vishnu*, iv, 2, 3.

[2] Kōsthalapura of the Allahabad inscriptions of Samudragupta?

[3] The address to the Buddha as 'the illustrious Ikshvāku' in a Nāgārjunakoṇda inscription and the inclusion of Suddhodana and Gautama in the Ikshvāku list of the Purāṇas introduce us to a still another branch of the glorious line of kings.

[4] Rice: *Mysore and Coorg from inscriptions*, p. 30; *E.C.*, vol. vii, sh. 4, 64. For Chōḷa descent see *E.I.*, xviii, p. 26. For Ilam Tiraiyan's pedigree see *Perumbānārrupadai*, lines 29–30.

Tiraiyar chief Toṇḍaman Ilam Tiraiyan of Kāñchi is given a similar pedigree by the poet. Trilōchana Pallava is said to have come from Oudh according to some traditions and has early associations with the Śri Śailam region. The pretensions of the Chāḷukyas to have come from Ayōdhya explain their anxiety to link themselves with its famous dynasty. The Kēkayas of the Deccan were proud of their marriage alliances with the Ikshvākus and the Räjarishis.[1] The Kadambas were Häritiputras and 'perhaps descended from Angiras, Angirasa Hāritas being of the Ikshvāku lineage'.[2] If we can rely on the tentative reading of the new inscriptions by the Madras Epigraphist, one of the earliest of the Chāḷukyas (called *Chaliki* there) married an Ikshvāku princess. An Ikshvāku princess is said by a Nāgārjunakoṇda inscription to have married the king of Vanavāsi, the capital of the later Kadambas. Neither the Śātavāhanas nor the Śakas (who seem to have been mainly responsible for the dismemberment of the Śātavāhana empire) were free from the attractions of the Ikshvāku family. For, in the surname and even in one or two of the Ikshvāku names found in the new inscriptions, one may perceive the hidden relationship between the Śātavāhanas and the Ikshvākus. Dr. Vogel[3] rightly guesses that Rudradhara Bhaṭṭarika of Ujjain, the Queen of Vira Purushadatta the second Ikshvāku of Āndhradēsa known to us was a Śaka princess. Above all, one fact is clear that the Ikshvākus were the most famous family of Āndhradēsa, north of the Krishna, in the third century A.D. This position they attained after the last Śātavāhana who has been assigned to the first quarter of the third century A.D.

The Ikshvākus and the Śri Parvata Āndhras

That the Śātavāhanas ruled over Āndhradēsa in the second century A.D. has been incontrovertibly established on sound numismatic and epigraphic evidences. So, the Ikshvākus must have expanded from Dakshina Kōsala southward after the extinction of the rule of their suzerains, the Śātavāhanas (225 A.D.). The celebration of the aśvamēdha by Chāntamūla, Mahārāja and

[1] *E.C.*, vol. xi, Introd., p. 5, *D.G.* 161.
[2] *Bomb. Gaz.*, vol. i, pt. ii, p. 287, f. n. 4.
[3] *A.B.I.A.* (*Leyden*) 1927, p. 11.

Vāsishṭiputra, was an assertion of his power and independence after the break-up of the Śātavāhana empire. While his capital is not definitely known,[1] the extent of his empire was limited by the Pallava dominion in the south, south-east and south-west and by the kingdom of the Bṛihatphalāyanas in the eastern half of the present Krishna district.[2] Chāntamūla is said to have annexed the great army of Vīrūpākshapati which may be taken to mean a defeat of the king of the western direction. If the great deed was accomplished by the Ikshvāku in his capacity as general of the Śātavāhana's army is more than what we can say at present. Nor can we answer precisely who the King was that was thus overthrown. For, the last of the Śātavāhanas, Puḷumāyi IV is said to have ruled the Bellary region, and according to the *Matsya*, a dynasty of Āndhras known as the Śri Parvata Āndhras began to rule even during the life-time of the parent Śātavāhana dynasty.

The only dynasty that we know of in the Śri Śaila *Prānta* in the post-Śātavāhana period is the Ikshvāku. The only dynasty that resembles the Śātavāhana in name and surname (*e.g.* Vāsishṭiputra and Mādhariputra) and is of the Āndhra country is the Ikshvāku. Like their overlords, the Ikshvākus were great patrons of Buddhist art and letters and this cannot be said of any other Śātavāhana feudatory, the Pallava or the Bṛihatphalāyana. In fact, the Ikshvākus took up the threads where they were left and continued to add to the spiritual lustre of their land by further beautifying Śri Parvata which has deservedly been mentioned more than once as a very sacred spot in the sacred Āndhra country in the *Ārya Manjusri Mūla Kalpa*.[3]

The Ikshvākus, thus, succeeded to the cultural inheritance of the Śātavāhanas, as they did, to a large part of their temporal

[1] Vijayapuri, east of Śri Parvata (Nāgārjunakoṇda) is mentioned in an inscription and there are remains of civil buildings there. So it is likely that the capital was not far from Nāgārjunakoṇda.

[2] There is no evidence other than tradition to show that there ruled any other than the Śātavāhanas in the earliest historical period in Āndhra. Nor is it definitely known if, at any time, the Ikshvākus held sway over the whole of Āndhra. There are, however, a few place names which may indicate Ikshvāku sway. Ikshupuri (Cherukūru) in Guntur district, Kākulam in Krishna and Ganjam districts, Kākandi in Nellore district, Kākandivāda (Cocanada) in Godavari district, Kākāni in Guntur district are some of them.

[3] Vol. i, p. 88; vol. iii, pp. 627, 628.

dominion and augmented the intellectual traffic along the Krishna with the outside world. So close seems to have been the affinity between the Ikshvākus and the Śātavāhanas and identical as are the Parvata of the Parvatiya Āndhras and the Parvata of the Ikshvāku inscriptions, as also the periods of their rule that the suggestion is irresistible that perhaps the Puranic Śaila Āndhras were the same as the Ikshvākus who undoubtedly ruled over the regions round Nāgārjunakoṇda and Jaggayyapēta in the second quarter of the third century A.D.[1]

Chāntamūla and Vīra Purushadatta

Three generations of kings are supplied by the inscriptions at Nāgārjunakoṇda.[2] From an inscription of the reign of Mahārāja Mādhariputra Śri Vira Purushadaṭṭa, we get to know of his father Mahārāja Vāsishṭiputra Sri Chāntamūla. The latter was a great vēdic sacrificer and performed the agnihotra, agnishṭoma, vājapēya and aśvamēdha. He also made the gifts hiranyakoṭi, gośatasahasra and halaśatasahasra and thus patronized the Brahmin. These acts reveal the great *vaidiki* in Chāntamūla who was thus a saint-king of the Ikshvāku race. Though there is no room to suspect any partial leaning in him to the religion of the Buddha, like most of the kings of old, even this *vaidiki* must have respected all the religions then existent as the members of his family have contributed much to the Buddhist buildings on Parvata.

Chāntamūla 'of unconquerable will' had a son Mahārāja Mādhariputra Śri Vīra Purushadaṭṭa, the only Ikshvāku hitherto known to us from his Jaggayyapēta inscriptions.[3] He has been immortalized in the splendid benefactions at Nāgārjunakoṇda by the members of his family to the Buddhist communities resident there. The reign of Vīra Purushadaṭṭa was a red-letter day in the annals of Āndhra Buddhism, as royal patronage of Buddhism was not found in such a large measure at any subsequent period. Most of the ornate Ikshvāku epigraphs are of his reign and also

[1] There is such a paucity of materials for the period that we cannot hazard much beyond the realm of hypotheses. It may also be borne in mind that we know of no earlier Ikshvāku of Śri Śaila region than Chāntamūla and that no Ikshvāku calls himself Āndhra.

[2] For ins. etc. see *M.E.R.* 1926 Ap. and p. 92 ; *M.E.R.* 1927 Ap. and p. 71 ; *A.R.A.S.I.*, 1925–6 ; *A.B.I.A.* (Leyden) 1926 and 1927.

[3] *E.I.*, vol. x, Ap. Nos. 1202 and 1203.

the large number of stūpas, chaityas and vihāras recently excavated at Nāgārjunakoṇda. In his reign lasting more than twenty years, he made Parvata not only the beauty spot but the fountain of learning also in Āndhra. Curiously, the inscriptions supply us with no definite evidence as to his own religion, but it may be presumed that all his efforts were concentrated on the glorification of the religion of the great Ikshvāku, Gautama the Buddha.

The whole site of Buddhist buildings was called Vijayapuri in Śri Parvata. But, every hill had a name as every stūpa, chaitya and vihāra. The adjoining hills were called Pushpagiri, Dēvagiri, Kantakaśaila and so on.[1] The *mahāchaitya* containing the relics of the Buddha was renovated by Chāntiśri, sister of Chāntamūla, wife of Kandaśri of the Pūkiya clan and the aunt of the reigning king Vīra Purusha in his ever memorable sixth year. The ladies of the royal house take the lion's share in the erection of the buildings. The same Chāntiśri gave 300 coins (*denari masaka*) to the '*mahāchaitya*' and bestowed her attention on other communities like the Śramanas, Brahmanas, Kavanas, and Vanijas. The two queens of Vīra Purusha, Bapisri or Chāntiśri his second aunt's daughter and Rudradhara Bhaṭṭarika of Ujjain vied with each other in making gifts.

The benefactions of an upāsika Bōdhiśri deserve special mention. Many chaityas, *mantapas* and *taṭākas* were dedicated by her. In all probability she was a princess before she became an *upāsika*. The vihāras mentioned in her long inscription are Chuladhammagiri Kulaha vihāra, Silaha vihāra, Dēverakana mahāvihāra, etc. There were, among other sects, the *Pūrva* and the *Avaraśailas*, the *Bahusrutiyas* and the *Mahisāsakas*. The construction of the buildings was supervised by Chandramukha Thēra, Dharmanandi Thēra and Nāga Thēra. Upāsika Bōdhiśri is said to have dedicated a temple to the fraternities of Ceylonese monks who had converted Kashmir, Gandhāra, China, Tosali, Aparānta, Vanga, Vanavāsi, Yavana, Damila,—lura, Ceylon, etc. This version of Dr. Vogel is slightly different from that of the Madras Epigraphist according to whom 'this hill (Śri Parvata) was sacred to pilgrims from Kāsmīra, Gandhāra, China, Aparānta,

[1] There is no reason for identifying Kantakaśaila with Ghanṭasāla near the mouth of the Krishna.

Vanga, Vanavāsi, Tāmbapanni, etc.' Be that as it may, it is clear that during the third century A.D. there was intercourse between Āndhra and the above countries which was fruitful of great results for the evolution of Āndhra culture. The home of Nāgārjuna must have attracted crowds of pilgrims from far and near and Buddhist culture flowed along the Krishna to the wider world outside.[1]

Of the hundreds of monks and nuns that lived during the heyday of the history of the Ikshvākus, Upāsika Bōdhiśri and Bhadanta Ānanda, a great scholar of the fraternity of Nandigāma (Krishna district) who consecrated the mahāchaitya stand out prominent. It is really strange that Nāgārjuna finds no mention in the inscriptions discovered thus far. According to *Ārya Manjuśri Mūlakalpa*, he was called Nāgāhvaya and he was well-versed in many *śāstras*, particularly in *mayūri-vidya*. He entered Śukhāvati and attained Buddhahood. Then, the work mentions a certain Śanghā and a certain Nanda, also distinguished Bhiksus.[2]

Bahubala

The son and successor of Vīra Purushadaṭṭa was Mahārāja Vāsishṭiputra Bahubala Chāntamūla. He may be roughly assigned to the last quarter of the third century A.D. In the second year of his reign, Bhaṭṭidēvi, probably his mother, erected the Dēvi vihāra and Kandabalisri his sister and Mahārāni of Vanavāsi honoured the ascetics with another vihāra.

Perhaps Ikshvāku rule continued for a time after Bahubala in Āndhra till it was displaced by the Śālankāyanas from one side and the Kadamba-Vākāṭaka expansion from the other. There is no evidence of any Pallava—Ikshvāku conflict and the existence of inscriptions in Ikshvāku script at Amarāvati is the only indication of Ikshvāku sway to the south of the Krishna along the coast. But, as yet it cannot be said with any degree of certainty that Ikshvāku rule did not once cover the lower valley of the Krishna up to the coast. The Ikshvāku-Pallava frontier along the Krishna was perhaps shifting from time to time.

Pallava-Kadamba rivalry on the one hand and Kadamba-Vākāṭaka conflicts on the other engross our attention after the

[1] Note the remark of Fahian that pilgrims came here from neighbouring countries ; p. 63, Giles.

[2] Vol. iii, pp. 626–7, 651.

meteoric descent of Samudragupta into the Deccan (A.D. 340). We are unable to identify the Ikshvāku among the kings the northern Emperor encountered in the Deccan.[1] It is quite possible that the rise of the Kadambas was helped by the Ikshvāku as Mayūraśarman is said to have fled to the forests of Śri Śailam to war against the Pallava. There was marriage relationship between the Ikshvāku and the dynasty of Vanavāsi in the reign of Bahubala, but it would appear that the Kadambas had not risen then into a ruling power.[2]

[1] We may look for the Ikshvāku in Svāmi*datta* and in Dhananjaya of *Kōsthalapura*. A later Vāsishṭiputra Śaktivarman of Pithapuram has a surname like the Ikshvāku and the Śatāvāhana. The later dynasties like the Kākatiyas who claim solar descent may be traced to the Ikshvākus.

[2] The new inscriptions introduce to us a number of new clans like the Pūkiyas, the Dhatakas, the Sagara, the Chaliki, etc., the last two being implicit in the names of some of the princes. The Ikshvāku must have married into the local families. Chāntiśri married her brother's *senāpati*, *mahātalavara* Vāsishṭiputra Śkanda Śri of the Pūkiya clan and their son was Śkanda *Sagaram* nāga. Purushadaṭṭa's sister married Śkanda *Visakha* nāga of the Dhataka clan, the *mahādandanāyaka* of her brother. Another princess is said to have married *mahātalavara* Śkanda *Chaliki* Kammanaga of the Hiramnaga (Ilam, Ceylon, nāga ?) dynasty. Apart from the peculiar significance of the name-ending nāga, the words sagaram and Chaliki seem to be of great import, as in all probability the Tamil Tiraiyar and the later Chāḷukyas lie hidden in them.

CHAPTER VIII

THE ŚĀLANKĀYANAS (ABOUT 275–450 A.D.)

The Bṛihatphalāyanas

THE Śālankāyanas (whose dominion comprised the modern Krishna and West Gōdāvari districts) probably succeeded to the kingdom of the Bṛihatphalāyanas who have left us but a single trace of their power in the Koṇḍamudi copperplates.[1] The epigraph is in prakrit and in archaic script similar to the early Pallava inscriptions of Sivaskandavarman. So, Mahārāja Jayavarman, Bṛihatphalāyana, belonged to the same epoch, more or less, as Mahārāja Sivaskandavarman of Kāñchi. While the Bṛihatphalāyanas ruled north of the Krishna along the coast, the Pallavas ruled south of the river and the Ikshvākus west of the Ghats and perhaps north of the Gōdāvari along the coast.

The Koṇḍamudi plates refer to the region round Masulipaṭnam, the Kūdūra of the inscription referring to Kūdūru near that town. Kūdūru cannot be identified with modern Gūdūr as the latter was then within the kingdom of the Pallava (and at some unknown period within the principality of the *Perum* Tiraiyan[2] according to early Tamil literature). The name Bṛihatphalāyana was perhaps a family name as such a *gotra* is not found in the extant lists.[3] Under the influence of Brahminism, the chiefs of the mixed tribes along the Krishna and the Gōdāvari assumed Brahminical *gotras*[4] and titles and adopted Brahminical rites. The Bṛihatphalāyanas were one such family and assumed the title of Mahārājas on the decline of Śātavāhana overlordship (225 A.D.). Jayavarman was a follower of Brahminism and a devotee of Śiva. What relations his family bore to the expanding Ikshvāku and the neighbouring Pallava and what happened to it after the reign of Jayavarman in the third quarter

[1] *E.I.*, vol. vi, p. 315.

[2] It is interesting to note the prefix *Bṛihat* to the Bāna, to this Tiraiyan and to the dynasty under notice.

[3] But, many *gotras* have been lost.

[4] In contrast to the Śātavāhanas.

of the third century A.D. are unknown. But, it may be presumed that the Bṛihatphalāyanas were succeeded by the Śālaṅkāyanas after about 275 A.D. to which date, more or less, may be assigned Vijayadēvavarman, Śālaṅkāyana and aśvamēdhin.

Śālaṅkāyana Genealogy

Śālaṅkāyana was a Vēdic *rishi* and his *gotra* was adopted by this dynasty of Vēngi. Visvāmitra, Śālaṅkāyana and Kausika are the three *pravaras* of the Visvāmitra *gana.*[1] Ptolemy[2] locates a tribe, the *Salakenoi* somewhere about the Oroudian mountains bordering the region of the *Maisoloi* but neither its exact locality nor its relation to the Śālankāyanas or to the Chāḷukyas can be ascertained at present. A similarity in the names of the Pallava, Bṛihatphalāyana, Śālaṅkāyana and other kings, the epithet *pitribhakta* which they bore and the emblem of the bull which they had, raise a presumption about the sameness of their stock.[3]

The history of the Śālaṅkāyanas has to be reconstructed from half-a-dozen copperplate charters.[4] Working from paleographic evidence and from the Samudragupta-Hastivarman synchronism supplied by the Allahabad Pillar inscription, we may arrive at a workable genealogy and chronology. The two prakrit grants must be given precedence in point of time to the Sanskrit grants. Thus, Vijayadēvavarman of the Ellore prakrit grant and Vijayanandivarman and his son Vijaya Buddhavarman of another prakrit charter (now lost) came prior to Hastivarman(340 A.D.)[5] mentioned

[1] Pargiter: Indian Historical tradition, p. 237. *M. R. College Magazine* (Vizianagram) October 1922, p. 46.

[2] p. 172, M'Crindle: Ptolemy, ed. by Majumdar.

[3] It is this similarity that has made some writers infer that the Pallavas were once rulers up to the Mahānadi. See Dr. V. A. Smith: Oxford History of India, p. 207.

[4] (*a*) Ellore Prakrit grant, *E.I.*, vol. ix, p. 56.

(*b*) Another Prakrit grant (unpublished), *I.A.*, vol. v, p. 175; vol. ix, p. 100.

(*c*) Pedda Vegi C. P. *Bhārati*, August 1924.

(*d*) Kollēru, C. P. *I.A.*, vol. v, p. 175.

(*e*) Kantēru, C. P., vol. ii. *M.E.R.* 1925, p. 73.

(*f*) Kantēru, C. P. *I.*, *M. E. R.*, 1925, p. 73, Also *M. R. College Magazine* (Vizianagram), October 1922.

[5] It is strange that even in the latest edition of Dr. Smith's *Early History* Hastivarman is called Pallava. Also Kurāla of Mantarāja is wrongly identified with lake Koḷḷēru which is near Vengi the Śālaṅkāyana capital.

by the Allahabad inscription and by the Pedda Vēgi plates (in the latter as the great grandfather of the donor). It is not possible to assign to the kings of the prakrit charters a fourth century datum as prakrit inscriptions were rare then. Nothing more is known of the second and third kings of the prakrit charters. Vijayadēvavarman may be supposed to have founded the Śālankāyana power in Vengi as he celebrated the aśvamēdha, half a century after the Ikshvāku Chāntamūla who had performed the sacrifice on a similar occasion.

The Pedda Vegi plates supply four generations of kings in continuous succession as father and son, Hastivarman, Nandivarman, Chandravarman and Nandivarman the donor. In this list, the first was the same as the Vengi foe of Samudragupta and the script of the charter would confirm the datum for Hastivarman. The Kollēru grant of Vijayanandivarman mentions the donor as the eldest son of Chandravarman. There are two reasons for identifying the two kings of this charter with similar names in the Peddavegi plates: (1) the Kollēru and the Peddavegi plates have the same *ājnāpti* Mulakūru Bhōjaka (though it is possible that the reference was to the official of Mulakūru and not to a proper name), and (2) it is impossible to identify this Nandivarman the donor with Vijayanandivarman of the Prakrit grant or with Nandivarman, son of Hastivarman, of the Peddavegi plates as the Kollēru donor calls himself the son of Chandravarman and not of Hastivarman. Again, the resemblance in script between the Kollēru and the Peddavegi plates has to be taken into account.

The Kantēru copperplates II may or may not be assigned to the donor of the Kollēru, Nandivarman. The epigraphist sees some slight paleographic difficulty in identifying the Nandivarmans, the donors of the Kollēru and the Kantēru II grants. Nandivarman of the latter may be the Nandivarman, son of Hastivarman. But, this does not vitiate our argument either as to the genealogy or the chronology of the period. Lastly, there is the charter of Vijayaskandavarman, Kantēru I. There is no place for him in the genealogy of the Peddavegi plates as they give a continuous succession for four generations. The script of Vijayaskanda's inscription is similar to that of the grants of Nandivarman, eldest son of Chandravarman. So, Vijayaskanda came sometime after Nandivarman. Perhaps, Vijayaskanda came immediately after Nandivarman as it may not be possible to allow chronologically any other successor besides.

Mahārāja Vijayadēvavarman (Ellore C. P.)
:
Vijayanandivarman (I)
|
son
Yuvarāja Vijaya Buddhavarman (a Prakrit C. P.)
:
Mahārāja Hastivarman, 340 A. D.
|
son
Mahārāja Nandivarman (II) (Kantēru C. P. II).
|
son
Mahārāja Chandravarman
|
eldest son
Mahārāja Vijayanandivarman III (Peddavēgi C. P. and Kollēru C. P.) — ? Mahārāja Vijayaskandavarman (Kanṭēru C.P. I.

Chronology and some events

Besides the paleography of the plates, the only other determining factor for the chronology of the Śālankāyana kings is the contemporaneity of Samudragupta and Hastivarman of Vengi (about 340 A.D.). From this sheet anchor, we may work backward and forward allowing about 25 years as the maximum for each generation. We may also bear in mind some other facts relevant to this chronological scheme. Vijayadēvavarman calls himself king of Vengipura and he was a mighty Mahārāja. He could not have assumed the lordship of Vengi (near Ellore) when the Bṛihatphalāyana Jayavarman ruled very near Vengi, i.e., in and round Masulipaṭnam. It is, again, unlikely that Vijayadēva performed a horse-sacrifice when the Ikshvāku power extended upto Jaggayyapētā in the reign of Vīra Purushadaṭṭa. So, Vijayadēva, Śālaṅkāyana, ascended the throne some time in the last quarter of the third century A.D. Arguing now from the Hastivarman datum, we must allow for *at least* two generations between Vijayadēva and Hastivarman and thus we arrive at the same date, more or less, for Vijayadēva.

Working forward from Hastivarman, we arrive at about 440 A.D. for the end of the rule of Vijayanandi, donor of the Peddavegi plates. His successor (brother ?) Vijayaskanda ruled for some time when his realm was invaded by the Pallava from the south and subsequently taken from him (or from the Pallava) by the Vishṇukuṇḍins who were rising into prominence to the west and to the north of the Śālaṅkāyana. Closely interwoven with the chronology of the Śālaṅkāyanas is that of the Vishṇukuṇḍins one of whose plates supplies a relationship with the Vākāṭaka chronology, the date of the last Vishṇukuṇḍin itself being determined by the arrival of Puḷakēśin II and his brother Vishṇuvardhana. In the genealogy and chronology of the Śālaṅkāyanas we have left some inevitable gaps but they have not stood in the way of arriving at approximate results as to the general scheme.

Mahārāja Vijayadēva the aśvamēdhin was the first to come out of obscurity and claim a high position among kings. Vengipura (represented to-day by the hamlets of Peddavēgi and Chinnavēgi, 6 miles from Ellore) was the capital of all the Śālaṅkāyana kings. The Bṛihatphalāyana power was destroyed; the Ikshvākus were on the decline and could not have clung to the Jaggayyapēta region on account of the new Śālaṅkāyana supremacy. There is no record, however, of Pallava-Ikshvāku or of Śālaṅkāyana-Ikshvāku conflicts. Vijayadēva was a patron of Brahmins and a devotee of Śiva and the Sun. At Peddavēgi are the ruins of a temple to the Sun which is reminiscent of Śālaṅkāyana associations.

Hastivarman is said to have won many military triumphs, over whom it is not stated. The Allahabad inscription reveals the utter dismemberment of Kaliṅga and Āndhra about the middle of the fourth century A.D. Hasti's war exploits may allude to his part against Samudragupta and to his victories, if any, over his neighbours of Pithāpuram, Pālakka and Kāñchi. The aftermath of Samudragupta's march seems to have been the weakening of the Pallava, the revival of the Chōḷa, and the rise of the Kadamba. So, the Śālaṅkāyana was supreme. While little is known of the son of Hasti, Nandivarman the Charitable, Chandravarman seems to have inherited the warlike qualities of his grandfather. Chandra was the master of his neighbours. The Pallava charters speak of the numerous wars that Vīravarman and Skandavarman his son had to wage (against their neighbours). Attempts at exercising control over his neighbours ceased with Chandravarman, as by the beginning of the fifth century, Pallava expansion had begun once more. Vijayanandi III is known to us only as a worshipper of Sūrya and Vishṇu, his Peddavēgi plates recording a grant to a temple of Vishṇu, lord of the three worlds.

The attention of the Pallava was first directed to the south from his homeland of Nellore and Guntur and Kumāravishṇu recaptured Kāñchi and his son drove out the Chōḷa forces at the end of the fourth century A.D. Pallava expansion northward is evidenced by the Māngaḍur grant of Siṁhavarman which donates a village in Vengōrāshṭra (Vengi). This Siṁhavarman was a contemporary, more or less, of the Śālaṅkāyana Vijayaskanda-varman of Vengi. So, the Pallava interregnum in the kingdom of Vengi took place in the time of the last-known Śālaṅkāyana. We do not know if the Śālaṅkāyana continued in Vengi as a tributary prince or if the Vishṇukuṇḍin conquered the kingdom of Vengi from the Pallava. Equally dark is the extent of the temporary Pallava sway in the northern districts in point of time as well as in point of territory. The rule could have lasted only for a short time as about the middle of the fifth century the Vishṇukuṇḍin became ruler of Vengi. Mādhava III the first Visṇukuṇḍin to rule along the coast has made a grant from his camp at Kudavāda in the Gōdāvari district, and his great grandson Vikramēndra has made a grant in the Krishna district. It may be plausibly argued that the Śālaṅkāyana held to Vengipura as the first mention of Lendulūru (modern Dendalūru) near Vengi as the Vishṇukuṇḍin capital occurs in an inscription of the great grandson of Mādhava III. But, it may be borne in mind that the last Śālaṅkāyana plates so far discovered cannot be placed in the sixth century and that the Śālaṅkāyanas and the Vishṇukuṇḍins could not have ruled side by side as Mahārājas for any length of time. It is equally difficult to assign a long period to the Pallava at Vengi between the last Śālaṅkāyana and the first Vishṇukuṇḍin rulers of the area.

Brahminical Revival

Within the small ambit of territory delimited by the kings of Kaliṅga north of the Gōdāvari, by the Pallavas south of the Krishna and by the Kadamba-Vākāṭaka war zone on the west, the Śālaṅkāyanas ruled with the proud and great title of Mahārāja, accelerating the revival of Brahminism and the resuscitation of Sanskrit language and literature. The threads of their policy were taken up by the Vishṇukuṇḍins and a new impetus was given to the rising tide of Brahminism by the protégé of the Vākāṭakas who were themselves in close touch with the classical revival of the Gupta age in the north.[1] Āndhradēsa is thus slowly lost to Buddhism with which her culture is saturated and the Kadambas, the Gaṅgas and the Pallavas of the south come within the sphere of the Gupta religious and cultural sway. The cult of sacrifices largely swept away its enemy into the sea and assumed great importance in the state. *Pūrvamimāmsa* was practised to a fault and the Brahmins, ever delighting in *yajnas*, lighted the sacred fires which slowly quenched the Buddhist and scorched the Jaina creeds to death. The mention in the inscriptions of the Śālaṅkāyana and other later dynasties of only Hindu temples and the reference in those records to Brahmins of various *gōtras* patronised by kings and *yajnas* celebrated by the rulers is a significant commentary on the relative positions of Buddhism and Brahminism. Kumārila Bhaṭṭa, Sri Śankarāchārya and the Bhakti cult were still to come with tempestuous force to Āndhradēsa to wipe away the two religions, Buddhism and Jainism, which had lost all vitality.

[1] Fahian remarks about the desertion of, and the Brahminical revival in *Poloyu* (Parvata).

D. 1518.

General View of the Rock-Cut Temple, Bhiravakonda, Nellore Dt.

CHAPTER IX

THE LATER PALLAVAS (ABOUT 340–610 A.D.)

Genealogy

THERE is little difficulty in putting together the lists of kings supplied by the following copperplates and in evolving a genealogical table agreeable to the paleographic evidence and the historical facts supplied by them :—Ōṁgōḍu I, Uruvapalli, Pikira, Ōṁgōḍu II, Māngaḍūr and Chūra grants.[1] The earliest of these is Ōṁgōḍu I which resembles the Prakrit grants in point of dating and which supplies the following kings :—

Kumāravishṇu, aśvamēdhin
son
Skandavarman, acquired a kingdom
son
Vīravarman, a great victor
son
Vijayaskandavarman, donor of the C.P. in his 33rd year.

The kings found in Pikira, Māngaḍūr and Ōṁgōḍu II copperplates are the same, Vīravarman, Skandavarman, Yuvamahārāja Vishṇugōpa and Siṁhavarman in continuous succession as father and son. So, this list may be tacked on without dispute to the above, identifying Vīravarman, son of Skandavarman of Ōṁgōḍu I and Vīravarman of the three later copperplates. Thus,

1. Kumāravishṇu
son
2. Skandavarman
son
3. Vīravarman
son
4. Vijayaskandavarman
son
5. Yuvamahārāja Vishṇugōpa
son
6. Siṁhavarman

[1] *a*. Ōṁgōḍu I (Guntūr district) *E.I.*, vol. xv, p. 246, issued from Tāmbrāpa (Chebrōlu) Guntūr district.

b. Uruvapalli (Nellore district) *I. A.*, vol. v, p. 50, issued from Palakkada (Nellore district).

c. Pikira (Nellore district) *E.I.*, vol. viii, p 159, issued from Menmatura.

d. Ōṁgōḍu II *E.I.*, vol. xv, p. 252 ; *M.E.R.* 1914, p. 82.

e. Māngaḍūr (in Vengi, Krishna district) *I.A.*, vol. v, p. 154, issued from Dasanapura (Nellore district).

f. Chūra, *M.E.R.* 1914, p. 82.

The Uruvapalli grant gives Nos. 2–5 in the above list, and No. 5, the donor Vishṇugōpa dates the charter in the eleventh year of the reign of a certain Siṁhavarman. Dr. Fleet identified this Siṁhavarman as the elder brother of Vishṇugōpa and Dr. Dubreuil has fallen in with the view of Dr. Fleet. While, Dr. S. K. Iyengar has identified him with No. 6 in the above list, the son of Vishṇugōpa on the ground that Vishṇugōpa did not ascend the throne as king. Apart from the improbability of the father being Yuvarāja in his son's reign, the Vēlūrpāḷaiyam plates refer to a king Vishṇugōpa before Nandivarman and he calls himself a great victor which shows that he took great interest in temporal matters and nothing seems to have prevented him from ascending the throne before his son unless it were the long reign of his elder brother Siṁhavarman. The Chūra plates add to the above list their donor Vijaya Vishṇugōpavarman, son of Siṁhavarman No. 6 and, curiously enough, call the father of Siṁhavarman, Mahārāja Vishṇugōpavarman.

So far, the arrangement is flawless. The primary difficulty arises in fitting in with the above list the line of kings found in the Chendalūr copperplates.[1] The difficulty is the greater as they are dated from Kāñchi while the half-a-dozen charters mentioned hitherto were issued either from Nellore or from Guntūr district. Skandavarman, Kumāravishṇu, Buddhavarman and Kumāravishṇu figure in the Chendalūr grant which is assigned in point of script to a period between 450–550 A.D.

Dr. Dubreuil has identified the first Kumāravishṇu of the Chendalūr grant with No. 1 in our list above. Thus, he added a Skandavarman above Kumāravishṇu and arrived at

Skandavarman
|
Kumāravishṇu
- Buddhavarman
  - Kumāravishṇu (donor of Chendalūr C.P.)
- Skandavarman
  - Vīravarman
    - Skandavarman (donor of Ōṁgōḍu I)
      - Siṁhavarman
      - Y. R. Vishṇugōpa (donor of Uruvapalli)

[1] *E.I.*, vol. viii, p. 233.

The difficulty in the above arrangement seems to be of a serious kind as the donor of the Chenḍalūr copperplates of about the fifth century is placed a generation earlier than Skandavarman, donor of Ōṁgōḍu I grant which, made in his 33rd year, was nearer the age of Prakrit grants in point of dating, etc. The French savant added Skandavarman and Nandivarman of the Udayēndiram grant below Siṁhavarman.[1]

Dr. S. K. Iyengār, whose arrangement was followed, more or less, by Mr. Gōpālan[2] solved the problem in a different way.

Skandavarman

son Siṁhavarman I	son Y. R. Vishṇugōpa (donor of Uruvappalli C. P.)	Kumāravishṇu I
son Skandavarman II	son Siṁhavarman II (donor of Pikira, Māngaḍur and Ōṁgōḍu II C. P.)	Buddhavarman
son Nandivarman (donor of Udayēndiram C. P.)	son Vishṇugōpa (donor of Chūra C. P.)	Kumāravishṇu II (donor of Chenḍalūr C. P.)
	Siṁhavarman III	

The obvious defect in the above scheme is chronological. How to provide for three sets of contemporaries, especially when the Doctor does not believe in the theory of two branches of the Pallava dynasty, has not been properly taken into account. Of the nine descendants of Skandavarman, not even one can be omitted from the ruling list (including his second son Yuvamahārāja Vishṇugōpa) as there is inscriptional evidence to prove that everyone was a Mahārāja. In assigning dates and places in succession for the kings of his list, Mr. Gōpālan passes on from one branch to another in an arbitrary manner and chooses kings in succession in no particular order. 'The probability seems to be that soon after the reigns of Siṁhavarman II and Skandavarman II . . . . the Pallava kings Kumāravishṇu II, who captured Kāñchi, Nandivarman I, Siṁhavarman III occupied the Pallava throne . . . .'[3] If it is assumed that all the three

[1] *S.I.I.*, vol. ii, p. 361.
[2] p. 59.
[3] Pp. 68-69. Very strange it is that Kumāravishṇu II is said to have captured Kāñchi expressly against the available evidence. Our arrangement

branches ruled from Kāñchi and if any of the branches is taken down to the end, as it must be done according to the inscriptions, then it will become too late for the earlier members of the other two branches to rule, if not to live. The point may be explained further. The Kumāravishṇu branch is placed earlier than Vishṇugōpa and others and next to Skandasishya in the Vēlūrpālaiyam plates [1] and it is assigned an early place in the Vāyalūr list [2] however confused it might be in other respects. However, to follow Dr. Iyengār and Gōpālan, let us place the Kumāravishṇu branch next to Skandavarman as they do. Then, Kumāravishṇu I who captured Kāñchi was followed by his son Buddhavarman according to the Chendalūr and Vēlūrpālaiyam plates and Buddhavarman by Kumāravishṇu II according to the Chendalūr plates. Is it reasonable then to assign the next places in the chronological scheme to Siṁhavarman and Vishṇugōpa of the two *senior* branches, the grandfathers of Kumāravishṇu II? Or, let us take the first line as succeeding Skandavarman. Then, Siṁhavarman

of the available facts must be based on a historical and logical basis. Was there no rule of succession? Similarly, Dr. S. K. Iyengār confounds the Kumāravishṇus on pp. xxiv–v. Compare the table on p. 59. On p. 53 Mr. Gōpālan assigns Skandavarman, son of Virakurcha and father of Siṁhavarman, Vishṇugōpa and Kumāravishṇu I, to 388 A.D.

[1] *S. I. I.*, vol. ii, pt. v.

Kālabhartr
|
son
Chūtapallava
:
Virakūrcha, *married* a nāga.
|
son
Skandasishya, took the *ghatika* of Satyasena
:
Kumāravishṇu captured Kāñchi
|
son
Buddhavarman, defeated the Chōḷas
:
Vishṇugōpa
:
Nandivarman
:
Siṁhavarman
|
son
Siṁhavishṇu

[2] *M. E. R.* 1908–9; Dubreuil: The Pallavas, p. 20.

must be followed by a Skandavarman according to the Penukonda plates and the spurious Udayēndiram grant.[1] And when we take down the line to Nandivarman, it will be too late for the earlier members of the other branches. Nor will it be possible to allow the brothers Siṁhavarman, Vishṇugōpa and Kumāravishṇu to succeed one after another and then pass on to the next generation and so on. The essential difficulty arises on account of the fact that all were Mahārājas who must be assigned places in succession to Kāñchi. Thus, chronological confusion results from this scheme into which three errors have crept: (*a*) the three sets of kings were contemporaneous, whereas it is clear that the Kumāravishṇu branch came earlier than the Vishṇugōpa line and it would appear that the first to capture Kāñchi was Kumāravishṇu after whom alone the rest of the later Pallavas of Kāñchi must have come, (*b*) there was only one Pallava dynasty ruling from Kāñchi and there was no other in the northern districts, though none of the charters of Vishṇugōpa's branch is dated from Kāñchi and there are as many as five of them, and (*c*) the identification of Siṁhavarman of the Uruvappalli plates and Siṁhavarman son of Vishṇugōpa and the consequent confusion of the two Siṁhavarmans and their achievements.[2]

[1] The grant supplies Skandavarman, his son Siṁhavarman a great hero, his son Skandavarman and his son Nandivarman. *S. I. I.*, vol. ii, p. 361; *I. A.*, vol. viii, p. 169, 213; *E. I.* iii, p. 142. For the Penukonda plates, see *E. I.* xiv, p. 331. *Note this Siṁhavarman a great hero had a son Skandavarman, while, another Siṁhavarman donor of three grants had a son Vijaya Vishṇugōpavarman.* The two Siṁhas are not identical. So it is reasonable to assume that the Penukonda plates refer to Siṁhavarman 'the great hero' and his son Skandavarman and not to Siṁhavarman II and Skandavarman II his successor of Mr. Gopalan's list, p.59; 68–69 of his book.

[2] Siṁhavarman brother of Vishṇugōpa has to be clearly distinguished from Siṁhavarman son of Vishṇugōpa. In our opinion the latter was not a king of Kāñchi though he was undoubtedly a great king and occupied temporarily the Śālankāyana kingdom. The first Siṁhavarman and his son Skandavarman are mentioned in the Penukonda C.P. The first Siṁhavarman was the contemporary of Dignāga of Kāñchi. He is mentioned in the *Lokavibhāga* as the ruler of Kāñchi. There was always the utmost friendliness between the two branches of the Pallavas and on more than one occasion the northern line supplied a king to Kāñchi. Probably it was during the Pallava

There is no reason why we should omit some kings arbitrarily from a chronological frame-work. When it is distinctly known that Kumāravishṇu and his son Buddhavarman were Mahārājas and distinguished ones too, it is not easily understood why they should be passed over and why only the donor of the Cheṇḍalūr plates should be selected as ruler in his branch. The succession from Siṁhavarman, son of Skandavarman, down to Siṁhavishṇu is more or less uninterrupted if the lists contained in the Penukonda, Vāyalur and Vēlūrpālaiyam plates are read together. Can it be contended that Kāñchi was captured by a Kumāravishṇu, and the Chōḷas were driven out by Buddhāvarman between Siṁhavarman and Siṁhavishṇu ? If Vishṇugōpa issued his Uruvappalli grant in his son's reign according to Dr. Iyengār and Gōpālan, then what was the place that Siṁhavarman and his son Skandavarman of their list were occupying then ?

All these difficulties are easily got over by Dr. Dubreuil's arrangement. By putting together the relevant parts of the Udayēndiram, Vēlūrpālaiyam and Vāyalūr inscriptions, he gives a continuous succession from Siṁhavarman to Siṁhavishṇu, thus.[1] The whole scheme is clear, logical, chronologically sound and paleographically unexceptionable save for the flaw we have referred to already.

interregnum in Vēṅgi that Dignāga went there and Buddhadatta was patronized. See Gōpālan, pp. 62, 69, for his identification of the two Siṁhavarmans.

[1] *The Ancient History of the Deccan*, p. 68.

Skandavarman I
- Kumāravishṇu I
  - Buddhavarman
    - Kumāravishṇu II
  - Skandavarman
    - Vīravarman
      - Skandavarman
        - Siṁhavarman I ac. 435 A. D.
          - Skandavarman II
            - Nandivarman
              - Siṁhavarman II
                - Siṁhavishṇu ac. 575
        - Y. R. Vishṇugōpa
          - Siṁhavarman
            - Vishṇugōpavarman
              - Siṁhavarman
                - Siṁhavishṇu ac. 575

In fitting in the Chenḍalūr copperplates with the Ōṁgōḍu I grant, the question may be asked, why should we not identify Skandavarman of the Chenḍalūr copperplates with the first Skandavarman of Ōṁgōḍu I grant? Then we will arrive at

Kumāravishṇu I aśvamēdhin
son
Skandavarman, acquired a kingdom

- son: Kumāravishṇu II captured Kāñchi
  - son: Buddhavarman defeated the Chōḷas
    - son: Kumāravishṇu III
- son: Vīravarman a great victor
  - son: Skandavarman a hero of 100 battles
    - son: Siṁhavarman ac. 435
      - son: Skandavarman
        - son: Nandivarman
          - : Siṁhavarman
            - son: Siṁhavishṇu ac. 575
    - Y. R. Vishṇugōpa
      - son: Siṁhavarman
        - son: Vishṇugōpa
          - : Siṁhavarman
            - son: Siṁhavishṇu

In the above scheme, the paleographic defect of Dr. Dubreuil's is avoided but we have to put in three kings of the name of Kumāravishṇu whereas even in the longest list in the Vāyalūr inscription there are only two of that name. Again, the chronological difficulty has to be overcome. In the above scheme, Kumāravishṇu, father of Buddhavarman, must be assigned to about 360 A.D. allowing 25 years for each generation backward from Siṁhavarman (ac. 435). Then, we come to the border of the Early Pallavas whom we have dealt with in an earlier chapter. While it is impossible at present to identify Kumāravishṇu and his son Skandavarman with the Early Pallavas (the early Skandavarman having ruled about the third quarter of the third century), unless we date the beginnings of Pallava rule at Kāñchi at the end of the third century A.D., it is equally difficult to assign two such distinguished predecessors to Kumāravishṇu, the captor of Kāñchi somewhere between 300 and

350 A.D. If we identify Skandavarman son of Kumāravishṇu in the above list with the Mahārāja Sivaskandavarman (ac. 250 A.D.), then it is untenable that a son of his should succeed in about 360 A.D. In fact, the relation between the Early Pallavas, Sivaskandavarman, Buddhavarman and Vishṇugōpa and the later Pallavas Skandavarman, Kumāravishṇu and others is not obvious though it is undoubted that the later Pallavas (of the Sanskrit charters) were lineally descended of the early Pallavas (of the prakrit charters).

Dr. Dubreuil, however, offers the following explanation for the paleographic defect in his scheme. 'If, instead of comparing the letters, we compare the general aspect of the writings, the Chenḍalūr plates appear to be a little irregular and disorderly which is a characteristic of the ancient documents, whereas, the plates of Uruvappalli, Māngaḍūr, Pikira possess the order and regularity that belong to more modern writings. However, I do not believe that, in general, a comparison of the alphabets can give us any very correct information. Not only the plates of the Pallavas but also those of the Gaṅgas and the Kadambas prove that the alphabets differ much according to the scribes who have engraved the plates; and the documents of the same reign do not sometimes resemble one another. Lastly, I think that there is no need to compare the Chenḍalūr plates dated from Kāñchipuram with those of Uruvappalli dated from Palakkada, Māngaḍūr dated from Dasanapura and Pikira dated from Mēnmatura: the towns Palakkada, Dasanapura and Mēnmatura were probably in the Gunṭūr district, that is, far away from Kāñchipuram and the difference of the countries fully explains the difference in the alphabets.'[1]

Chronology

There is only one definite date in Pallava history, that given by *Lōkavibhāga*[2] according to which a certain Siṁhavarman ascended the throne of Kāñchi in about 435 A.D. This Siṁhavarman was the father of a Skandavarman according to the

[1] *The Ancient History of the Deccan*, p. 65.

[2] Mys. Arch. Rep. 1909–10, p. 45; *J.R.A.S.* 1915, p. 471. Mr. Krishṇa Śāstri does not agree with the *Lōkavibhāga* datum (*E. I.* xv, p. 252) because it does not agree with certain astronomical particulars mentioned in Ōṁgōḍu C. P. ii. But, the Siṁha of *Lōkavibhāga* was not the Siṁha of Ōṁgōḍu.

Udayēndiram grant and both are mentioned in the Penukonda plates of Mādhava Gaṅga as having successively crowned two Gaṅga kings. Another datum of which we may be sure, more or less, is that of Siṁhavishṇu, a contemporary of Vishṇuvardhana and the poet Bhāravi.[1] Working from the chronology of the western Chāḷukyas, we arrive at the same date, the last quarter of the sixth century A.D. for Siṁhavishṇu. If we include Vishṇugōpa, after Siṁhavarman there ruled five kings between 435 and 575 A.D. and allowing for an interruption after Nandivarman on account of an apparent break in succession and perhaps on account of Kadamba troubles also, the average for each reign is not high. Three more generations before Siṁhavarman would take us back to about 360 A.D. for Kumāravishṇu the Captor of Kāñchi.

Were there two branches?

The Early Pallavas described in Chapter VI were the ancestors of the Later Pallavas. But, the link between the two is not clear at present. Originally it was the custom to inscribe in Prakrit but Prakrit gave way to Sanskrit in course of time.

As only the Chenḍalūr plates among Pallava inscriptions of the fifth and sixth centuries mention Kāñchi and connect the Pallavas with the city, we have to infer that the other Pallavas who date their copperplates from places in Nellore and Gunṭūr districts were not connected with Kāñchi at all. If they had been related to Kāñchi, they would have clearly said so, as the Early Pallava and the Chenḍalūr grants say. Again, the order of succession and chronology of the plates dated from Nellore and Gunṭūr districts are without any gap and the kings of the Chenḍalūr and Udayēndiram grants cannot be fitted into the list. In whatever order we may arrange the kings of these Pallava grants, we have to confront two lines of contemporary kings after the time of Vishṇugōpa (340 A.D.) A certain Ugravarman of Palakka (Palakkada ?) mentioned as a contemporary of Samudragupta sounds like a Pallave name. And a pillar inscription at Amarāvati in early Pallava script contains a Pallava dynasty.[2] These would lead us to infer there was another branch of the Pallavas in the Telugu districts as different from the

[1] Proc. of the Oriental Conference, 1922 and 1926.

[2] *S.I.I.* vol. i, p. 25; *E.I.* vol. xviii, p. 148.

Pallavas of Kāñchi. Howsoever we may arrange the genealogy, a separate line of kings from Vīravarman down to Vishṇugōpa of the Chūra plates not connected in any way so far known with Kāñchi, has to be postulated and they were cousins of the main line. To assign the kings of the two branches places in succession to the same kingdom of Kāñchi will lead to chronological impossibilities.[1] The northern branch succeeded to Kāñchi when Siṁhavarman son of Skandavarman and, later, Siṁhavishṇu ascended the throne in the south.

Was there a Chōḷa Interregnum? [2]

The Pallavas of Kāñchi had to contend against the Chōḷas when they occupied Toṇḍai, for Kāñchi was within easy reach of only that Tamil dynasty, and was prized by the ambitious Chōḷas and made a part of their empire. The Chōḷas were the only foes the Pallavas could have had in the third century A.D. to threaten their dominion of Kāñchi.

From the inscriptions of Mahārāja Sivaskandavarman it is clear that the Pallava sway round Kāñchi was undisputed. Some time after Vishṇugōpa must have occurred one of the epochs of Chōḷa revival. For, Kumāravishṇu the aśvamēdhin who may be assigned to about 360 A.D. is said to have captured Kāñchi. And what is more, his son Buddhavarman is said to have fought hard against the Chōḷas. The probabilities are that the Chōḷas invaded and took the Pallava capital and a little later, the Pallava recaptured it.

Karikāla the great Chōḷa emperor is connected by tradition with a Trilōchana Pallava. Karikāla is said to have punished Trilōchana for having disobeyed his orders. In early Tamil poems containing references to the great deeds of Karikāla, this

[1] Probably, there was another branch somewhere in the Ceded Districts, where the Nolamba-Pallavas were found later and where the Hirahadagalli plates mark an early Pallava sway.

[2] *A.R.A.S.I.* 1906-7, p. 224 and *S.I.I.*, vol. ii, p. 503 for a Chōḷa interregnum. But, Gōpālan argues against an interregnum, see p. 63. It may be that Karikāla did not live so late but that cannot stand in the way of Chōḷa invasion. Mr. Krishna Sastri suggests the Kadambas or the Chōḷas as the usurpers, *E.I.* vol. viii, p. 28 and xv, p 249. On p. 65, Gōpālan suggests the possibility of a Kadamba *interregnum*. On p. xxiii of Mr. Gōpālan's book, Dr. Iyengār says that the 'Chōḷas' whom Buddhavarman fought were the Kalabhras, the Kalambas of Buddhadatta. There is no certain evidence for the equation. The Chōḷas were too weak to invade Kāñchi in the fifth century.

exploit against Trilōchana is conspicuous by its absence? The Chōḷa conquered the *Oliya nagās* and the *Aruvālar* of Toṇḍai, the *Vadavar* (Telugus ?) and the *Poduvar.*[1]

Attempts have been made to pitchfork Karikāla into the Pallava period. There appear two interregnums in the Pallava history of Kāñchi, before Kumāravishṇu I and after Nandivarman.[2] But neither of these periods would be suitable for Karikāla. According to the late inscriptions of the Telugu Chōḷas who claimed descent from Karikāla, Karikāla II grandson of his great namesake founded one branch of the Telugu Chōḷas, Dasavarman the second grandson conquered Pākarāshṭra with its capital Potappi and Toṇḍamāna the third grandson became lord of Toṇḍai.[3] Neither in the second half of the fourth century A.D. nor at the beginning of the sixth century A.D. would it have been possible for Karikāla and his grandsons to plant their power in the Telugu districts. Karikāla did not encounter the Pallava as he conquered only the *Oliya nāgas* and the *Aruvalar* in Toṇḍai. This stage of tribal states in Toṇḍai was pre-Pallava.

The troubles to the Pallava in the fifth and early sixth centuries came from the Kadambas. In spite of repeated Kadamba attacks, the Pallavas like Kumāravishṇu II, Siṁhavarman, Skandavarman and Nandivarman were powerful. In the reign of the last king, the Kadamba trouble was at its height and the Chōḷa fortunes were at a low ebb. Buddhadaṭṭa of the fifth century speaks of his contemporary Kalamba king in Chōḷanādu, enough evidence for proving the sad state of the Chōḷas.

Telugu traditions and late Telugu inscriptions equate Trilōchana Pallava and Vijayāditya the first Chāḷukya king in point of time. And since Karikāla and Trilōchana are alleged to be contemporaries as stated above, the date of Karikāla is sought to be established thereby. Vijayāditya was the grandfather of

[1] Paṭṭinappālai, lines 274–82.

[2] For full references on Trilōchana Pallava, see my note *Was Karikāla a contemporary of Trilōchana Pallava?* pp. 383-8 in the History of the Tamils by Mr. P. T. Srinivasa Iyengar (Madras, 1929) and Trilōchana Pallava and Karikāla Chōḷa by Dr. Venkataramanayya (Madras, 1929). If the Chāḷukyas were in the Deccan in the third century A D., the story of the invasion of Vijayāditya their first king will have to be revised. Neither Pallava nor Western Chāḷukya inscriptions speak of Trilōchana and of his exploits against the Chōḷa and the Chāḷukya.

[3] *S.I.I.* vi, No. 628 ; No. 650. See also *M.E.R.* 1900, p. 17 (22 August).

Puḷakēśin I (ac. 550 A.D.) and so Karikāla lived in the fifth century A.D. But, it has already been demonstrated that the state of the Chōḷa then was far from enviable and there was a contest for supremacy between the Kadamba and the Pallava. At any rate, the traditional Trilōchana-Vijayāditya synchronism helps us little in fixing the age of Karikāla in the fifth century. The continuous traditions about Trilōchana from about the seventh century and the ambition of many small Telugu dynasties of a later day to link themselves with him prove at best that he was an ancient and famous Telugu sovereign. The rise of the Chāḷukyas into a big power might have been attempted at his expense in the Śri Śailam region. But it is not possible to locate the rise of the Chāḷukya, the existence of a powerful Telugu state under Trilōchana Pallava and the glorious expansion of the Chōḷa state under Karikāla (which was more powerful than Trilōchana's kingdom) either before Kumāra-vishṇu I or after Nandivarman.

The Pallava-Kadamba rivalry

After Buddhavarman's defeat of the Chōḷas, the centre of the storm that was brewing to swoop over the whole south was in the west, in the kingdom of the Kadambas of Vanavāsi.[1] In the Pallava-Kadamba hostilities, the Gangas of Mysore were the subordinate allies of the Pallavas.[2] The Pallavas lived to see the decline of the Kadambas and the rise and fall of another rival, the Early Chāḷukyan family.

The Tāḷaguṇḍa inscription,[3] the most valuable for Kadamba history, relates that the Kadambas rose into power under a certain Mayūraśarman who carved a kingdom for himself at the expense of the Pallava. Whatever the relation of Mayūra's dynasty to its predecessor,[4] the zeal of the founder left its stamp on all his successors and the policy of war and death to the Pallava initiated by him (Mayūra) was followed with varying success. Kadamba expansion from its home, Kanara, was north-eastward across the present Ceded Districts, the

[1] The Kadambas were pirates. (*Padirruppaṭṭu* 11-12, lines 1-3, 12-13. See Majumdar's M'Crindle: Ptolemy p. 46. In *gotra* and in descent from Hāriti, the Kadambas resemble the Chāḷukyas.

[2] Penukonda C.P.

[3] *E.I.*, vol. viii, p. 24.

[4] *E.I.*, vol. x. Ap. 1195 Luders's list.

cockpit of many a conflict, traditional and historical, between aspirants to political hegemony in the Deccan. The greatness of Kadamba expansion in the course of half a century (350–400 A.D.) can be gauged from the fact that the Vākāṭakas had to expand in the Deccan by defeating them and from the value attached to the Kadamba marriage alliance by the Vākāṭakas (the Guptas).

The Kadambas were perhaps the first to succeed in dislodging the Pallavas from a large part of the Ceded Districts, [1] defeated them several times and kept them at bay from their new capital at Uchangi in Bellary. After Kumāravishṇu I the aśvamēdhin and captor of Kāñchi, there were two branches of the Pallavas, the senior branch ruling from Kāñchi and the junior ruling the northern districts. There was close friendliness between the two lines and they united against their common foes the Kadambas. While Buddhavarman was engaged in wars against the Chōḷa, his cousin Vīravarman 'the victor,' 'the bravest,' 'the only hero on earth' and 'the subduer of many kings' was engaged in wars with his neighbours. Kumāravishṇu II of Kāñchi probably ruled jointly over both the parts of the Pallava kingdom as his Chenḍalūr charter makes a grant in Gunṭūr district. When Skandavarman, son of Vīravarman, ascended the throne of the northern Pallava principality, he had to continue the traditions of warfare bequeathed to him by Kumāravishṇu II and his own father. Skandavarman was 'the hero of 100 battles'. His younger son Vishṇugōpa was again 'a great victor.' His elder son Siṁhavarman succeeded to the throne of Kāñchi and he and his successors had their share of wars as we learn from Kadamba inscriptions. Once the northern branch took the aggressive against the Śālankāyana as Siṁhavarman (son of Vishṇugōpa) 'who subdued an assemblage of kings' has made a grant in Vengorāshṭra. The Kadambas were the mighty enemy of the Pallavas during the epoch. Their trouble reached the highest pitch in the fifth century. Baffled by the Vākāṭakas in their attempts at northern expansion, the ambition of the Kadambas was directed against the Pallavas and their allies the Gaṅgas. The relative positions of the Pallavas and the Gaṅgas

[1] Rice; Mysore, II. Mayūra the founder attacked the Pallava in the forests of Śri Śailam.

may be understood from the crowning of the Gaṅga Āryavarman and Mādhava by Siṁhavarman 'the unrivalled hero'[1] and his son Skandavarman. The Gaṅgas were in subordinate alliance with the Pallavas possessing as much territory in Mysore as could be held against the aggressive Kadambas and the suzerain Pallavas.

The numerous Kadamba inscriptions present to us a vivid picture of the martial activities of the dynasty mainly directed against the Pallavas. Raghu was a great hero. Kākusthavarman (ac. 425 A.D.) uprooted the Gaṅgas, destroyed the Pallavas and boasted of his imperial connections.[2] Mrigēśavarman (ac. 475 A.D.) was 'a veritable fire of destruction' to the Gaṅgas and the Pallavas.[3] Ravivarman (ac. 500 A.D.) uprooted Chandadanda of Kāñchi and re-established the Kadamba family. The Pallava fomented dissensions in the Kadamba family by siding Vishṇuvarman against his cousin Ravivarman.[4] Vishṇuvarman was the son of Krishnavarman who waged a disastrous war with the Pallava king.[5] Ravi rose to the occasion, slew his rival and dethroned the Pallava.[6]

From the Pallava and Kadamba inscriptions of the fifth century, it may be easily gathered that a most disastrous and unceasing war was being carried on between them, fortune now favouring one and at another time, the other. Perhaps, once or twice the Pallava had to abandon his capital, but as often he carried the war home to the Kadamba. The territory of the Ceded Districts, more or less, was the bone of contention in all the rivalries in that area but it was the plaything of fortune. A late reference to Nandivarman Pallavamalla's succession to Kāñchi from somewhere that region shows that the Pallava stuck to some portion of it. The reduction of the Kadamba who had reached the zenith under Krishnavarman II (ac. 550 A.D.) 'lord of Dakshināpatha' and who befriended the Gaṅga by a marriage alliance was no easy task.[7] The Chāḷukyas alone could do it and the very tiger of the family 'with the boar crest', Puḷakēśin II reigned supreme over them. Even before him, Puḷakēśin I

[1] Udayēndiram C.P.
[2] Taḷagunda ins.
[3] Halsi *C. P. I. A.*, vol. vi, p. 25.
[4] *I. A.*, vol. vi, p. 29.
[5] *E. C.*, vol. v, *B. L.* 121, vol. xi, Introd., p. 5 and *D. G.* 161.
[6] *I. A.*, vol. vii, p. 30, Rice, *Mysore and Coorg*, p. 24.
[7] Dubreuil A. H. of the Dec., p. 106.

(ac. 550 A.D.) captured Palāsika (Hālsi) and Triparvata and Kīrtivarman I defeated Krishnavarman II. Kīrtivarman was in fact 'a very choice elephant of a king who broke to pieces the Kadamba tree'. Thus, the Kadambas were reduced to vassalage and the Gaṅgas were separated from the Pallavas. A new power rose in the Deccan, the Chāḷukyas to continue Kadamba politics with the Pallavas and conquer at a sweep the bulk of the Telugu country.

With this change in the Deccan came a change in the Pallava succession. After Nandivarman the victor came Siṁhavarman, father of Siṁhavishṇu belonging to the northern branch according to the Vāyalūr inscription. Siṁhavishṇu (ac. 575 A.D.) easily made himself master of the Tamil country and started an illustrious age in the annals of Tamil religion and arts.

The Ānanda Gōtra

We do not know for certain whether the Kadambas at any time extended their rule towards the Āndhra coastal districts. But the Ānanda Gōtra founded early in the sixth century A.D. has the *Kapidhwaja* like the Kadambas[1] and it had its dominion in a part of Guntūr district. Kandara[2] the first of the Ānanda Gōtra so far known is said to have fought with his enemies at Dhānyakaṭaka. The latter brought in their army a number of elephants which he routed.[3] Defeating Bennānātha (the lord of the Krishna),[4] Kandara captured *Āndhra Sundari* and drove a wedge between the Pallava and the Vishṇukuṇḍin kingdoms. But the family was not independent for long. The grandson of Kandara was a feudatory of Mahēndravikrama, Vēgavatisanātha[5] (lord of the Vēgavati i.e. of Kāñchi ?) perhaps Mahēndravarman I[6] (ac. 600 A.D.)

[1] Rice : *Mysore and Coorg*, p. 24.

[2] *Bombay Gazetteer*, vol. i, pt. ii, p. 334—Dr. Fleet writes thus : 'The name Kandara is a variant of Krishna ; and this suggests that we may possibly have here an early Rashtrakūta record'. Probably Kandarapura (Kanteru) in Guntūr district was named after Kandara.

[3] *S.I.I.*, vol. vi, 155 of 1899, ins. at Chējrāla.

[4] Was he a Pallava or a Vishṇukuṇḍin that Kandara had to deal with ? Probably the latter.

[5] *S.I.I.*, vol. vi, p. 155 A of 1899, ins. at Chejrāla.

[6] Could it have been Vikramēndra I the Vishṇukuṇḍin (end of the fifth century) ? There is evidence for the sway of the Vishṇukuṇḍin round Dhānyakaṭaka. M.E.R. 1925-6—Ins. at Vēlpūru near Amarāvati on the right bank.

Two more names of the Ānanda Gōtra are known to us, Mahārājas Dāmōdaravarman and Hastivarman.[1] Their grants were made in the same district and it is obvious that they did not expand beyond it. Dāmōdara was a devotee of the Buddha, performer of Brahminical rites and patron of the Brahmins. People and princes were generous to all religions in those days and Dāmōdara was a typical product of the times.

The Ānanda Gōtra claimed to belong to Dhānyakaṭaka and Trikūṭaparvata (perhaps near Nāgārjunakoṇda). From their names ending in *varman* and their bull seal, they were considered as belonging to the Pallava stock.

Obscured for some time by the hoar-frost of Kadamba expansion, the sun of Pallava glory shone again with undiminished lustre from Kāñchi to the Krishna. The epoch of the great Pallavas beginning with Siṁhavishṇu was ushered in and together with it a new political rivalry. But, the Pallavas were not destined to be the masters for long of any part of the Telugu country. The Chāḷukyan invasion left Mahēndravarman I son of Siṁhavishṇu only a few Telugu titles (as a painful reminder of his northern dominion) and ample scope to expand to the south where his family carved for themselves an immortal name.

[1] *E.I.*, vol. xvii, p. 327; *M.E.R.* 1920, p. 95. *I.A.* ix, p. 102. The Maṭṭepād (Ōngōle taluk) plates of Dāmōdara are in Sanskrit and prakrit and suggest for him a date earlier than the sixth century. The numbers in the plates are like those of the Ellore prakrit grant of Śālaṅkāyana Vijayadēva. For the Telugu surnames of Mahēndra Pallava see *M.E.R* 1909, p. 75.

CHAPTER X

THE VISHṆUKUṆḌINS (ABOUT 350–610 A.D.)

Original Home

HARDLY had the Pallavas overthrown the last of the Śālankāyanas of Vēngi when a new power came from the west to succeed to the Śālankāyana heritage. This dynasty was the Vishṇukuṇḍin, new to Vēngi but apparently not a stranger to Āndhra as its earliest associations were with Śri Śailam and as all its charters have been found in the Telugu districts. A fresh impulse was given to the religious revival by the Vishṇukuṇḍins, the protégé of the Vākāṭakas who were in close touch with the classical renaissance in Northern India. With the entry of the Vishṇukuṇḍins into Vēngi (about 460 A.D.), the Vākāṭaka power reached its grand climax and since the Guptas were related to the Vākāṭakas, the Gupta political and cultural influences were felt as far as the Krishna valley.[1]

The earliest mention of the Vākāṭakas is in the inscriptions of Amarāvati of the second century A.D. As a dynasty of rulers, the Vākāṭakas appear in the Central Provinces about the middle of the third century A.D. They rose after the decline of the Śātavāhana empire and began to expand south along the track of Ikshvāku progress when the Ikshvākus had declined. It was in Āndhra west of the Ghats that the Vākāṭakas came into conflict with the Kadambas, and the Vishṇukuṇḍins, when they appeared on the scene, were perhaps the palatine rulers of the Vākāṭaka empire in the south.

The Vishṇukuṇḍins[2] claim to belong to Trikūṭa[3] and Malaya and according to their earliest charter, Ipūr copperplates II

[1] For the Vākāṭakas, see V. A. Smith in *J.R.A.S.* 1914, p. 317; Dubreuil, *Ancient History of the Deccan*; S. K. Iyengār: *The Vākāṭakas* issued as a supplement to his *J.I.H.* (Madras).

[2] *I.A.*, vol. xii, p. 239 for the Vishṇuvridha gōtra (a branch of the Bhāradwāja) of the Vākāṭakas. Vishṇu also is a recognized *gōtra*. Vishṇukuṇḍin is not in the extant *gōtra* list. The town of Vinukoṇḍa (Gunṭūr district) is connected by some with Vishṇukuṇḍin.

[3] Kūṭa is corrupted into gūdem as in Pullareddigūḍem.

their capital was (Ama)rapura. These three places have been identified with Tagara, Mahēndragiri (Gañjam district) and Amraoti (Central Provinces) respectively. But evidence is lacking for locating the dynasty originally in the Central Provinces. None of their inscriptions discovered so far belongs to the Central Provinces. The third king of the Vishṇukuṇḍins, the donor of the earliest grant Ipūr II calls himself a devotee of the God of Śri Śailam which is none other than the place of the same name in Kurnool district. The Vishṇukuṇḍins had the lion-crest like the Kadambas. Their Trikūṭa and Malaya may be identified with places in the hilly Śri Śailam regions and (Āma)rapura may be only another place hard by.[1] It is not unlikely that this dynasty temporarily expanded upto Amarāvati in the teeth of the opposition of the Pallavas. But, it was only for a very short time that the Vishṇukuṇḍins held sway in the Amarāvati region south of the Krishna as Pallava supremacy over the district of Guntūr was undoubted and undisputed in the reigns of Kumāravishṇu III and Skandavarman, son of Vīravarman. Also the donor of the next grant Ipūr I (found in Tenali taluk) refers to his capital as Trivaranagara (not (Ama)rapura) and makes a grant in the district of East Gōdāvari. Thus, it is possible that the Vishṇukuṇḍins succeeded to the place of the Ikshvākus in the Śri Śailam region and they were found and retained as such by the Vākāṭakas who successfully fought with the Kadambas and rolled back the tide of their invasion. Though they were apparently unsuccessful in their first entry into the coastal region on account of strenuous Pallava opposition, the Vishṇukuṇḍins allied themselves by marriage with the Vākāṭakas and invaded and conquered the coastal region north of the Krishna (about 460 A.D.).

Genealogy

There are five copperplates of this dynasty which serve as the source of its history.[2] There are stray references to

[1] The Ānanda gōtra claims to have belonged to Trikūṭaparvata. Triparvata was a Kadamba capital. *J.R.A.S.* 1905, p. 566 for Trikūṭa. See Rice: *Mysore and Croog*, p. 24, for Kadamba lion crest.

[2] (*a*) Ipūr *C.P.* II, (Tenali taluk) *E.I.*, vol. xvii, p. 337 ; *M.E.R.* 1920, p. 98.

(*b*) Ipūr *C.P.* I, *E.I.*, vol. xvii, p. 334 ; *M.E.R.* 1920, p. 98.

Mādhavavarman IV in a work on prosody known as *Janāṣrayi* (Janāsraya was another name of Mādhavavarman IV)[1] and to another of the same name in a later inscription.[2]

The inscriptions have been arranged thus in paleographic order: Ipūr II, Ipūr I, Rāmatīrtham, Chikkulla and Gōdāvari grants. Ipūr II grant has:

Mādhavavarman, aśvamēdhin and lord of many vassals
|
son
Devavarman, a powerful king
|
son
Mādhavavarman, a devotee of Śri Śailam, capital (Ama)rapura

Ipūr I grant supplies.

Govindavarman I, devotee of Śri Śailam
|
son
Mādhavavarman, capital Trivaranagara performed 1,000 agnishtomas made a grant in East Gōdāvari district.

The Mādhavavarman of Ipūr I cannot be identified with Mādhavavarman II of Ipūr II, as the latter was the son of Dēvavarman and had a different capital. Nor can he be identified with Mādhavavarman I of Ipūr II grant as the epigraphist places Ipūr I later than Ipūr II in point of time. Next come the three other plates, the dynastic lists in which it is not difficult to put in order.

(*c*) Rāmatirtham C.P. (Vizianagram taluk), *M.E.R.* 1909, p. 110; *E.I.*, vol. xii, p. 134; *M.E.R.* 1913–4, p. 102.

(*d*) Chikkulla C.P. (Tuni taluk), *E.I.*, vol. iv, p. 193; *M.E.R.* 1920, p. 93.

(*e*) Gōdāvari C.P., *M.E.R.* 1914, p. 102, E. I. xviii. This grant also known as Pulimbūru was found together with one of the E. Chāḷukya Jayasimha I (633–66 A.D.) showing thereby that the Vishṇukuṇḍin rule was closely followed by the Eastern Chāḷukyan. Rudra Sarma the donee of Jayasimha's C.P. was the son of Siva Śarma donee of Madhava IV's C.P. and the son's ownership was confirmed by the new king.

(*f*) *M.E.R.* 1925–6, p. 3 a stone ins. at Vēlpūru, 12 miles west of Amarāvati, which mentions Mādhavavarman the Vishṇukuṇḍin.

[1] *Nitidwishashtika*, ed. by V. Prabhākara Sāstri. Preface by M. Rāmakrishna kavi, p. xiii (Madras, 1928).

[2] *M.E.R.* 1901, p. 81, also 1910, p. 81, for a Mādhavavarman's association with Bezwāda in tradition.

Rāmatīrtham C. P.
Mādhavavarman, devotee of Śrī Śailam, aśvamēdhin.
|
son
Vikramendravarman, ornament to both families.
|
son
Indravarman, won victories in the east.

Chikkulla C. P.
Mādhavavarman, *Md.* a Vākāṭaka, aśvamēdhin, overlord.
|
son
Vikramendravarman
|
son
Indrabhaṭṭāraka, warrior, conqueror of the East.
|
eldest son
Vikramendra

Gōdāvari C. P.
Vikramendravarman.
|
son
Govindavarman.
|
son
Mādhavavarman, conquered the East.

Mādhavavarman of the Rāmatīrtham grant must be identified with Mādhavavarman of Ipūr I copperplates. This king is the best known of the Vishṇukuṇḍins as having married a Vākāṭaka princess and conquered the coastal region. Thus, we arrive at

Mādhavavarman I
|
son
Devavarman
|
son
Mādhavavarman II
:
Govindavarman I
|
son
Mādhavavarman III, the first king of Vēngi.
|
son
Vikramendravarman I
|
son
Indrabhattāraka
|
son
Vikramendravarman II
|
son
Govindavarman II
|
son
Mādhavavarman IV *alias* Janāsraya.

Chronology and Events

There is no evidence for the statement that the Pallava was lord of Vēngi when the Chāḷukya king Puḷakēśin II led an expedition into the Telugu country. Mādhavavarman IV Vishṇukuṇḍin was the king of Vēngi at the time and according to his Gōdāvari plates, he was not confined to his kingdom but attempted to conquer the east, *i.e.*, north of the Gōdāvari. Dating the last year of the reign of Mādhavavarman IV in about 610 A.D. and the starting year of the reign of Mādhavavarman III (the conqueror of Vēngi) *in the kingdom of Vēngi* in about 460 A.D., *i.e.*, sometime after the last Śālankāyana, we get about 150 years for six kings. Mādhavavarman III is said to have married a Vākāṭaka princess probably in the reign of Pravarasēna II the grandson of Chandragupta II of Magadha (ac. 380 A.D.). The Ipūr Plates I are dated in the 37th year of Mādhavavarman, the Rāmatīrtham plates in the 27th year of Indrabhaṭṭāraka and the Gōdāvari or Pulimburu grant in the 48th year of the last Mādhava. So, three of the six Vishṇukuṇḍins of Vēngi had long reigns.

The dynasty must have been founded *at least* four generations before Mādhavavarman III and Mādhavavarman I must therefore be assigned to the middle of the fourth century A.D. It is curious that the earliest Pallava emperor coincides in point of time with the earliest Ikshvāku emperor Chāntamūla, the aśvamēdhin. The next aśvamēdhin we hear of is the Śālankāyana Vijayadēvavarman. About three-quarters of a century later, just perhaps after Samudragupta's *digvijaya*, two more aśvamēdhins appear in Mādhavavarman I of the Vishṇukuṇḍins and Kumāravishṇu I of the Pallavas.

Mādhavavarman I Vishṇukuṇḍin performed 'eleven aśvamēdha and other sacrifices' and had 'a number of vassals'. His son was the 'powerful' Dēvavarman. Dēvavarman's son was Mādhavavarman II who from his residence at (Ama)rapura issued the Ipūr plates II found in Tenali taluk. He ruled over Trikūṭa and Malaya and was a great devotee of the Śiva of Śri Parvata. His reign lasted not less than (4) 7 years.

With the expansion of the Vākāṭakas, the Vishṇukuṇḍins came to be prominent. From modern Berar, the Vākāṭakas expanded between 250 A.D. and 395 A.D. over the Deccan as far as the Krishna. Prithvisēna I, the first to come South (ac. 350 A.D.) is said to have conquered Kuntala over which the Kadambas of Vanavāsi had extended their sway.[1] He ruled long and his son was Rudrasēna II, son-in-law of Chandragupta II (395 A.D.).[2] The reign of Prithvisēna I brought about the powerful relationship with the Vishṇukuṇḍins. Pravarasēna II, son of Rudrasēna II, further strengthened the Vishṇukuṇḍins by marriage and enabled them to expand towards the Coast.

[1] *A. S. W. I.*, vol. iv, pp. 53, 124 and 129.

[2] From *Kuntalēsvara Dautyam*, it may be learnt that Chandragupta II extended his influence over the Deccan through his devoted son-in-law. See Dr. S. K. Iyengār: The Vākāṭakas. Kuntala proper was Southern Mahārāshṭra and S. W. Hyderabad, though it was loosely used to designate the whole of the Deccan. 395 A.D. is the date assigned by Dr. V. A. Smith to the marriage. *J.R.A.S.* 1914, p. 326. The date is accepted by Dr. Dubreuil.

The Vishṇukuṇḍin Mādhava II was hitherto confined to his inland kingdom. Mādhava III, son of Gōvinda I, donated from his camp at Kudāvāda, a village in Guddādi vishaya [1] (East Gōdāvari district) round Drākshārāma, and he should have obviously extended his kingdom to the Coast. He performed 11 aśvamēdhas and 1,000 agnishṭomas. His capital was Trivaranagara and he was a devotee of the lord of Śri Parvata. The Chikkulla plates call him 'lord of many vassals' and the husband of a Vākāṭaka. From his donation in the Gōdāvari district, it may be inferred that Mādhava III destroyed the Śālankāyana dynasty of Vēngi which had been, in all probability, superseded by the Pallavas under Siṁhavarman, son of Vishṇugōpa (about 450 A.D.).

Vikramēndra I, son and successor of Mādhava III, was undisputed master of Vēngi. He was the ornament of both the families, the Vākāṭaka and the Vishṇukuṇḍin. Vikramēndra's son was *Rāja* Indrabhaṭṭāraka, the donor of the Rāmatīrtham plates from Purāni saṅgama. Indra was a great warrior, conqueror of the east and distributor of large charities.

From the time of Indrabhaṭṭāraka, a keen struggle for supremacy took place between the Vishṇukuṇḍins and the kings of Kaliṅga, which ended finally in the defeat of the former. But, Indrabhaṭṭāraka was successful against his foes as his grant was near Chipūrpalle (B. N. Ry.)

Kaliṅga was united and powerful under its kings Chandravarman, Umāvarman and Nandaprabhañjanavarman in the fifth century and a thorn on the side of the Vishṇukuṇḍins and of the Śālankāyanas before them.[2] Indrabhaṭṭāraka was the first to carry the war into the enemy's country and expand up to or beyond Chipūrpalle. The encounter between Indrabhaṭṭāraka and his foes is vividly described in the Gōdāvari plates of Prithvimūla,[3] a vassal of Kaliṅga. Indra of Kaliṅga formed a confederacy, according to Dr. Dubreuil, in which even Harisēna the Vākāṭaka joined and led his allies against Indra the

[1] Ipūr C. P. I. Guddādi was also known as Guddavādi.

[2] It is not likely that the Vishṇukuṇḍins expanded from the region round Mahendragiri southward as the Madras epigraphist suggests. This inference rests upon the identification of Malaya over which the donor of Ipūr II is said to have ruled. But he was a devotee of Śri Śailam and there is no reason why the place should be identified with any other than the place in Kurnool though Rāmatīrtham too is referred to as *Saila* in an ancient inscription on a seal found there.

[3] *J. B. B. R. A. S.*, vol. xvi, p. 116.

Vishṇukuṇḍin who put up a stiff fight against the mighty elephant forces of the North. Indrabhaṭṭāraka of Vēngi seems to have conquered as his Rāmatīrtham plates testify.

The Ajanta inscription of Harisēna, the great grandson of Pravarasēna II speaks of the conquest of Kuntala, Kaliṅga, Kōsala, Āndhra, etc. Harisēna Vākāṭaka was a contemporary more or less of Vikramēndra and Indrabhaṭṭāraka. The significance of the inscription should not be missed as it is clear from it that the Vākāṭaka was still the suzerain of the Deccan though it is not clear if Harisēna acted as an ally of Indra of Kaliṅga. The establishment of the Vishṇukuṇḍins on the coast by the Vākāṭaka was to create a buffer state as it were with the twofold object of keeping in check the Pallava in the south and the kings of Kalinga in the north as Kadamba alliance had been secured by the marriage of Kadamba Ajittabhaṭṭārika and Narendrasēna, son of Pravarasēna II.[1] This function of sentinel the Vishṇukuṇḍins eminently fulfilled for two generations though they had to be warned of their subordinate position by Harisēna. The assumption of the simple title of Rāja after Mādhava III is perhaps an indication of their subordinate position. When the last Vishṇukuṇḍin assumed the title of Mahārāja, external influences ceased to operate for a time over Āndhra. The Vākāṭaka power had declined. The Guptas and the Maukharis boast of victory over the lord of the Āndhras[2] who possessed thousands of rutting elephants but their influence passed away like that of the Vākāṭakas. And Kaliṅga and Āndhra again became independent sometime about the first quarter of the sixth century A.D. But, Āndhra independence was shortlived, as the Chāḷukyan expansion had already begun in the west to sweep her into the net later on.

The son of Indrabhaṭṭāraka was Vikramēndra II 'embellished with all royal virtues in childhood'. He granted the village of Regonram on the Krishna to a temple of Śiva. Two more generations of kings are supplied by the Gōdāvari plates. Their donor Mādhava, son of Gōvinda,[3] also known as Janāsraya,

[1] *E. I.*, vol. ix, p. 268.

[2] Gupta inscriptions, p. 228; *E.I.* xiv, p. 110; *I.A.* xlvi, p. 125.

[3] It is not possible to identify this Gōvinda with the Gōvinda of Ipūr I C.P. whose son had his capital at Trivaranagara. The Epigraphist considers the Gōdāvari C.P. as the latest palæographically. Again, Janāsraya is a special surname of Mādhava IV and it is not found in any other C.P.

crossed the Gōdāvari to conquer the east and made a grant in Guddavādi Vishaya. In other words, he had to defend himself against the aggressive king of Kaliṅga. For, already in the time of Indrabhaṭṭāraka, the Vishṇukuṇḍin empire extended up to Chipurpalle or about that region.

Their Capital and Coins

The capital of the Vishṇukuṇḍins was Lendulūru near the famous Vēngi, the capital of the Śālankāyanas. There are now extensive ruins on the sites of ancient Vēngi and Lendulūru. Eight miles north of Ellore there are the hamlets of Peddavēgi and Chinnavēgi removed from each other by half a mile and five miles to the north is Dendalūru, once Lendulūru with a number of villages round it. There are now a large number of Śiva temples in ruins and extensive mounds.

Coins with the lion and vase attributed to the Vishṇukuṇḍins have been found in the district of Vizagapatnam.[1] Some of their seals exhibit the lion.[2] The lion and vase motifs (so profusely found at Amarāvati) in some of the rock-cut caves at Undavalli and Mogalrājapuram are also noteworthy. Dr. Dubreuil places these and similar caves at Sitanagram and Bezwāda in the age of the Vishṇukuṇḍins.[3]

The devotion of this dynasty to the lord of Śri Śailam is repeatedly mentioned in the copperplates and is but one of the many indications of a rapid Brahminical revival under royal patronage. The shrine referred to is that of the famous Mallikārjuna rearing its hoary head off the Buddhist Parvata sanctified by Nāgārjuna.

[1] E. J. Rapson. *Indian Coins* (vol. iii, Ency. of Indo-Aryan research), also Dubreuil: A. H. of the Deccan, p. 92; also V. A. Smith: E. H. of India Plate, coin No. 16.

[2] *M. E. R.* 1909; *E. I.*, vol. iv, p. 193; vol. xii, p. 133.

[3] These temples have a simple plan in origin. They are cut out of the face of a rock and contain a cell and a porch the latter supported on pillars. Plenty of this type are found in Dravida or Tamilaham and they are attributed to Mahendra I Pallava. So the Vishṇukuṇḍin style was the same as the Early Pallava style. The Madras Archaeological Department considers these early Āndhra rock-cut temples as Pallava. Curiously the Madras Epigraphist (*M.E.R.* 1909, p. 74), thinks that they belong to the early centuries of the Christian era. The cell, halls, etc. of Undavalli are similar to the early Orissan cave style and remind us of the Buddhist epoch. Undoubtedly they are pre-Chāḷukyan as the E. Chāḷukyas made no rock-cut temples, says the Epigraphist.

D. 139.

General View of Cave Temple, Undavalli, Guntur Dt.

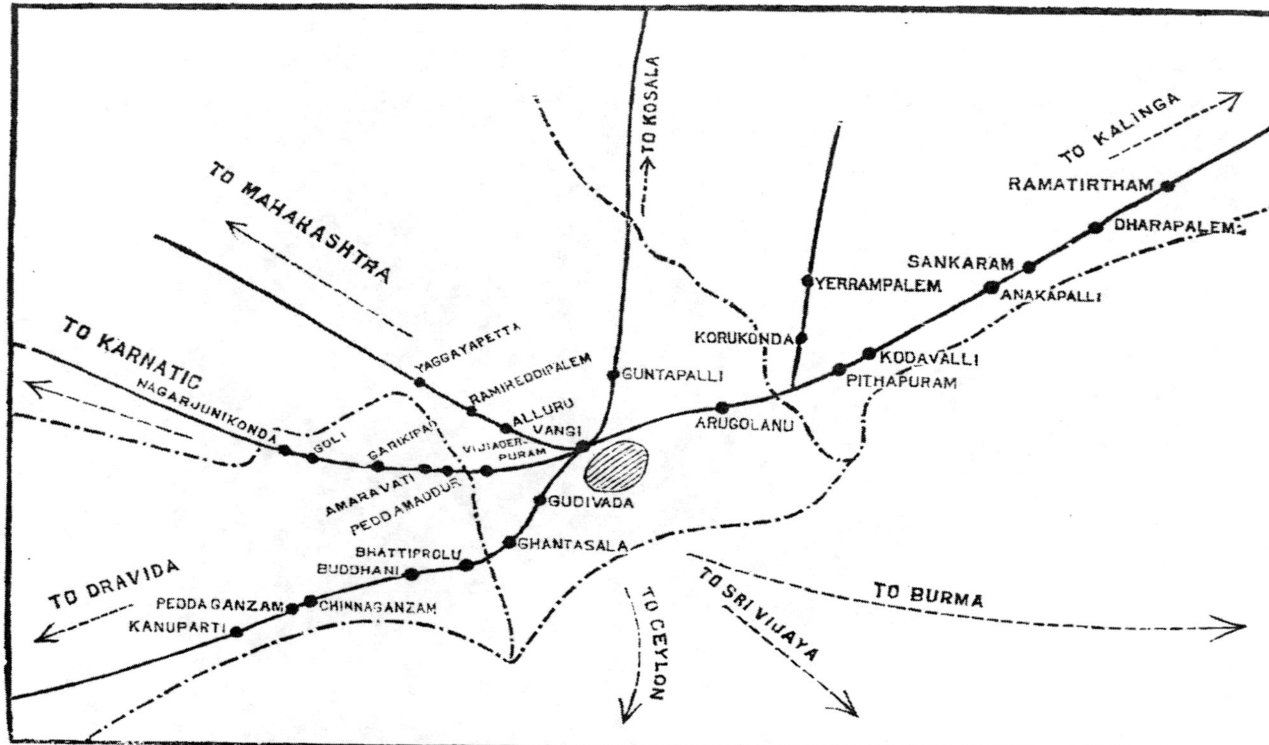
TO KALINGA
RAMATIRTHAM
DHARAPALEM
SANKARAM
ANAKAPALLI
YERRAMPALEM
KORUKONDA
KODAVALLI
PITHAPURAM
TO KOSALA
GUNTAPALLI
ARUGOLANU
TO MAHARASHTRA
YAGGAYAPETTA
RAMIREDDIPALEM
ALLURU
VANGI
TO KARNATIC
NAGARJUNIKONDA
GOLI
GARIKIPAD
VIJJADER-
PURAM
AMARAVATI
PEDDAMADDUR
GUDIVADA
GHANTASALA
BHATTIPROLU
BUDDHANI
TO DRAVIDA
PEDDA GANZAM
CHINNAGANZAM
KANUPARTI
TO CEYLON
TO SRI VIJAYA
TO BURMA

CHAPTER XI

THE KINGS OF KALIṄGA

THE extent of Kaliṅga has varied between the mouths of the Ganges and the Gōdāvari from time to time. Originally Dravidian as far as Tamuluk, Kaliṅga was more rapidly Aryanized than Āndhra. Kaliṅga seems to have been always divided among three or more kings from before the time of the Jātaka stories. In course of time, the name came to be appropriated by the present South Gañjam and Vizagapatnam districts, more or less. According to Hiuen-Tsang Kaliṅga was south-west of Konyodha[1] (the present North Gañjam District). But in later inscriptions, Bhōgapuram and Yellamanchili in the Vizagapatnam district were included in Kaliṅga.[2] The Odras appear to have seized the northern parts of Kaliṅga before the time of Hiuen-Tsang, driving the Kaliṅga Rajas south into the northernmost outpost of the Telugu country in Vizagapatnam and a bit of Ganjam district.

There is no evidence to show the condition of Kaliṅga after Śātavāhana rule. No trace of Ikshvāku rule has been found in the country north of the Gōdāvari down the Ghats. Nor is there any relic of Pallava rule in the area, though the names of some of the Kaliṅga kings, Chandravarman and Nandaprabhanjavarman (5th century A.D.) resemble Pallava names and they called themselves *pitribhaktas* like the Pallavas and the Śālaṅkāyanas. Indeed, from the earlier evidence of the Jātakas, the Rājas of Kaliṅga may be said to have had the flag with the bull emblem and belonged to the Bhāradwāja Gōtra.[3] But, the data are quite insufficient to venture any conclusion on the point.

The veil is lifted by the Allahabad Pillar inscription of Samudragupta in the middle of the fourth century A.D. The *digvijaya* before the aśvamēdha would not be complete if the southern direction were left out. In the Deccan there was no

[1] *E.I.*, vol. vi, p. 136.
[2] *M.E.R.* 1909, pp. 105, 108 ; *E.I.*, vol. xii, p. 212.
[3] *Jātakas* trans. Ed. by Cowell, vol. iii, No. 301 and iv, No. 479.

strong and united empire in the middle of the fourth century A.D. There was no king so powerful, as Gautamiputra Śātakarni or the later Puḷakēśin II. The Kadambas had not yet risen. Perhaps the Vākāṭakas had not yet begun to expand southward as the first to do so was Prithvisēna I whose son married the daughter of Chandra Gupta II.

Some of the places and kings of Dakshiṇāpatha contained in the Allahabad inscription have not yet been identified. The great Emperor is said to have captured and liberated (1) Mahēndra of Kosala, (2) Vyāghrarāja of Mahākāntāra, (3) Maṇṭarāja of Kaurāḷa, (4) Mahēndra of Paishṭāpura, (5) Svāmidatta of Kauttura on the hill, (6) Damana of Airaṇḍapalla, (7) Vishṇugōpa of Kāñchi, (8) Nīlaraja of Āvamukta, (9) Ugrasena of Palakka, (10) Hastivarman of Vēngi, (11) Kubēra of Dēvarāshṭra, (12) Dhanañjaya of Kusthalapura and all the other kings of the region of the south.

Whether it was a mere funeral oration[1] of the court poet Harisēna glorifying his lord in the usual style, none has ventured to suggest. And even if it were such, there was nothing to prevent him from mentioning all the kings who actually ruled in the Deccan; but it is doubtful if a panegyric would have omitted the kings of the Western Deccan out of the list, specially when there was no mighty monarch there. According to Dr. Dubreuil, all the states of the Deccan in the Allahabad inscription belonged to the East Deccan as Airaṇḍapalla[2] (Āmudālavalasa B.N.Ry.) and Dēvarāshtra[3] were in Gañjam and Vizagapatnam districts according to later inscriptions. But the states are not found in the inscription in any geographical order. Samudragupta's march across W. Deccan would give a completeness to his expedition and the location of five kings between the Mahanadi and the Gōdāvari, three of them so near one another was not so likely.

Next to Mantaraja of Kaurala which has been identified with the lower valley of the Mahanadi is mentioned the king of Pithapuram, Mahendra by name. '*Paishṭapurakamahendragiri Kauṭṭurakasvāmidatta*' has to be split into Mahendra of

[1] The inscription is not posthumous, says V. A. Smith who quotes Dr. Buhler, *J.R.A.S.* 1898, p. 386.

[2] *E.I.*, vol. xii, p. 212.

[3] *M.E.R.* 1908-9, p. 109.

Pithāpuram and Svāmidatta of Koṭṭūru on the hill.[1] Koṭṭūru is about 11 miles from Parlākimedi and has some ancient remains. So between the Gōdāvari and the Mahānadi were two states with their capitals at Pithāpuram and Koṭṭūru. Between the Gōdāvari and the Krishṇa was the kingdom of Vēngi then ruled by Hastivarman. South of the Krishṇa were Ugrasēna of Palakka (Palakkada, Nellore District) and Vishṇugōpa of Kāñchi. Nīlarāja of Avamukta[2] is unidentified, while, Kubēra of Dēvarāshtra and Damāna[3] of Airaṇḍapalla may be identified as kings of Mahārāshṭra and Kandesh respectively. Dhanañjaya of Kusthalapura is again unidentified.

Samudragupta had a triumphant progress through the Deccan after which he celebrated the aśvamēdha. True it is, however, that the Empire of Samudragupta did not comprise the Deccan, but that is beside the point for a *digvijaya* before a horse sacrifice. Raghu is said to have desired victory only for the sake of justice and took possession of no land. Samudragupta had no peer in the land from the Himalayas to Cape Comoṛin and was a true *Samrat*. The Hindustan and Deccan were in disintegration. His expedition seems to have led on to two alliances as far as we know, one with the Vākāṭaka in his son's reign and another perhaps with the king of Pithāpuram even in his own time. In all probability, these were the two states in the Emperor's opinion which had a glorious future. The later Vākāṭaka-Vishṇukuṇḍin alliance brought the south within the sphere of Gupta culture. The Pallava seems to have been paralysed after this time and this led to the rise of the Kadambas and to the revival of Chōḷa power. The use of the Gupta era[4] in Gañjam as late as the seventh century is reminiscent of earlier Gupta political sway and likewise the phrase 'ornament of the

[1] Another interpretation is that Svāmidatta was king of Pithāpuram and Mahendragiri Koṭṭūru. The *Raghuvamsa* places the capital of Kaliṅga near the coast. So the question of identifying Koṭṭūru (there is one on the coast also) teems with difficulties. According to the poem Kaliṅga was very powerful and Mahendragiri was in Kaliṅga. According to the inscription Kaliṅga was divided. If Mahendra was lord as far as Koṭṭūru in Parlākimedi where are we to locate the kings of Airaṇḍapalla and Devarashtra?

[2] See an interesting note on Ava in Āndhra in *J.B.O.R.S.*, vol. xiv, pt. i, p. 150.

[3] A familiar ending in the name of the Saka satraps of the Rudṛadāman line.

[4] *E.I.*, vol. vi, p. 143.

Magadha family' in Śaktivarman's copperplate. A curious vestige of Samudra's invasion along the coast is a gold coin of the Emperor found in Saṅghārāma.

It is a relief to find a supreme lord of Kaliṅga in Vāsisṭiputra Śaktivarman whose Rāgholu plates[1] are in early southern alphabet and were issued from Pithāpuram. The grant was made in Kaliṅga Vishaya. Much importance need not be attached to the word *Vishaya* though it is undoubted that Śaktivarman ruled over a larger area than Kaliṅga. He is said to have been an ornament of the Magadha family. Perhaps he was related to the Guptas. The surname of Vāsishṭiputra has not been found outside the Āndhra and Ikshvāku dynasties. Whether Śaktivarman was in any way related to Mahēndra of Pithāpuram or Svāmidatta of Koṭṭūru is not known but he was the Mahārāja of Kaliṅga. Nor is it possible to say why he was called the ornament of the Magadha family.

In the fifth century, a new dynasty attains pre-eminence over Kaliṅga. It is represented by Chandravarman, Umāvarman and Nandaprabhañjanavarman. They have no metronymic like Śaktivarman, call themselves *pitribhaktas*, the phraseology of the plates is the same and therefore they might have belonged to the same dynasty. They do not call themselves Gaṅgas or date their charters in any era. Nandaprabhañjanavarman[2] had his capital at Sārēpalle (near Vizianagaram).[3] As his name indicates, he must have fought hard with Vākāṭaka expansion on the west, and the dynasty of Śaktivarman on the south. The capital of Chandravarman,[4] and Umāvarman[5] was Simhapura, modern Singavarman near Chicacole. All the three were Mahārājas of Kaliṅga who must be dated sometime after Śaktivarman and before Indra the Vishṇukuṇḍin.

The last stray king we come across in the early history of Kaliṅga is Rāja Indra whose vassal Rāja Pṛithvimūla[6] (son of Prabhākara who ruled from Kandāli) has issued the Gōdāvari plates. Indra Ādhirāja, son of Mitavarman, ruled from Manalkudi[7] and was the great foe of Indrabhaṭṭāraka the Vishṇukuṇḍin

[1] Modern Rākaluva in Gañjam district *E.I.*, vol. xii, p. 1.

[2] *I.A.*, vol. xiii, p. 48.

[3] There is another in Parlakimedi Taluk.

[4] *E.I.*, vol. iv, p. 143.

[5] *E.I.*, vol. xii, p. 4.

[6] *J.B.B.R.A.S.*, vol. xvi, p. 114 ; *I.A.*, vol. x, p. 244.

[7] The name sounds Tamil.

according to the inscription. While the Śālankāyanas rarely bestirred themselves out of their kingdom, the Vishṇukuṇḍins came into conflict with the kings of Kaliṅga in their coastal expansion. It was during the spread of Vishṇukuṇḍin sway along the Gōdāvari that the dynasty of Pithāpuram was overthrown. The expansion of the Vishṇukuṇḍins took rapid strides under Indrabhaṭṭāraka who waged a fierce war with Indra of Kaliṅga.[1] Though the victory is claimed by the Rāja of Kaliṅga, the Vishṇukuṇḍin seems to have really won in the war. For, his Rāmatīrtham grant proves it very clearly. The Vishṇukuṇḍin-Kaliṅga hostilities continued till the next reign after Indrabaṭṭāraka. Harisēna Vākāṭaka, a contemporary of Indrabhaṭṭāraka, claims conquest of Āndhra and Kaliṅga thereby showing that he was overlord of the Deccan. Harisēna's dynasty began to decline with his death. After Indrabhaṭṭāraka, the Vishṇukuṇḍins were on the path of decline.

It was sometime about this epoch of Vākāṭaka-Vishṇukuṇḍin decline that the Gaṅga dynasty was founded together with the Gaṅga era. The Nadagām plates of Vajrahasta[2] represent the beginnings of Gaṅga rule as founded on the destruction of the sway of Bālāditya (ac. 467 A.D.). But how far this late story may be believed we cannot say, as there is no record of Gupta rule in Kaliṅga.[3] So also, the view that the Gaṅga era began sometime after Samudragupta's invasion is equally wrong as none of the fifth century Kaliṅga inscriptions is dated in an era and as neither Chandra nor Uma nor Nanda calls himself a Gaṅga. And the earliest Gaṅga inscriptions dated in the Gaṅga era do not afford any scope for a fourth century datum for the beginning of the dynasty. Therefore, the Gaṅga era was founded just after the decline of Vākāṭaka power in the Deccan and the Vishṇukuṇḍin rule in Kaliṅga, i.e., sometime after the year 27 of Indrabhaṭṭāraka, about the beginning of the sixth century A.D.

[1] Dr. Fleet held that the Ādhirāja Indra (of Maṅalkudi) was the first or second Mahārāja Indravarman of the Gaṅga dynasty of Kaliṅganagara. His foe was, according to him, Indrabhaṭṭāraka the Eastern Chāḷukya (666 A.D.). But, Dr. Dubreuil on valid grounds identifies the latter with the Vishṇukuṇḍin of the same name. See *Bombay Gazetteer*, vol. i, pt. ii, p. 334.

[2] *E.I.*, vol. iv, p. 185.

[3] Samudragupta also perhaps was called Bālāditya, p. 347, V. A. Smith (1924).

There is no sure foundation for the view that the Gaṅgas of Kaliṅga were descended from the Gaṅgas of Mysore.[1] There are two charters of the early Gaṅga kings one of the 80th year of Hastivarman *alias* Ranabhīta Rājasimha, Lord of Kaliṅga,[2] a *pitribhakta* and a devotee of Gōkarna and the other of Indravarman[3] *alias* Rājasimha, dated in the 87th year, a *pitribhakta*, devotee of Gōkarna, an Ādhirāja and a great victor. Both are styled as the founders of the family of the Gaṅgas, though as a matter of fact, the family or the era of the family had been founded 80 years before Hastivarman's grant.

Hastivarman issued his grant from Kaliṅganagara 'comfortable in all seasons'. He acquired sovereignty over the whole country by wielding his sharp sword. That Indravarman was the successor of Hastivarman is proved in two ways : (1) the former dates his grant in the 87th year while the latter dates his in the 80th year, (2) the two edicts were written by the same Vinayachandra, son of Bhānuchandra. The boast of Hastivarman and Indravarman of founding the Gaṅgas may mean only the

[1] Rice : *Mysore and Coorg*, p. 30. The Gaṅgas were so called after the river. The *Gangaridae Calingae* of Pliny may contain a clue to the early habitat of the Gaṅgas. In some inscriptions they call themselves Yādavas and in some Ikshvākus. *I.A.*, vol. xviii, p. 165 ; *E.C.* inscriptions from Humcha, Purala and Kallur-Gudda.

[2] *Pravardhamana Vijaya Rajya Samvatsvara* in earlier Kaliṅga inscriptions on which Mr. Rāmadās relies for dating the Gaṅga era about 350 A.D. is found in the Pedda Vēgi C.P. of the Śālankāyanas : See *J.B.O.R.S.*, vol. ix, p. 398, for his article on the Gaṅga era. See *E.I.*, vol. xvii, p. 330, for Hastivarman's inscription. The view of Mr. Subba Rao, R., of Rajahmundry, (*Q.J.A.H.R.S.*, vol. ii, p. 146), that the Gaṅga era began about 450 A.D. is equally untenable. According to his view Indravarman of Achyutapuram and other plates has to be assigned to about 540 A.D. He was the Ādhirāja Indra contemporary of the Vishṇukuṇḍin Indra Bhaṭṭāraka. But, the Vishṇukuṇḍins were still very powerful even over parts of Kaliṅga. And Yasodharman of Malwa claims conquest up to Mahendra in about 528 A.D. Secondly, if Indravarman was the same as Indra of Prithvimula's plates then Indravarman successor and (perhaps son also) of Hastivarman of Kaliṅganagara must be put as the son of Mitavarman of Manalkudi which is an absurd proposition. It is clear then that the Vishṇukuṇḍin Indra must have fought with some other Indra of Kaliṅga, a predecessor of the great Indravarman. Perhaps he it was that founded the era after Indra the Vishṇukuṇḍin's death. It is possible that Indra the founder of the era was the same as the donor of the Jirjingi plates *Q.J.A.H.R.S.*, iii, p. 49. Some time after him came Hastivarman and his successor Indravarman.

[3] *E.I.*, vol. iii, p. 127.

strengthening of the foundations already laid. The great enemy of Hastivarman and Indravarman was the eastern Chāḷukya on the southern frontier. Within fifty years after the rise of the Gaṅgas, the whole Deccan was shaken by the tempest of Chāḷukyan invasion. Kaliṅga escaped being annexed but struggled continuously for independence with Konyodha under Harshavardhana (a strong military outpost on one side) and with the eastern Chāḷukyas of Vēngi on the other. Speaking of Konyodha which extended from the hills of the coast Hiuen-Tsang remarks that its towns were strong, there was a gallant army which kept the neighbouring countries in awe and there was no powerful enemy. Hiuen-Tsang's life mentions the expedition of Harsha to Konyodha which might have been the south-eastern military outpost of Harsha's empire. Puḷakēśin apparently could not dislodge him from it though he claimed victory over Kaliṅga and Kōsala.

Indravarman was also donor of the Tekkali (87 year) and Parlākimedi plates.[1] By the power of his sword he acquired Ādhirājya and established the Gaṅgas. In other words, he and his predecessor also must have given a decisive set back to the advance of the Eastern Chāḷukyas who seem to have expanded at first as far as Chipurpalle. The wars which the Gaṅgas had to wage decimated the population of Kaliṅga besides natural calamities to such an extent that Hiuen-Tsang was sadly impressed with it. The frontier of Harshavardhana on the coast did not extend south of Northern Gañjam district, due to the mighty efforts of the Gaṅgas of Kaliṅga. Rising with the Chāḷukyas, the Eastern Gaṅgas continued to rule for more than 500 years eternally warring with their southern and northern neighbours. During the long rule of these devotees of Gokarnēsvara, Brahminical religion was rehabilitated and re-established and Buddhism and Jainism became past memories.

[1] *I.A.*, vol. xvi, p. 131—91 Yr. written by Vinayachandra, son of Bhanuchandra. There is another Indravarman, perhaps the grandson of the donor of the above three plates. The former has issued the Chicacole Grant in the year 128 and from the inscription we may learn that he was not so great as his grandfather. The Chicacole plates were written by Āditya son of Vinayachandra.

CHAPTER XII

THE EXPANSION OF THE CHĀḶUKYAS

THE curtain drops with the entrance of the Chāḷukyas into Āndhra. No power since the Śātavāhanas had held sway from sea to sea as the Chāḷukyas in the seventh century A.D. Āndhra had been dismembered by the Ikshvākus and the Pallavas, the former giving way to the Śālaṅkāyanas and the Vishṇukuṇḍins in turn. The Kadambas had many a side thrust in Āndhra along the coast and expanded into Āndhra west of the Ghats till they were pushed back by the Vākāṭakas. The Vākāṭakas once held a part of Āndhra through their vassals the Vishṇukuṇḍins. But, more enduring than Pallava and Vākāṭaka rule was the Chāḷukyan. The beginning of Telugu literature which, in course of time, was bound to integrate all the diverse factors and give a unity to Āndhra can be distinctly traced in the Chāḷukyan period. Some of their earliest grants refer to Brahmins well versed in all ancient books and to a *ghaṭika* or college of learning at Asanapura.[1] The cultural contact between Karnāṭa and Mahārāshṭra on the one hand and Āndhra on the other snapped asunder after the Śātavāhana rule was restored under the aegis of the Chāḷukyas of Bādāmi who rose to be the unquestioned masters of the Deccan. The swelling tide of Brahminism and Purāṇic Hinduism rolled over the land under the aegis of the Chāḷukyan monarchs. Kumārila paved the way for the triumphant progress of Śankara. The usual story is told of this terror of Buddhism and Jainism, a son of Kaliṅga, how he was once a Buddhist, then converted with himself the king of the land and aided the persecution of the unvedic religions. This late story in Mādhava's *Śankara Vijaya* may not be wholly credible, but it is sufficient to establish that the un-Brahminical religions had already lost support and fallen on evil days.[2] The acme of political greatness was reached when the ancient home

[1] Chipurpalle C.P. and a grant of Jayasimha I, *M.E.R.* 1917, p. 115; *E.I.*, vol. xviii, p. 55.

[2] *J.B.B.R.A.S.*, vol. xviii.

of the Pallava in Nellore and Gunṭūr districts was usurped and when hard blows were dealt to the rising Gaṅgas on the other side of Chipurpalle.

Origin

Much credence need not be given to the northern origin of the Chāḷukyas.[1] Some scholars see in the Chāḷukyas the Tamil Vēḷir[2] a chief of which was Āy Āndiran of Podiyal. The Chāḷukyan metronymic Hāritiputra reminds us of the Kadambas and the Śātavāhanas. The Chāḷukyas and the Kadambas not only belong to the same Mānavya gōtra but also claim to have been nourished by the 'seven mothers'. The name Chāḷukya has no proper Sanskrit root, the story of the Chāḷukyan origin from *Chuḷuka* being of a later origin.[3] The '*Chaḷiki*' in the Nāgārjunakoṇda inscriptions of the third century A.D. shifts back the age of the Chāḷukyas in the Deccan to a period far anterior to that of their supposed migration from the north. Again, there is a reference by Ptolemy to a tribe the *Salekenoi* not far from *Maisolia* which may afford a clue to the existence of the Chāḷukyas (also called Saḷukki, Chaḷiki, etc.) in the Deccan from still earlier times.

History

The Chāḷukyas get into prominence under Pulakēśin I (550 A.D.) an aśvamēdhin. His capital was Vātāpi or Bādāmi in the Bijapur district. He must have raised the fabric of his power over the destruction of the Kadambas who ruled from Hālsi. His two sons Kīrtivarman and Mangalēsa spread the sway of the dynasty. The Mahākūṭa inscription[4] credits him with victories in Vaṅga and Aṅga, Kaliṅga, Mūshaka, Pāṇḍya, Dramila, Āḷuka, Vaijayanti, etc. According to the Aihōle inscription[5] (634 A.D.) he was 'a night of death' to the Nalas, the Mauryas (of Konkan) and the Kadambas. The upshot of the *praśasti* is clear. Kīrtivarman was a great conqueror and drove out the old dynasties, ushering in the new supremacy. Mangalēsa

[1] Rice, *Mysore and Coorg*, pp. 61–3. *I.A.*, vol. iii, p. 305; vol. vi, p. 363; vol. x, p. 58; *J.B.B.R.S.*, vol. x, p. 348.

[2] M. Raghava Iyengar: Velir Varalaru (Tamil).

[3] Rice, *Mysore and Coorg*, pp. 15, 23, 61–4.

[4] *I.A.*, vol. xix, pp. 7–15. Āndhra is not in the list.

[5] *E.I.*, vol. vi, p. 1.

(ac. 597 A.D.) proved a worthy successor to Kīrtivarman I, as he added to his conquests by the defeat of the Kālachūris. When he resolved to usurp the kingdom for his own son and thus keep out Pulakēśin the son of his brother Kīrtivarman, he lost both his kingdom and his life to his illustrious nephew.

Pulakēśin II ascended the throne in 609 A.D., began a career of expansion, and was cut off in full meridian of glory by death at the hands of his deadliest foe, the Pallava. Even then, he could boast of the lordship over the Deccan limited by the Vindhyas (beyond which he repulsed Harshavardhana[1]) and by the Pallava to the South whom he vanquished and kept at bay many a time. The Kadambas and Gaṅgas were routed. Mahārāshṭra and Lāṭa bowed to the inevitable. Kaliṅga and Kōsala were defeated.[2] Pithāpuram tossed between the Vishṇukuṇḍins and the Rājas of Kaliṅga was captured. A terrible fight took place on the Kollēru, very near the seat of Āndhra power. The Pallava hid himself behind the walls of Kāñchi laying his home dominion at the feet of the conquering hero.[3] There are no grounds for assuming that the Pallava was the ruler of the Krishṇa-Gōdāvari doab though it is just possible, as already stated, that the Śālaṅkāyanas and their successors the Vishṇukuṇḍins were affiliated to the Pallava group of kings.

[1] One of the poems of Mayura credits Harsha with the conquest of the south, p. 234. The Poems of Mayura by Quackenbos (Colombia Univ. vol. ix). This fact is apparently confirmed by an epigraph in Mysore which has 'when Siladitya came conquering and Mahendra fled in fear'. See p. 83, Mysore Arch. Rep. 1923; *J. R. A. S.* 1926. Hiuen-Tsang says that only Mahārāshṭra was not conquered by Harsha. So it is possible that Harsha led an expedition into the south imitating Samudragupta and the Great Mauryas but met with a fate different from theirs. In continuation of the policy of expelling Harsha, Pulakēśin must have conquered and strengthened his weak frontiers especially in Kaliṅga in the east where Harsha seems to have had a strong military outpost.

[2] They are said to have 'effected the humbling of the pride of other kings' in the Aihole inscription. The same record has it that Pulakēśin 'dismissed the subjugated Kings with honor' which resembles the phrase 'captured and liberated' of Samudragupta's inscription but is not true as the Kopparam plates of Pulakēśin II (611 A.D.) in Guntūr district testify unless it is assumed that Āndhra had been conquered before Pulakēśin II which is not possible as Āndhra does not figure in Kīrtivarman's list of conquests.

[3] *M.E.R.* 1909, p. 75—Mahendra's Telugu birudas.

In 609 or 610 A.D.[1] Kubja Vishṇuvardhana, the brother of Pulakēśin II, was made viceroy of the Telugu country along the coast.[2] His first capital was perhaps Pithāpuram from which he dates his Chipurpalle grant.[3] His Chipurpalle copper-plates[4] prove the extension of his power as far as that place, while the mention of Vishamasiddhi in an inscription at Chējrāla[5] and of places in the Guntūr district in a grant of Jayasimha I[6] raises the presumption that the Eastern Chāḷukyan rule extended over the Guntūr district. Later inscriptions speak of Kubja Vishṇuvardhana's kingdom as Vēngi. The independent dynasty founded by this prince in or about 618 A.D. flourished for more than four and a half centuries till it merged into the Chōḷa during which long epoch Āndhra came to her own and took rapid strides in cultural advancement. Bhāravi,[7] a great Saiva

[1] The date for the beginning of Vishṇuvardhana's rule has been calculated from the data supplied by the Eastern and Western Chāḷukyan inscriptions. *See* Fleet: *I.A.*, vol. xx, 1 ff.

[2] The Koppāram plates of Pulakēśin II in Guntūr district in 611 A.D. clearly prove that Chāḷukyan rule was well established in Āndhra by the date while Dr. Fleet stated that Chāḷukyan rule was established before 612 A.D. Dr. V. A. Smith went further and fixed it in 609 A.D. or so. From his Satara C. P. it may be learnt that Kubja was Yuvaraja till 618 A.D. the date of that grant. The duration of the reigns of the E. Chāḷukyan kings is given in their charters and in some of them the saka date is given. To take one instance Amma II (*I.A.*, vols. xix, p. 102 ; xx, p. 23) ascended the throne in 868 saka and roughly 338 years had passed since the accession of Kubja. So Kubja became ruler in about 608 or 609 A.D. A copperplate of Pulakēśin II dated 535 saka refers to his victories over hostile Kings. (*I.A.*, vol. vi, p. 72).

[3] According to Hiuen-Tsang Pingchilo was the capital of Āndhra which has been generally identified with Vēngi. Later Eastern Chāḷukyan inscriptions refer to Vishṇuvardhana as of Vēngi. Dandin locates the Āndhra capital somewhere there.

[4] *I.A.*, vol. xx, pp. 3, 15 ; *see* also *E.I.*, vol. iv, p. 317, for Timmapuram C. P. an early Eastern Chāḷukyan inscription (from Sarvasiddhi taluk, Vizagapatnam district, which mentions Pithāpuram as capital. *M.E.R.* 1908, p. 60). *I.A.*, vol. xx, p. 97, for Jayasimha's kingdom extending to Udaya Pura, Nellore district. The separate mention of Pithāpuram in the Aihole inscription and references to it as a capital city elsewhere show that there was a separate kingdom between the Gōdāvari and Kaliṅga proper.

[5] *M.E.R.* 1917 ; *S.I.I.*, vol. vi, 154/2 of 1899.

[6] *E.I.*, vol. xviii, p. 55 ; and the Kopparam C.P. of Pulakēśin II in *A.B.O.R.I.*, Poona, vol. iv, part i.

[7] Avantisundarikatha, *See Q.J.M.S.*, vol. xii, p. 10 ; and summary of papers of the Fourth Orien. Conference, p. 44.

9

and author of *Kirātārjuniya*, was patronised by Vishṇuvardhana. The rich and fertile soil and abundant crops of the Āndhra country noticed by Hiuen-Tsang supported a large population and maintained a flourishing commerce. A keen observer as he was the pilgrim notes the emotional nature of the inhabitants and their love for arts which have earned for the Āndhra a niche in the temple of Indian History and have survived to this day.

The genealogy of the early Chāḷukya rulers is gathered from their inscriptions and from some of the inscriptions of the Eastern Chāḷukyas of Vēngi. An approximate chronology may be worked out from them.

In 611 A.D.

We may thus sum up the political situation of the Deccan in 611 A.D. The Chāḷukyas were the only big power in the Deccan occupying it from sea to sea and between the Vindhyas and the Tungabhadra with an uncertain border on the Pallava side. The independence of the Gaṅgas of Kaliṅga was ever threatened by the Eastern Chāḷukyas whose martial enthusiasm could only be quenched by the proverbial '108 battles with the Gaṅga and the Rāṭṭa'. But the Gaṅgas could not be shaken out of their kingdom. The Chāḷukyas had already overthrown the Kadambas and the Gaṅgas of Mysore in the reign of Puḷakēśin I from their base and capital Bādāmi. The Kadamba power which held its enemies at bay for wellnigh two centuries and boasted of imperial marriage alliances had spent itself out. The Gaṅgas of Mysore, hedged in between the expanding Kadambas and the ambitious Pallavas had to consent to be crowned by their Pallava masters and submit their crowns to the rising Chāḷukyan power. The Vākāṭakas once expanding as far as Ajanta and absorbing parts of Kuntaḷa withdrew into their mountain fastness after leaving some of the finest memorials of art and are heard of no more. Their protégé and feudatory, the Vishṇukuṇḍins cured for a time of their refractoriness by the hard blows of Harisēna, pushed out of their northern extension by the sturdy and puzzling Gaṅgas and kept within narrow limits by the Pallavas, assumed the title of Mahārāja, only to lose it in the surging wave of the new supremacy.

The *digvijaya* of Pulakēśin II, so beautifully described by Ravikīrti, was but the culmination of the efforts of his predecessors. In the whole of the Deccan and South India, only two powers were left, the Pallava and the Chāḷukya, even the Empire of the former being overrun by the latter. The old big dynasties had become small and the ancient obscure houses obscurer. We no longer hear for two centuries of the independent Tamil kingdoms except as vassals among whom the Pāṇḍya played Mrs. Partington to the ocean of Pallava fame. We read hereafter of the Gaṅgas and the Kadambas only by the side of the Chāḷukyas bearing their arms in war and distributing their charities in peace. The Āndhras and Āndhra-bhṛityas had become historic dynasties, the Vākāṭakas and the Vishṇukuṇḍins moribund.

According to legend, the Chāḷukya rose into prominence at the expense of the Pallava. The glory of the two 'natural enemies' would not have shed so much lustre without the shedding of blood. In fact, the Pallava-Chāḷukya rivalry was a priceless legacy from Mukkanṭi Kāduveṭṭi whose traditional fight with the invading Vijayāditya for his hearth and home in the modern Ceded Districts ran in the blood of his descendants. But, neither could subdue the other completely though each carried the war into the heart of the other's capital. And both were exhausted by about the middle of the eighth century, the Chāḷukya falling a prey to the Rāshṭrakūṭas and the Pallava being worn out by the incessant conflicts and machinations of the Pāṇḍyas.

CHAPTER XIII

ĀNDHRA CULTURE ABROAD

Rivers and Coastline

THE history of the commercial and colonial activities of the Āndhras reads like a romance. With an extensive sea-board stretching from Kaliṅgapaṭnam to Pulicat, Āndhradēsa had convenient and profitable facilities for adventure and foreign commerce. Communication by sea was easier in those days when the land, specially north of the Gōdāvari, was not yet denuded of forests and when heavy goods could be carried with less facility along the few good roads than by sea.

The Vamsadhāra, the Gōdāvari, the Krishna and the Pinākini (N. Pennār) offered safe anchorage for the vessels of those days and were navigable up to a certain point. The two bigger rivers served as highways of commercial and passenger traffic throughout the Āndhra Empire. In the age of the *Periplus of the Erythrean Sea* (about 80 A.D.) and the *Geography* of Ptolemy (about 140 A.D.), ships are said to have sailed eastward from the mouths of the Krishna and the Gōdāvari.[1] Pliny (about 80 A.D.) remarks that ships assembled near the mouth of the Gōdāvari and then sailed up to the places on the Ganges.

Endowed with these arteries of communication, the Āndhras ventured early enough into the wider and more stormy regions of the salty deep. The people living along the coast and on the banks of the big rivers accustomed to navigation from childhood and bred up as fishermen to eke out their livelihood took risks in their distant fishing voyages, when storms, a common enemy of mariners but the best ally of discoverers, would land them at times in strange countries. Sometimes thus by chance and sometimes by design, actuated by love to brave the perils or by curiosity to see strange lands or by the desire to reach *El Dorado*, the stout hearts of old constantly put out to sea to discover new lands and opened the way to foreign commerce.

[1] Schoff: The Periplus of the Erythrean Sea, p. 46.
Gerini: Researches on Ptolemy's Geography, p. 743.

ĀNDHRADĒSA
AND
GREATER INDIA
Canton
Chinese Sea
Tamarlipti
Sawankalok
R. Iravati
Mahendra
Sailor's mark
Puri
Ganjam
Kalingapatnam
Prome
Pegu
Ayodhya
R. Mekhong
AMARAVATI
Vijaya
Visakhapatnam
Point Godavari
Masulipatnam
Funan
Kauthara
Champa
Panduranga
Nellore
Pulicat
Mahabalipuram
Nagapatnam
Pulo Condore
Ligor
Patani
Gulf of Siam
BAY OF BENGAL
Nicobars
Kacha
Wel-lesley
BORNEO
SUMATRA
Singapore
Malaya
Koti
Pambuan
Palembang
Sri Bhoga
Kalinga
Sri Bhoga
KALINGA
Borobudur
Brambanam
Madura island
Bali island
JAVA
INDIAN OCEAN

Colonization followed commerce and culture flowed in the wake of colonization. Added to this native enthusiasm was the stimulus of western traders who swarmed the coast of India for sharing in her valuable trade and of the enterprising *yavanas* and others[1] who seem to have advanced by land as far as Āndhra and influenced her economic and cultural history. According to Col. Gerini, there were Dravidian colonists in Burma as early as the seventh century B.C. The earliest traditions in Greater India connect the beginnings of its civilisation with the Gōdāvari-Krishna deltas. Two kinds of vessels were noted by the author of the *periplus*, one for coasting, and the other for overseas, voyages, the latter being naturally bigger and stronger.

The rivers of Āndhra, while facilitating internal and external communication, have also fertilised the land by bringing rich deposits of alluvium from the hills and by raising the level of the plains and rendering them thereby fit for cultivation. For, before exchange could begin, there must be goods to be exchanged. The products of the forests, the fields, the looms and the mines which formed the chief items of merchandise from Āndhra required a large measure of civilisation for their manufacture.[2]

Āndhra commerce ancient

The inscriptions of Bhaṭṭiprōlu point to the high level of economic progress reached by Āndhra.[3] Āndhra was famous for its weaving according to the *Bhimasēna Jataka.*[4] The *Periplus* refers to the large stores of ordinary cottons, many sorts of muslins and mallow-colored cottons in the markets of Tagara and Paithan whither they were carried by boats, carts or pack bullocks from Maisolos (the present Krishna and Gōdāvari districts).[5] The land traffic grew in volume after the establishment of the Śātavāhana Empire as the goods destined to the

[1] The Sakas, Pahlavas and Yavanas seem to have crossed the high seas from the mainland and planted their rule in Further India. For Dravidian Colonists of Burma, see Gerini, pp. 29-33.

[2] For the mines of Āndhra see Sewell: Lists of Antiquities in the Madras Presidency (Madras, 1882), vol. i, p. 45, 63 f.n. *Krishna District Manual*, pp. 169, 202, 222, 247. The diamond mines of Pārtiyāla, the copper mines of Vinukoṇḍa, the lead mines of Palnād, the marble quarries of Palnād and Sattenpalle were worked in early times.

[3] See the Chapter on the monuments of Āndhra.

[4] Cowell: Trans.

[5] Schoff, pp. 51, 62.

western countries were despatched more safely, cheaply and speedily across the Deccan than by the distant sea route doubling Cape Comorin. And goods intended for Ujjain and further caravan trade were also sent to Paiṭhan which occupied a position of commercial as well as strategic vantage. Masūlipaṭnam and Sopatma not far from it[1] are the only two Āndhra ports mentioned by the *Periplus*, if we leave out Podouke which only Lassen and Yule have identified with Pulicat.

Ptolemy is more informing about the economic history of Āndhra. The mouth of the Pinākini, Manarpha,[2] Kottis,[3] the mouth of the Krishna,[4] Konta Kossyla,[5] Koddura,[6] Allosgyne[7] the point of departure for Chryse are some of the ports and marts mentioned by the Greek. A large number of inland cities are also mentioned by him which have not been properly identified. The trade from the banks of the Ganges passed along the Āndhra coast to the far-off Tamil Nāḍu whose extensive commerce can be gauged from the *Paṭṭinappālai*[8] and other poems. Into the ports of Podouke, Melaṇge[9] and Sopatma flowed all the goods from Egypt and the farther west for distribution to the eastern countries. The spices, sandal and pearls of the south, the *aghil* and gold of Takola (in Malaya) and Kalaha (Sumatra), the coral of the eastern seas, and the camphor, silk and other products of China were familiar in the markets of Āndhradēsa, as Ptolemy's book proves that there was extensive commercial relationship with these countries.

The discovery of Roman Coins in Vinukoṇda, Nellore and Cuddappah (chiefly cotton areas[10]) and the evidence of a recently discovered inscription of the third century A.D. at Nāgārjunakonda clinch the argument that Āndhradēsa was well-known

[1] Somewhere about the mouth of the Swarnarēka or where Pedda Gañjam stands to-day. See pp. 66–7, M'Crindle: Ptolemy edited by Majumdar.

[2] At the mouth of the Manneru in Nellore district.

[3] Probably Allūr Kōṭṭapaṭnam in Guntūr district.

[4] The Krishna is called the Maisolos by him.

[5] Ghanṭasāla near Masulipaṭnam.

[6] Kūḍūru near Masulipaṭnam.

[7] Point Gōdāvari.

[8] *The Pattuppāṭṭu* ed. by Mah. V. Swaminathaiyer (Tamil).

[9] Melange has been severally identified with Mahābalipur, Krishnapaṭam and Bandar Mālanga.

[10] *J.R.A.S.*, 1904, p. 599.

from China to Rome. On such a broad commercial basis must have been reared the glorious colonial and cultural structure of Greater Āndhra. Among the numerous places mentioned by Ptolemy in Further India, two deserve special attention—Trilinga capital of Arakan[1] and Kākula in the Gulf of Siam which might have been so named after the places in the mother country by loyal colonials. Pānduranga, Amarāvati, Vijaya and Kauthara (Kottura), Takola (near Rangoon), Ligor (lit. city) and Simhapura (Singapore), Kaliṅga and Bhōga (or Bhōja) are some other names[2] which may serve, at any rate, to confirm our hypothesis that the culture of Further India had its main source in Āndhra-Kaliṅga. The ship coins of Yajña Śri and the Pallavas have a peculiar significance as vestiges of a lost chapter of Āndhra's maritime greatness and the small village of China at the mouth of the Krishna, bearing an inscription of Yajña Śri from the second century A.D., must have silently witnessed for centuries the flow of the Āndhra culture into the wide ocean of strange and distant realms. Āndhra like Ancient Greece looked to the east where tradition has located the 'golden' Burma and Sumatra, 'silver' Arakan and 'copper' Champa (Indo-China).[3]

The decline in trade with the Roman Empire, the disintegration of the Śātavāhana dominion and perhaps a severe periodic storm ruining some of the ports[4] at about the commencement of the dark age of the *Paurānika* must have adversely affected the golden age of Āndhra economic history. But a temporary eclipse should not be mistaken as a permanent catastrophe. The Ikshvākus maintained and added to the Śātavāhana traditions. The Pallavas who were originally of the Āndhra country—none

[1] Gerini : pp. 29-33.

[2] Bhōja (Palembang) was also known as Andhala, see Gerini, pp. 611-12 Gerini assumes some relationship between Mōṭuppalle (Krishna district) and Pentapolis between the Brahmaputra and Arakan (see p. 35) and between Balongka in Malaya and Malanga (see p. 113).

[3] M'Crindle : Ptolemy's Geography edited by Majumdar (Calcutta, 1927).

For Sumatra see Itsing's observations. Ava is still called Golden frontier. The Rangoon mouth is still called Golden river.

[4] There are traditions and other indications to that effect at several places like Pavitri in *Kadalkonda* Kākandinādu (Gudur tk.), Kanuparti, Peddagañjam and Masulipaṭnam.

The disintegration of the Śātavāhana empire and the invasions of the foreign hordes might have contributed to emigration to some extent.

disputes the point—continued to plough the deep seas and sow the seeds of their culture far and wide. Eminent savants like Burnell and Vogel would fain affiliate the dynasties of the South Sea islands with the Pallavas of the mainland. In fact, the intercourse begun in misty antiquity was kept up as late as the eleventh century A.D.; for, the coins of Śaktivarman and Rājarāja II of the Eastern Chāḷukyan dynasty have been found in Arakan and Siam.[1]

Burma

The names Kaliṅga (for the coast of Pegu) and Utkala (to the north-west of it) given for two parts of Burma[2] after their Indian prototypes well justify the title 'Lord of the Sea' given to the Kaliṅga king by the poet Kāḷidāsa.[3] Phayre quotes traditions that Indians from the mouths of the Krishna and the Gōdāvari settled in Pegu.[4] He would connect the *Tailangs* of Burma with Telingāna, as Ptolemy's Trilingon or Triglypton would suggest a similar derivation for the name of the settlers. 'Intercourse with the east coast of India may be assumed as natural, and is confirmed by the presence of Sanskrit words in Old Talaing and the information about Southern India in Talaing records. Analogies have also been traced between the architecture of Pagan and Southern India. . . . The earliest Talaing alphabet is identical with the Vēngi alphabet of the fourth century A.D.'[5]

There is an inscription of the first century A.D. in South Indian alphabet in Prome district.[6] A very valuable discovery[7] in the 'land of gold and teak' is reported of a stūpa of the sixth or seventh century A.D. This find throws fresh light on the nature of the inter-relations between Burma and Eastern Deccan. In old Prome was found a stūpa with a relic chamber 'a veritable

[1] *I. A.*, vol. xix, p. 79. Burnell: *South Indian Paleography.* Vogel: *Inscriptions of Mūlavarman.*

[2] Gerini.

[3] *Raghuvaṁsa*, vol. vi, p. 57.

[4] Phayre, *History of Burma*, p. 24.

[5] Eliot, *Hinduism and Buddhism* (London, 1921), vol. iii, p. 51.

[6] *E.I.*, vol. v, p. 101.

[7] *The Times of India* (Weekly Illustrated), Bombay, April 8, 1928, p. 16. See also Hackman: Buddhism as a Religion, p. 68 and Bode: The Pāli Literature from Burma, p. 8.

wonder-house of archæological treasures. Round the top of the stūpa is an inscription in mixed *pyu* and pāli in a script closely related to Kannada-Telugu script of South India.' A manuscript of twenty thin gold leaves with short extracts in pāli of the Dharma in an early South Indian script of the same type as above, gold and silver images of the Buddha, a number of inscribed silver and gold finger-rings, ear ornaments, *miniature boats*, terra-cotta reliefs, coins of various value, beads, precious stones—speak volumes of the source whence Burmese religion and culture were imported. After the mission of Asoka, every boat from Āndhradēsa (which to-day can boast of the most extensive Buddhist remains) must have carried the Gospel of the Enlightened One. It is a fact, however, that Buddhaghosa began the revival in Burma and supplied her with the scriptures he assiduously worked at in Ceylon, Burma in due course passing them on to Siam.[1] As Buddhaghosa speaks of Āndhra and of the Gōdāvari with familiarity and mentions two kingdoms on her banks, it may be assumed that he resided for a time in the sacred land.[2] As Rhys Davids would make Dharmapāla and Buddhaghosa university mates and as Dharmapāla is said to have absconded from a festive home and lived sometime in a *mountain* monastery,[3] it is likely that the future savants studied together for a while in Āndhra.

A far-reaching suggestion has been recently made that the Śālankāyanas of Vēngi (Krishna Dt.) were responsible for the introduction of Buddhism into Burma. 'The *Śāsanālamkāra* makes Buddhadatta and Buddhaghosa co-contemporaries of the *Talaing* king San Lan Krom who ruled in modern Pagan. This San Lan Krom was in all probability a member of the Śālankāyana dynasty of kings . . . noted for their naval power and maritime commerce. It is also noteworthy that this same San Lan Krom is credited with the introduction of Buddhism into Burma.' Again, 'Buddhadatta was invited by the Kings of Vēngi whose patronage had set the Buddhist school at Kāñchi on a sound basis. It is not unlikely that Buddhadatta was consulted, if not actually deputed, in connection with introducing Buddhism

[1] Gray, Buddhaghosauppatti, p. 31.
[2] B. C. Law, Buddhaghosha (Calcutta), *J.R.A.S.* 1923, p. 269.
[3] Ency. of Religion and Ethics, vol. iv, p. 701. Beal: Life of Hiuen-Tsang, pp. 138–9.

into Burma where the kings of Vēngi, the Śālankāyanas had made more or less permanent settlements.'[1]

Curiously enough, in the post-Śātavāhana period we know only the Ikshvākus, Dāmodara of the Ānandagotra, and a stray Simhavarman Pallava as patrons of Buddhism. Curiously enough, we know of the Śālankāyanas only as devotees of Śiva, Sūrya and Vishṇu. About Buddhadatta's relation with Āndhradēsa or Burma, little is known as the scholar refers only to the Tamil country.

Malay Peninsula

Throughout Further India, all immigrants from the coast of the *Coromandel* were called *Kḷings* probably because the earliest and the most familiar colonists went from Kaliṅga which was vaguely used to denote the country extending from the Mahānadi to the Gōdāvari. The Malay Peninsula was known as golden Chersonese and parts of it were from time to time included politically under Burma, Java and Siam. According to tradition, Ligor on the east coast was founded by a descendant of Aśōka,[2] Prince Dantakumāra of Dantapura who was wrecked on the Malay coast.[3] In the Hindu art of Ligor may be traced the influence of the art of Ellora and Mahābalipuram in 'the accentuation of the limbs and charm of rhythmical movement.'[4] In Ligor and Wellesley are found inscriptions of the fourth century A. D. proving that Buddhism was already well-established on the coast. Takola on the west coast was the medium of communication between the mainland and Indo-China where another seed of Indian civilisation had been planted in the dim past. The bronzes of Sawan Kolak (*Swargaloka*)[5] with their 'ovoid form, boldly modelled locks, eyebrows like raised crescents, hooked nose and smiling mouth' have their Indian prototype in the images of Buddhāni in Gunṭūr district.[6] The images of Buddhāni and Amarāvati represent the same school of art combining

[1] J.O.R. (Madras), vol. ii, part ii, pp. 112-14.

[2] There is an Asoka among the earliest ancestors of the Pallavas, see the Vāyalur Ins.

[3] Gerini, pp. 107-8 ; p. 109.

[4] Salmony : Sculpture in Siam, pp. 5 and 14.

[5] Gerini, p. 178.

[6] *J. R. A. S.* 1895, pp. 617–37 by Sewell.

in itself the best of the native and foreign styles and the marble and metallic Buddhas of Āndhra were in great demand in distant countries following the *Dharma*.

Indo-China

Thanks to the French savants, much is known of the cultural affinities of Indo-China which is loosely used to denote a number of kingdoms which rose and fell in succession. The kingdom of Champa was founded evidently by colonists from India as early as the second century A. D. It comprised what is now called Annam and included the provinces of Amarāvati, Vijaya, Kauthara and Panduranga. The Vocan stone inscription [1] of about the third century A. D. traces the ruling dynasty to a certain Śri Māra. The epigraph is of unusual interest as it is in Sanskrit in the same script as the Girnār inscription of Rudradāman and the Kanhēri inscription of Vāsishṭiputra Śātakarṇi. The script must have travelled *via* Āndhra-Kaliṅga to Indo-China. More noteworthy is the evolution of the Indo-Chinese script *pari passu* with that of the Deccan script which could not have happened but for close intercourse with the Deccan. The Vocan epigraph has been considered Buddhist though there is little evidence of the prevalence of the religion till long after. King Bhadravarman I 'learned in the four Vēdas' calls himself Dharma Mahārāja[2] like some of the Pallavas (400 A. D.) and scholars are not wanting who trace all the dynasties of Further India which have royal names ending in *varman* to the Pallava stock.

Funan was west of Champa and at the height of its power comprised Cochin-China, Cambodia, Siam and parts of Malaya. The kingdom of Funan dates back to the first century A. D. when Kauṇḍinya, a Brahmin from India, is said to have Hinduised the country, married a nāga princess and founded a dynasty. The inscription of 658 A. D.[3] continues to say that he planted the javelin received from Asvathāman, son of Drona.

[1] Ancient Indian Colonies in the Far East, vol. i, Champa, by Dr. R. C. Majumdar (Lahore, 1927) Book iii, p. 1. For full references see Eliot: chap. iii, pp. 100 and 137.

[2] Dr. Majumdar, p. 27.

[3] Dr. Majumdar: Book iii, p. 16—Myson Stelae Ins. of Prakasadharma d. 579 Saka.

The story bears a family resemblance to that of the Pallava who obtained a kingdom by a nāga marriage, who was descended from Asvathāman and a nāgi and who belonged to the Bhāradwāja gōtra. There was constant intercourse with the mainland as Chandravarman sent an embassy to India (250 A. D.) and as in the next century another Kauṇḍinya arrived from India in Funan and reformed the people. Chandravarman, Dēvavarman and Jayavarman of Indo-China [1] remarkably enough, have their namesakes in the dynasties of Vēngi while Indravarman, so largely figuring in the history of Champa, is a familiar name among the Gaṅga Kings of Kalinga. Buddhist embassies were despatched to China by the kings of Funan from time to time.

About the sixth century A.D. the vassal state, Kamboja (Cambodia) began to assert itself and soon destroyed the power of Funan. Bhavavarman's inscription is said to be like that of Mangalēsa of the Western Chālukyan family (end of the sixth century A.D.)[2] Buddhism of the Mahāyāna form was popular in Kamboja. Siam (Sukho-daya) was first under Cambodia and became independent about the thirteenth century A.D.

All the inscriptions of Indo-China are in Sanskrit and the script is Chāḷukyan or Deccani. In the later inscriptions after the sixth century, the Śaka era is used. As the era was popular only in the Deccan, it must have crossed to Indo-China from that country. Though the era is not used by the dynasties of the East Coast till very late, it has been rightly conjectured that Indo-Chinese civilisation had its source in the lower valleys of the Mahānadi, the Gōdāvari and the Krishna and her ruling families were related to those of the same regions. Emigrants to Indo-China from Western Deccan, it must be remembered, generally cut across the country and embarked from the Āndhra Coast. The close correspondence between the Eastern Chāḷukyan script of Āndhradēsa and the script of Indo-China bespeaks the continuous influence of the one on the other.

As early as the fourth century A.D. there was an elaborate system of worship of the Hindu deities in Indo-China. This, together with the custom of deification of kings, queens and

[1] Dr. Majumdar: pp. 32–3.

[2] The Hindu Colony of Cambodia by Prof. P. N. Bose (Madras, 1927), p. 78. Eliot: vol. iii, p. 106 and f.n. 4. Dubreuil's A. H. of the Deccan, p. 85.

other great personages, was Dravidian, perhaps largely Tamil in origin. The bronze image of the Buddha as a *Guru* showing unmistakeable Greek influence in dress is of the same type as the images discovered in Amarāvati and was undoubtedly imported from that region.[1]

The architecture of Indo-China owes much to the Pallava style the best representatives of which are found at Mahābalipuram. The styles of the pagodas are mostly an evolution from the pre-existing Buddhist forms of architecture found in plenty in Āndhra. In the words of Dr. R. C. Majumdar, 'the characteristic feature of a Cham temple with its storeyed roofs of several stages is derived from the Dravidian style which made its appearance in India as early as the seventh century A.D. in the Māmallapuram *rathas* and the temples of Kāñchi and Bādāmi '.[2] Even in the intricate floral designs and in the lotus and *makara* motifs in sculpture, the influence of the mainland is traceable.

Ceylon

There are some Buddhist stories connecting Āndhra and Ceylon like those relating to the relics of Rāmagrāma and to the tooth-relic of Dantapura. Duttagāmini obtained some relics from Āndhra which he enshrined with great pomp. The assembly that he held on the occasion was attended by Mahādēva and by thousands of monks from Pallavabogga which may be identified with Palnād in Āndhra. With the relics must have travelled to Ceylon the art of Āndhra as the ancient dāgabas of the island were in the Āndhra style.[3] Structural edifices of the same type as the rock-cut monastery at Undavalli (Guṇṭūr district) are found in Ceylon as well as in far-off Cambodia.

Pilgrims and scholars used to go to and from Ceylon as that island had a good collection of the scriptures. Nāgārjuna[4] and Āryadēva are associated with the island, while Buddhaghosa and Buddhadatta of a later day laboured hard in her libraries.

[1] The Influences of Indian Art (The India Society, London, 1925), p. 121. Mazumdar: Champa, pp. 211-13.

[2] Mazumdar, p. 272-73.

[3] Rea: *South Indian Buddhist Antiquities* (Arch. Sur. of India N. I. Series, 1894), pp. 39-40.

[4] See the Chapter on Nāgārjuna Bodhisattva, the King of Monks.

The 'island of pearls and precious stones' had large commerce with the mainland and with the Spice Islands.

The Spice Islands

Sir Stamford Raffles was the pioneer in the field of Javan antiquities and his noble work has been ably continued by the Batavian Society and Dutch scholars.

The islands of the South Seas, Sumatra, Java, Borneo, Bali, and Madura are other fields bearing the stamp of Pallava expansion. The grandest and biggest stūpa at Borobudur (which was modelled on the stūpa of Sangharama in its mighty design with countless dāgabas and that of Amarāvati in its numerous and elegant sculptures) and the temple to the Trinity at Prambanam (another monumental work) bring the most important of the islands, Java, into intimate contact with Āndhra.[1] The Pallava temples were generally for the Trinity like the one at Prambanam. The stūpa of Borobudur shows the astounding range and audacity of the artists who have chiselled a mountain into a paradise of beauty. The history that began with Bhārhut and passed through Amarāvati in meridian splendor closed in Borobudur in picturesque glory. In dimensions, it is unparalleled; in beauty of conception, it is unequalled; in the sculptures of its galleries 'which would extend over three miles if arranged consecutively', it is unique.

Java or *Yavadwipa* was sometimes indifferently applied to Sumatra as well as to Java. The references of Ptolemy, Fa-Hian and Itsing are to the former rather than to the latter. Java of to-day was known as Kaliṅga and possessed two towns of the same name and another named Śri Bhōga or Bhōja (Bhōgavati, *Tamil* Nāgapuram).[2] There are traditions of colonisation by a certain Ādi Śaka, by the peoples of Telingāna and by the peoples of Kaliṅga.[3]

The *Kawi* poems of Java and Bali are like the South Indian artificial poems.[4] The inscriptions found in Java and Borneo are in Pallava or early southern script.[5] The style of the Javan

[1] Fergusson: Indian and Eastern Architecture, ii, p. 318.

[2] Takakusu: Itsing, p. xlvii.

[3] *Madras Journal of Literature and Science*, vol. xvi, p. 132. Sir S. Raffles: *History of Java*, vol. ii, p. 73; *Gerini*, p. 591.

[4] Burnell: S. I. Paleography.

[5] *I.A.* iv, p. 355.

architecture is southern or Pallava. Pūrnavarman of the Javan inscriptions like Mūlavarman of Borneo was apparently of the Pallava stock. In the *dvārapālas,* in the figures in the niches, in arches and in sculptures in relief, the same Pallava influence is clearly traceable. The use of the Śaka era by the later kings of Java shows again the influence of the Deccan rather than of the Tamil country.

In the fourth century A.D. Fa-Hian noted the decline of Buddhism in the islands. From the next century we get the Brahminical inscriptions of Pūrnavarman. In the seventh century, Itsing remarks about the popularity of Buddhism, the importance of Śri Bhōga in Sumatra as a centre of learning and the common intercourse between China and India which is testified to by Ptolemy and Fa-Hian. The new impetus must have come from the Brahminical revival all along the coast from which the Buddhists might have escaped by sailing to the islands.

In Borneo, the Yupa inscriptions of Mūlavarman [1] reveal the prevalence of Vēdic Brahminism in the fourth century A.D. From the script and from the name of the king, Mūlavarman has been pronounced as of the Pallava lineage. According to his inscription, Ādirāja Āditya Dharma of Sumatra was a devotee of the Buddha and erected a seven-storeyed vihāra (656 A.D.). According to Itsing, Sumatra was very rich with its gold and spices. The type of the Buddha found in these islands is similar to that of Amarāvati with *usinisa*, short curls, full robes, etc. Pallava influences are visible at every turn in the monuments of the isles.

Results

The period when Buddhism was popular was one of restless activity as the religion was a missionary one. Prominent religious centres were also of great economic importance.

Increased commerce led to greater economic activity, more wants, more luxuries and a fuller life. Things largely available in one country were brought to another and thus production increased all round in all countries. More commerce meant more wealth and more leisure for finer arts and literature. In short, civilisation grew by leaps and bounds.

[1] By Dr. Vogel of Leyden.

The colonial expansion of Āndhra civilised savage tribes in Greater India, gave them a new religion, art and literature and created a zest in them for a higher life. For the emigrants, it gave new experiences and brought a wider scope for intellectual and economic activity. The mother country derived the benefit of oversea trade and had additional training ground for her religious teachers. Her literature spread and was added to by her children abroad. Some of the inscriptions of Indo-China are good literature; they mention some of the rare literary works of the mainland and are relics of a considerable literary output by the colonials. There was, on the whole, more of movement, activity, enterprise and initiative under the favourable conditions of a busy commercial and colonial life.

CHAPTER XIV

THE ADMINISTRATION

A WELL-ORGANIZED administration with ministers and local governors and subordinate officials, more or less, on the Mauryan model, was in existence under the Śātakarṇis. This is learnt from their inscriptions which mention some of their officials and from those of their erstwhile feudatories, the Pallavas. There is no reason to think that in empire building and administrative organization the Śātavāhanas were not inspired by the northern models and literature on Politics. The Śātavāhana empire was of the same kind as the Mauryan with an order of governors who, like Skandanāga, combined the function perhaps with that of a general of the king. The extent of the empire depended on the capacity of the king and was not dictated by racial affinities or linguistic considerations. In India, an empire by its very nature was short-lived. It aimed, not at exploitation but at glory and gave a sense of pride and a position of privilege to the emperor. Very rarely the native dynasties were rooted out, and never did the empire stop the even tenor of the local life. The empire was but a fulfilment of higher life but never the whole life itself. It was not one well-knit organism but a combine of organisms with independent life throbbing in the several local capitals.

Local Divisions

Even a small kingdom requires for a proper discharge of its functions a division and separation of power. Just as a loose imperial organization was the rule in the history of India, so a self-contained local life was a general feature. A certain number of villages constituted a *vishaya* or district which had a central official for looking to the two primary duties of collecting the revenues of the king and maintaining his authority. Looking after the king's charities and deciding disputes were also matters within his competence. The *rāshṭra* or province was found only in an empire. Or, if an independent kingdom was reduced to subjection, it often bore the name *rāshṭra* to remind, as it were, its former freedom. Thus, Mundarāshṭra, Karmarāshṭra and Vengorāshṭra were kingdoms once. It may be remembered that the country of the Āndhras who now naturally look forward to a province of their own was only occasionally under one umbrella and even then the power of the local Rājas and chiefs was not inconsiderable. The districts of Guṇṭūr, Krishṇa and Gōdāvari were invariably under three independent dynasties.

The Officials

The king the head of the kingdom was the supreme authority. He made no new laws but only administered the customs and the Brahminical laws. He rarely interfered with local life or with the people's. He had his advisers on whom devolved the bulk of his duties. Sometimes, like Jayavarman, the king would himself sign a grant of lands. Often, he would go out on camp to inquire into the welfare of his subjects, visiting the holy spots and dispensing charity to Gods and Brahmins. Many of the charters of the Pallavas of the northern branch were issued from such camps. Some kings like Skandavarman and his son Yuvarāja Vishṇugōpa were famous scholars. The Yuvarāja was associated with the administration and Yuvarājas like Siva-skandavarman and Vishṇugōpa have made grants on their own authority. Manchyanna the Vishṇukuṇḍin prince was an *ājnapti* of a grant and Yuvarāja Vishṇugōpa led the army into the field. We have no idea at present what part, if any, the queen played in the administration. The freedom and equality of the women of those days are impressed upon us by the Āndhra sculptures which contain panels of local kings and queens holding court together. Instances are not wanting of queens like Chārudēvi and princesses like Chāntiśri making grants. The growing Brahminical influences must have operated on the relations between the sexes to the disadvantage of the fair.

All the officials of the king's court are not mentioned in the inscriptions which are our only source for this subject. The royal princes are addressed by the Hirahadagalli plates[1] from

[1] They are also addressed to 'the generals, rulers of districts, prefects of countries, ministers, military officers,' etc. For Śātavāhana officials and administration see *E.I.*, vol. i, p. 95 ; x, Ap. No. 1279 ; xviii, p. 316 ; xiv, p. 153. In the Śātavāhana and post-Śātavāhana periods there must have been a fairly organized military department. Elephants are mentioned more than once as an important limb of the army. All big villages and capital towns were fortified. There is no evidence, however, to show if the state owned ships for war and other purposes if we omit the reference to the Śātavāhana boats in a Tamil epic.

which the inference may be drawn that they were viceroys. The same grant is signed by Bhaṭṭisarman the privy councillor (*rahasadhikata*). Another grant of the same age, the Kondamudi plates of Jayavarman, mentions the Mahārāja's *vyāprita* (executive officer) and *Mahādandanāyaka* (general in chief). In the *mahātalavara* of the Ikshvāku sovereigns may be seen a high official of the sword. Ministers and governors of the king are mentioned by the Kollēru grant of Nandivarman Śālankāyana and Arjunadatta was *āmātya* of Vāsishṭiputra Saktivarman, Mahārāja of Kalinga who ruled from Pithāpuram. The Peddavēgi plates mention *dēsādhipatya*, *ayuktaka*, *vallabha*, *rāja-purushas*, etc. (governors, revenue officers, favorites, princes, etc). Except the duties of the *mahādandanāyaka*, those of the other advisers of the king cannot be defined and the former often occupied only a second place in command as the king himself led the forces to battle. The existence of a record office and of a special officer in charge of it are suggested to us by the word 'seen' that is engraved on the charters. Generally, a big officer signed the grant and executed it issuing the necessary letters for the purpose. It would be absurd to imagine that an organized administration in such a civilized epoch went on without regular records, chronicles and accounts. In more than one record, e.g., in the Pikira and Uruvappalli benefactions royal favorites are mentioned. These were presumably a distinguished order scattered throughout the kingdom who were honored by the king with private audience and personal friendship and who thus constituted a bulwark of the monarchy as did the Brahmins whose learning and piety were at the service of the State in return for its benefactions to them. The inscriptions of the period of our study and the long Eastern Chāḷukyan inscriptions indicate the preservation at the courts of royal genealogies and some of the important events.

The local divisions had their officials like the *niyogas*, *niyuktas*, *āyuktakas* and the *vishayapati* of the Kantēru grant II, and the *adhikrita* and *āyuktakas* of Karmarāshṭra of the Ōṁgōḍu grant I. Mention has already been made of princes who were viceroys. The Mayidavōlu grant is addressed to the royal representative ruling Āndhrapatha from Amarāvati. Thus, the Pallava had two or more viceroys in the third century A.D. Under him were the district and other officials. Even the Śālankāyana of Vēngirājya seems to have had governors according to the Kollēru grant. Provincial and local chiefs (*Rathika* and *Bhojaka*) appear as early as Kharavēla's inscription (2nd century B.C.). The Hirāhadagalli and the Uruvappalli plates of two centuries later mention rulers of districts and prefects of counties. Below the district heads were the heads of villages. A village headman is known from the Bhaṭṭiprōlu inscriptions of the third century B.C. and in the *Bhōjaka* of the inscriptions of this period may be seen a slightly higher limb of power. Thus, Kavachakāra *Bhōga* was a subdivision of Karmarāshṭra.[1] The viceroy or governor seems to have had his own advisers and departmental heads for his province. The overseers of the Pikirā plates were inspectors of modern times who toured about and kept up the efficiency of the administration. In the same document are found mentioned messengers who were charged with special tasks, while the roaming spies of the Hirahadagalli plates remind us of Kautilya's *Arthasastra* which deems them indispensable as the eyes and ears of the king. The mention of generals, guards and military officers in the same valuable document warrants the inference that the king's army was divided and stationed in different and vulnerable parts of the kingdom.

The political divisions of Āndhra

The Āndhra country contained, among others, the following divisions :—

(1) Sātāhani rāshṭra of the Myākaḍoni[2] and the Hirahadagalli inscriptions. It was the region in and round Adōni to the east of the natural boundary of the Sandur hills, but if it extended eastward as far as the later Rēnāḍu in Cuddappah is not known.

(2) Bālikulanāḍu, the land of the Bānas which lay west of the Āndhrapatha or Vadugavali 12,000. This nāḍu comprised parts of the modern Cuddappah and Chittoor districts. There is no early reference to the Bāna except that in the Ṭāḷaguṇḍa inscription. A part of the Balikuḷa nāḍu was in later Pākarāshṭra which comprised parts of Cuddappah and Nellore and had Pottappi as its capital (Pullampet taluk), the city figuring in many later Telugu Chōḷa inscriptions. This dynasty affiliated to the Tamil Chōḷas was found here as early as the seventh

[1] *E.I.*, vol. viii, p. 233.

[2] *E.I.*, vol. xiv, p. 153.

century according to Hiuen-Tsang and inscriptions and this link between Āndhra and Dravida must have influenced Telugu religion and literature from Karikāla's days.

(3) Muliki *nāḍu* or Muriki *nāḍu* which appears as Mulaka in the Nāsik inscription of the second century A.D.[1] It comprised a goodly portion of the present Kurnool district and a part of south-east Hyderabad and was dominated by Sri Parvata. There are innumerable references to it in later inscriptions.[2]

(4) Munda rāshṭra of the Pikirā[3] and Uruvappalli Plates.[4] Why it was so called is not known. It comprised the present Nellore district, more or less. It was once an independent kingdom and perhaps Ptolemy's *Arvarnoi* extended so far. For long it was the home province of the Pallavas together with the Guntūr district. Pākanāḍu or *Vishaya* appears later as a division of this *rāshṭra*.[5]

(5) Karma rāshṭra north of Munda rāshṭra.[6] It was also originally an important division and possessed the most famous and magnificent Buddhist establishments. It was also known as Karmanānḍu[7] or Kammanānḍu and is as old as the Jaggayyapēṭa inscriptions of the third century A.D. It is surmised that Kammamet in Hyderabad had some connection with Karmarāshṭra. This country was later on known as Velanānḍu or Velanāḍu (round Rēpalle) Krornāḍu (new country, round Amarāvati) and so on. The *Vishaya* of Kantēru, Kandēruwādi was a well-known one in this province.[8]

(6) Vēnginādu or Vengorāshṭra, north of Karmarāshṭra. It was the *doab* between the Krishna and the Gōdāvari and indefinitely extended up to the Ghats to the west. It was the very heart of Āndhra for long. The Kudūrāhāra Vishaya round Masulipatnam of this Nāḍu is very well known from the third century A.D.[9]

[1] *E.I.*, vol. viii, p. 61.

[2] *E.I.*, vol. iii, p. 24. Parts of Anantpūr were in later Nalavādi and Nulambapādi both of which can be traced back to the seventh century.

[3] *E.I.*, vol. viii, p. 159.

[4] *I.A.*, vol. v, p. 50.

[5] *E.I.*, vol. iii, p. 24.

[6] *E.I.*, vol. xv, p. 246; *E.I.*, vol. viii, p. 233.

[7] *Nāndu* or *Nāḍu* does not occur in the inscriptions of our period.

[8] *E.I.*, vol. xviii, p. 55.

[9] *I.A.*, vol. v, p. 154; *S.I.I.*, vol. i, p. 47 f. n.; *I.A.*, vol. v, p. 176; *E.I.*, vol. vi, p. 315.

(7) Prōlnāḍu, north of the Gōdāvari, occurs first in an eighth century inscription. It was the country round Piṭhāpuram. The name of the country between Rajahmundry and Piṭhāpuram is not known though it contained the *vishaya* of Guddādi[1] round Drākshāramā and Chellur.

(8) Dēvarāshṭra occurring in a late inscription as the name of the country in which Yellamanchi Kaliṅga was, i.e., round modern Yellamanchili (M.S.M.Ry.). Dēvarāshṭra occurs in the Allahabad inscription of Samudragupta as the kingdom of Kubēra though it is uncertain if the reference is to the Telugu Dēvarāshṭra and not to the Mahārātta.

(9) Plakirāshṭra[2] in and round Rāmatīrtham (Vizagapatnam district) occurs in the Vishṇukuṇḍin inscription of Rāmatīrtham and in the Chipurpalle inscription of Kubja Vishṇuvardhana. North of this began Kaliṅga Proper though undoubtedly Kaliṅga extended its sway indefinitely as far as the Gōdāvari as opportunities occurred. About the seventh century and onwards, it expanded over a large part of modern Vizāgapatnam district. The Rāgholu plates of Śaktivarman call the country round Chicacole Kaliṅga Vishaya and they perhaps belong to about 400 A.D. Besides Kaliṅga, Kośala encroached upon Āndhra from time to time to the west of the Ghats.[3]

In all the inscriptions between 200 and 600 A.D., there is no suggestion of any rule other than that of one man. Committees and *nigamas* with president and treasurer appear in the early Bhaṭṭiprōlu inscriptions as well as in those of Amarāvati and Buddhist *sanghas* with their own functionaries to supervise their works, their meetings, etc., must have existed in large numbers.[4] But, how far the self-governing guilds and *sanghas* may be taken as reminiscent of extinct political and judicial *sabhas* it is very

[1] *E.I.*, vol. xviii, p. 58; vol. iv, p. 33; vol. xvii, p. 334. The origin of Guddādi may be traced to Guddi (blind, Andhaka).

[2] *E.I.*, vol. xii, p. 133; vol. ix, p. 317.

[3] *E.I.*, vol. xii, p. 1. The *vaidikis* of Kosalanāḍu are a distinct branch of the Telugu Brahmins.

[4] The *sangha* was the governing body of each monastery. It was democratic and well regulated. It owned property, had officers and periodic meetings for religious and administrative business. It was no easy matter to provide a big establishment with food, etc. There was communal life. See D. R. Bhandarkar: Carmichael lectures (Calcutta Univ.) for the rules of the *sangha*. But the laity had no share in the *sangha*.

difficult to say, though the Hathigumpha inscription warrants to some extent the prevalence of local self-government in Kaliṅga.[1] A stray reference to the place of the village assembly as a boundary mark in an inscription of Amma II is, however, very suggestive.[2]

Revenues

The revenues of the state were drawn from various sources. The mainstay of Public finance has always been land revenue. In addition, numerous imposts were levied. There were duties on articles of merchandise and special customs officers were appointed by the Pallava for the purpose. The king had a share in all the products grown and manufactured.[3] Thus, he was entitled to a percentage of milk, buttermilk, sugar, salt, vegetables, etc. In all likelihood, the custom originated in the supplies made to the king during his tours. The king had the rights of purveyance and pre-emption against which the Magna Charta provided in England. Men and oxen could be forced into royal service. Grass, wood, vegetables, etc., were required to be supplied to the king. In course of time, all these dues must have been consolidated as the total revenue from the village. Thus, the Komarti plates of Chandravarman of Kaliṅga[4] speak of the grain and gold due from a village gifted away to a Brahmin. The grain was the share of the land revenue and the gold, the other imposts. The donee never interfered with the agricultural or other organization of the village, but, thereafter what used to go to the royal treasury went into his hands.

Charities

Out of the revenues, the king maintained his household and establishment. He celebrated *yajnas* which benefited the poor and gave lands to Brahmins and Gods, the former being the custodians of learning, the high priests of religion who kept

[1] *Paura* and *Janapada* occur in the inscription. The *Janapada* of Kanṭeru (Guntūr district) is mentioned in an inscription of the Ānanda Gōtra. The *Janapada* of Sātavāhani ahāra occurs in the Myakadōni inscription.

[2] *I.A.*, vol. viii, p. 76 ; *E.I.*, vol. v, p. 138.

[3] This had its origin in tribal kingship when the king was entitled to the best that was produced and to a share of all products.

[4] *E. I.*, vol. iv, p. 142.

the calendar and propitiated the gods and the holders of the balance of justice which was done according to the customs and *Sāstras*. One king, the father of Sivaskanda Pallava gave ox-ploughs for cultivation, perhaps after clearing wasteland. Lands given to Brahmins enjoyed the rights of a *Brahmadēya* while those gifted to temples those of a *Dēvabhoga*. Both tenures were exempt from the vexatious dues to the king which were eighteen in number. Thus, the Mayidavolu grant gives the donee exemption from diggings for salt, supply of bullocks, entrance of soldiers, supply of boiled rice, water-pots, cots and dwellings, etc. Thus, he was entire master of the dues he derived from the gift lands. The royal officers are asked by the charters not to interfere with such lands, which suggests an elaborate Land-revenue routine according to which officers inspected and reported on crops, etc. From these inscriptions, we learn incidentally that there were serfdom[1] and forced labor and also the quartering of soldiers in the villages. Besides these gifts to Gods and Brahmins, kings built temples, dug tanks and did other kinds of public good. The *rājataṭāka* of Chāru-devi's grant was perhaps the gift of a king.

[1] *E. I.*, vol. i, p. 2.

BIBLIOGRAPHY

PART I

CHAPTER I

Aitreya Brahmana.

Ahananuru.

A.B.O.R.I. Vol. i (Poona).

A.S.W.I. Vols. iv, v.

Bhandarkar R. G. Early History of the Deccan.

Buhler. Indian Brahmi Alphabet.

C.I.I. Vol. i, Inscriptions of Asoka.

Cowell. Jatakas (trans.)

Cunningham. Ancient Geography of India. Ed. by Majumdar, Calcutta, 1924.

Dandin. Dasakumaracharitra.

Daladavamsa. (trans.) Adyar Library.

Epigraphia Indica. Vols. i, ii, iii, vi, viii, x, xiv, xviii, xxii.

Epigraphia Carnatica. Vols. ii, vii.

Geiger. Mahawamsa.

Grierson. Linguistic Survey, Vols. i, iv.

Hindu. (Illus.) Weekly, 18th May 1930.

Indian Antiquary. Vols. iv, ix, xv, xvi, xxii, xxiii, xxxii, xlii.

Indian Historical Quarterly. (Calcutta), Vol. i, No. 3.

J.A.S.B. Vols. vi, xvii.

J.P.T.S. 1888, 1889, 1904.

J.R.A.S. 1891, 1892, 1906, 1907, 1910, 1926.

Kathasaritsagara.

Kathavastu. (Oxford Univ.)

Mahabharata.

Mahavagga. (Trubner).

Manusmriti.

Manjusri Mula Kalpa. 3 vols. (Tri. SKT. Series).

M.A.R. 1910–13, 1917–18.

Matsya Purana.

M.E.R. 1904, 1906–7, 1910, 1924, 1927.

Nellore Inscriptions. 2 vols. by Butterworth and Venugopal Chetty.

Pargiter. Dynasties of the Kali Age.
Purananuru.
Q.J.M.S. (Bangalore), 1928.
Raja Raja Pattabhisheka Sanchika. (Rajahmundry).
Rapson. Indian Coins.
Rice. Mysore Inscriptions.
Rice. Mysore and Coorg from Inscriptions.
Silappadhikaram. Ed. by Mah. V. S. Iyer.
Schoff. The Periplus of the Erythrean Sea.
Smith, V. A. Asoka (Rulers of India), Oxford, 1901.
Smith, V. A. Early History of India.
South Indian Inscriptons. Vols. iii, v, vi.
Srinivasa Pillai. Tamil Varalaru, Pt. i.
Subramanian, K. R. The Origin of Saivism and its history in the Tamil land (Madras Univ. Jour.)
Taylor. Mackenzie MSS. 3 vols.
Thurston : Castes and tribes in the Madras Presidency.
Turnour. Mahawamsa.
Wilson. Mackenzie MSS.
Watters. Ywan Chwang, 2 vols.

CHAPTER II

A.B.I.A. (Leyden) 1926 and 1927.
A.R.A.S.I. 1905–6, 1906–7, 1907–9, 1910–11, 1919–20, 1925–6.
Bhattacharya. Indian Bud. Iconography.
Burgess. Buddhist Stupas of Amaravati and Jaggayyapeta.
Beal. Buddhist Records of the W. World, 2 vols.
Dubreuil, J. The Pallavas.
Dubreuil, J. Pallava Antiquities.
E.I. Vols. ii, viii, x, xv.
Fergusson. The Cave Temples of India.
I.A. Vols. i, iv, xii.
Indian Historical Quarterly. Vol. iii, Nos. 2, 3 ; iv, No. 4.
J.B.O.R.S. 1930.
J.R.A.S. 1895.
Longhurst. Umbrella on Indian Architecture.
Manjusri Mula Kalpa. Vol. i.
M.A.R. 1888–1889, 1892–4, 1902–4, 1906–11, 1916–21,
M.E.R. 1900, 1906–8, 1914, 1919, 1921–27.
Q.J.A.H.R.S. Rajahmundry, Vol. iii, p. 58.

Ramachandran, T. N. Marbles of Goli (Madras).
Rea. South Indian Buddhist Antiquities.
S.I.I. Vols. i, v, vi.
Times of India. (Illus.) Weekly, March 25, 1928.
Venkataramanayya : South Indian Temple (Madras Univ.).
Watters. Ywan Chwang, 2 vols.

CHAPTER III

A.R.A.S.I. 1903–4, 1905–6, 1908–9.
Burgess. Buddhist Stupas of Amaravati and Jaggayyapeta.
Cambridge History of India. Vol. i.
Codrington. Ancient India.
Coomaraswamy, A. Indian and Indonesian Art.
E.I. Vols. iii, vi, viii, x, xv.
Fergusson. Tree and Serpent Worship.
Fouchier. The Beginnings of Bud. Art.
Grunwedel. Buddhist Art in India.
Griffiths. Ajanta.
Havell. A Handbook of Indian Art.
M.A.R. 1888–9, 1905–10.
M.E.R. 1897.
Rea. South Indian Buddhist Antiquities.
Rūpam. (A Journal on Indian Art), all the volumes.
Seshagiri Rao, B. Studies in South Indian Jainism.
Sewell. Lists of Antiquities in Madras Presidency, 2 vols.
Sewell. Report on the excavation of the Amaravati Stupa (1877, London).
Smith, V. A. History of Fine Art in India and Ceylon.
Watters. Ywan Chwang, 2 vols.

CHAPTER IV

Alberuni. India, vol. i.
A.B.I.A. (Leyden) 1926, 1927.
Burgess. Stupas of Amaravati and Jaggayyapeta.
Beal. Buddhist Records of the W. World, 2 vols.
Beal. Life of Hiuen-Tsang.
Fahian. Travels. Trans. by Giles.
Geiger. Mahawamsa.

Giles. History of Chinese Literature.
Hastings. Encyclopædia of Religion and Ethics, Nagarjuna.
I.A. Vols. iv, ix, xvi.
Itsing. Travels. Trans. by Takakusu.
Journal and Text of the Buddhist Text Society. Vol. iii (1897).
J.A.S.B. Vol. li, Pt. i.
J.R.A.S. 1918.
J.P.T.S. 1883, 1886.
Kern. Manual of Buddhism.
Krishna District Manual.
Manjusri Mula Kalpa. Vol. i.
M.E.R. 1926, 1927.
Nanjio. Catalogue of Chinese Tripitaka.
Nariman. Literary History of Sanskrit Buddhism.
Ray, P. C. History of Ancient Indian Chemistry, 2 vols.
Stein. Rajataramgini, 2 vols.
Taylor. Mackenzie MSS.
Vidyabushan, S. C. History of Indian Logic.
Wallescr. Nagarjuna from Chinese and Tibetan sources.
Watters. Ywan Chwang, 2 vols.

PART II

CHAPTER V

Atlas of the Madras Presidency (Districts), (Madras Survey Department).

A.B.I.A. (Leyden) 1926 and 1927.

Bhandarkar, R. G. Ancient History of the Deccan.

District Gazetteers and Manuals. (With maps).

Dubreuil. A. H. of the Deccan.

E.I. Vols. vii, viii, x, xiv.

Gazetteer of India.

Hunter, W. W. Orissa, vol. i.

J.R.A.S. 1903.

Journal and Text of the Buddhist Text Society 1893, vol. i.

Pargiter. Dynasties of the Kali Age.

Rapson. Andhra Coins (1908).

Smith, V. A. Catalogue of Coins.

Vaidya, C. V. Mediæval Hindu India, vol. i.

Wilson. Catalogue of Mackenzie MSS.

CHAPTER VI

Ahananuru. 85, 340.

A.R.A.S.I. 1906–7.

Dubreuil. Ancient History of the Deccan.

E.I. Vols. i, ii, iii, vi, viii, xv.

Foulkes. The Pallavas.

Geiger. Mahawamsa.

Gopalan. The Pallavas of Kanchi.

Iyengar, S. K. Some Contributions of S. India to Indian Culture.

Iyengar, P. T. S. History of Tamil Culture (Madras)—My note on Trilochana.

Iyengar, M. Srinivasa. Tamil Studies.

I.A. Vols. v, lii.

J.I.H. Vol. ii.

J.R.A.S. 1907.

Kanakasabai. The Tamils 1800 years ago.

Lists of Villages in the Madras Presidency.
M.E.R. 1900.
Pattuppattu. Ed. by Mah. V. S. Iyer.
Ptolemy, by M'Crindle. Ed. by Majumdar.
Periyapuranam.
Rapson. Catalogue of Coins of the Andhra Dynasty.
Rapson. Indian Coins.
Rangachari, V. Inscriptions of the Madras Presidency, 3 vols.
S.I.I. Vol. ii, Pt. v.
Sewell. Lists of Antiquities, 2 vols.
Smith, V. A. Early History of India.
Subramanian, K. R. Origin of Saivism, etc. (Madras Univ. Journal, vol. ii).
Subramania Iyer, K. V. Historical Sketches of Ancient Deccan.

CHAPTER VII

A.R.A.S.I. 1925–6.
A.B.I.A. (Leyden) 1926 and 1927.
Bombay Gazetteer, Vol. i, Part ii.
Dubreuil. Ancient History of the Deccan.
E.I. Vols. x, xviii.
E.C. Vols. vii, xi.
Fahian. Trans. by Giles.
I.A. Vol. ii.
Indian Historical Quarterly. Vol. i, No. 1 (on the Kosalas).
Manjusri Mula Kalpa. 3 vols.
M.E.R. 1926 and 1927.
Matsya Purana.
Pattuppattu. Ed. by Mah. V. S. Iyer.
Rice. Mysore and Coorg from Inscriptions.
Vayu Purana.
Vishnu Purana.

CHAPTER VIII

Bharati. 1924 August.
E.I. Vols. vi, ix.
Early History of India, by V. A. Smith.
Fahian. Giles.

Fleet. Gupta Ins.
I.A. Vols. v, ix.
M.E.R. 1925.
Maharaja's College Magazine (*Vizianagaram*). October 1922.
Oxford History of India, by V. A. Smith.
Ptolemy. Trans. by M'Crindle, ed. by Majumdar.
Pargiter. Indian Historical Tradition.
Q.J.A.H.R.S. Rajahmundry, vol. i, p. 92.

CHAPTER IX

A.R.A.S.I. 1906–7.
Bombay Gazetteer. Vol. i, Pt. ii.
Dubreuil. Ancient History of the Deccan.
Dubreuil. The Pallavas.
E.I. Vols. iii, viii, x, xiv, xv, xvii, xviii.
E.C. Vols. v, xi.
Gopalan. The Pallavas of Kanchi.
I.A. Vols. v, vi, vii, viii, ix.
Indian Historical Quarterly. Vol. ii, No. 3.
Iyengar, S. K. Pallavas. J. I. H., vol. ii.
Iyengar, P. T. S. History of Ancient Tamil Culture—my note on Trilochana Pallava.
J.R.A.S. 1915.
M.E.R. 1900, 1908–9, 1914, 1920, 1925–6.
Mysore Archæological Report. 1909–10.
Pattuppattu. Ed. by Mah. V. S. Iyer.
Padirruppattu. Do.
Proceedings of the Oriental Conference. 1922, 1926.
Ptolemy, by M'Crindle, ed. by Majumdar.
Rice. Mysore, 2 vols.
Rice. Mysore and Coorg from Inscriptions.
S.I.I. Vols. i, ii, Pts. v, vi.
Venkataramanayya, Trilochana Pallava and Karikala Chola.

CHAPTER X

A.S.W.I. Vol. iv.
Dubreuil. Ancient History of the Deccan.
Dubreuil. The Pallavas.
E.I. Vols. iv, ix, xii, xiv, xv, xvii, xviii.

Gupta Inscriptions. Ed. by Dr. J. F. Fleet *C. I. I.* Vol. iii.
I.A. Vols. xii, xlvi.
Iyengar, S. K. The Vakatakas (*J. I. H.* supplement).
J.B.B.R.A.S. Vol. xvi.
J.R.A.S. 1905, 1914.
M.E.R. 1901, 1909, 1910, 1913–14, 1914, 1920, 1925–6.
Nitidwishashtika.
Pargiter. Dynasties of the Kali Age.
Rapson. Indian Coins (1898, Strassburg).
Rice. Mysore, 2 vols.
Rice. Mysore and Coorg.
Smith, V. A. Early History of India.
Vishnu Purana.

CHAPTER XI

Bombay Gazetteer. Vol. i, Pt. ii.
Cowell. Jatakas, trans.
E. Carnatica.
E.I. Vols. iii, iv, v, vi, xii, xiii, xiv, xvii.
Gupta Ins. by Fleet.
I.A. Vols. x, xiii, xvi, xviii.
Indian Historical Quarterly. Vol. i, Nos. 2, 4.
J.B.O.R.S. Vols. ix, xiv.
J.B.B.R.A.S. Vol. xvi.
Kalinga Sanchika. (Telugu) published by the A.H.R.S., Rajahmundry.
M.E.R. 1908, 1909.
Q.J.A.H.R.S. Rajahmundry, vol. i, p. 49 ; vol. ii, p. 146 ; vol. iii, p. 49 ; January 1931.
Raghuvamsa.
Rice. Mysore and Coorg from Inscriptions.
Smith, V. A. Early History of India.

CHAPTER XII

A.B.O.R.I. Vol. iv.
Beal. Buddhist Records of the Western World, 2 vols.
E.I. Vols. iv, vi, xviii.
Fourth Oriental Conference. Summary of Papers.
I.A. Vols. iii, vi, ix, x, xix, xx.

J.B.B.R.A.S. x, xviii.
J.R.A.S. 1926.
Mysore Archæological Report. 1923.
Mayura, Poems of, (Columbia Univ.)
M.E.R. 1908, 1909, 1917.
Q.J.M.S. xii.
Raghava Iyengar, M. Velir Varalaru.
Rice. Mysore and Coorg from inscriptions.
S.I.I. Vol. vi.

CHAPTER XIII

Beal. Life of Hiuen Tsang.
Bode. Pali literature from Burma.
Bose, P. N. Ancient Indian colony of Siam.
Do. ,, ,, of Champa.
Burnell. South Indian Paleography.
Coomaraswamy. Mahayana Buddhist Bronzes, *J.R.A.S.* 1909.
Cowell. Jatakas. Trans.
Dubreuil. Ancient History of the Deccan.
Eliot, Sir Charles. Hinduism and Buddhism, 3 vols.
E. I. Vol. v.
Foucher. Indian art in Cambodia (Sir A. Mukerjee Memorial, iii.)
Fergusson. Indian and Eastern Architecture, 2 vols.
Gerini. (*Col.*) Researches in Ptolemy's Geography.
Gray. Buddhaghosuppati.
Hackmann. Buddhism as a religion.
Hastings. Encyclopædia of Religion and Ethics, iv.
Itsing. A record of Buddhism in India etc. Trans. by Takakusu.
I.A. Vols. iv, xix.
Indian Historical Quarterly. Vol. i, No. 4 ; ii, Nos. 2, 4.
Influences of Indian Art. Lectures on (India Society, London).
J.R.A.S. 1895, 1904, 1923.
J.O.R. II (Madras.)
Krishna District Manual.
Law, B.C. Buddhaghosha.
Majumdar, R.C. Champa.
Madras Journal of Literature and Science. Vol. xvi.
Madras Manual of Administration. 2 vols.
Phayre. History of Burma.
Ptolemy by M'Crindle. Ed. by Majumdar.

Pali Text Society. Sasanavamsa.
Pattuppāttu. Ed. by Mah. V. S. Iyer.
Raffles. History of Java.
Rea. S. I. Buddhist antiquities.
Raghuvamsa.
Schoff. The Periplus of the Erythrean Sea.
Sewell. Lists of antiquities in Madras Presidency, Vol. i.
Salmony. Sculpture in Siam.
Times of India. (Illus.) Weekly, 8 Ap. 1928.
Taylor. Mackenzie Manuscripts, Catalogue of.
Vogel. The Yupa Inscriptions of King Mulavarman from Koetei.
Warmington. Commerce between India and the Roman Empire.
Wilson. Catalogue of Mackenzie MSS.

CHAPTER XIV

Bhandarkar, D. R. Carmichael Lectures (Calcutta).
E.I. Vols. i, iii, iv, v, vi, vii, viii, ix, x, xii, xiv, xv, xvii, xviii.
I.A. v, viii.
M.E.R. 1899.
S.I.I. i. vi.

GENEALOGICAL TABLES

I. SOUTHERN ĀNDHRA

(A large part of Guntur, Nellore and a large part of the Ceded Districts).

PALLAVAS

(See pages 76 and 100)

Father of Siva or Vijayaskandavarman
(ac. after 225 A.D. Married a *Nāga* ?)

|
son

Siva or Vijayaskandavarman
(ac. about 250 A.D. Aśvamēdhin. Donor of Mayidavolu and Hīrahadagalli plates)

|
son

(Yuvarāja) Buddhavarman
(married Chārudevi, donor of Kandukuru C. P. Ikshvaku sway in Amarāvatī ?) About 275 A.D.

|
son

Buddhyankura (ac. about 300 A.D.)

:

Vishṇugopa (340 A.D. contemporary of Samudragupta)

:

Chola interregnum
Rise of the Kadambas

:

Kumāravishṇu I (Aśvamedhin, captured Kāñchi 360 A.D.)

Kāñchi

|
son

Buddhavarman (ac. 385 A.D. fought with the Chōḷas

|
son

Kumāravishṇu II (ac. 410 A.D. donor of the Chendalūr C.P., ruled up to the Kṛishṇa)

Northern

|

Skandavarman (acquired a kingdom)

|
son

Vīravarman (a great victor)

|
son

Skandavarman (a hero of 100 battles and donor of Omgōḍu I. C. P.)

Kāñchi

|

Simhavarman (ac. 435 A.D. according to *Lokavibhāga*, crowned the Gaṅga and warred with the Kadamba who had imperial relations)
son

|

Skandavarman (crowned the Gaṅga and warred with the Kadamba)

|

Northern

|

Yuvarāja Vishṇugopa
(donor of Uruvappalli C. P.)

|
son

Simhavarman (donor of Pikira, Māṅgadur and Omgōḍu II. C. P. conquered Vēngi. (ac. about 450 A.D.)

|

I. SOUTHERN ĀNDHRA--(*contd.*)

son
Nandivarman (warred with the Kadamba. Ananda Gotra founded now? donor of Udayēndiram grant)
:
:
Simhavarman
|
son
Simhavishnu (ac. 575 A.D. contemporary of Kirtivarman Chāḷukya
|
son
Mahēndravarman (the great, lost his Northern possessions, ac. 600 A.D.)
|
son
Narasimhavarman (contemporary of Hiuen Tsang. Killed Puḷakēśin II)

son
Mahārāja Vishnugopavarman (donor of Chūra C. P.)
|
son
Simhavarman
|
son
Simhavishṇu (ascended the throne of Kāñchi)

II. CENTRAL ANDHRA

(Parts of Eastern Hyderabad, Krishna and West Godavari Districts).

I. IKSHVĀKUS

(Ruled Northern Āndhra and parts of Guṇṭūr District also).

Chāntamūla (Aśvamēdhin, perhaps contemporary of Nāgārjuna. Ac. after 225 A.D.)
|
son
Mādhariputra Śrī Virapurushadatta (Ac. about 250 A.D. Conquered parts of Guṇṭūr and Krishṇā Districts. Married a Śaka of Ujjain. Beautified Nāgārjunakoṇda. Inscriptions there. Marriage alliance with the *Chaṭiki*)
|
son
Bahubala (Ac. about 275 A.D. Inscription at Nāgārjunakoṇda. Marriage alliance with the Mahārāja of Vanavāsi
:
Rise of the Śālaṅkāyanas, Kadambas and the Vākātakas. Invasion of Samudragupta 340 A.D.

II. ŚĀLAṄKĀYANAS

(Ruled Krishṇā and West Godāvarī Districts).

Vijayadēvavarman. (Ac. end of the III century A.D. Aśvamēdhin Conquered the Bṛihatphalāyana kingdom ? Conquered parts of the Ikshvāku kingdom ? Donor of Ellore Prakrit C. P.)
:
Vijayanandi, donor of a lost Prakrit C. P.
|
son
Yuvaraja Vijaya Buddhavarman
:

II. ŚALAṄKĀYANAS—(*contd.*)

Hastivarman (340 A.D. contemporary of Samudragupta. A warrior)

|
son

Nandivarman, donor of Kanṭēru C. P. II

|
son

Chandravarman (a warrior)

|
son

Nandivarman (donor of Peddavēgi and Kolleru C. P.)

:

Brother of above ?

Vijayaskandavarman (donor of Kanṭēru C. P. I. Temporary Pallava sway in Vengi. Vishṇukuṇḍin conquest of Vengi (about 460 A.D.)

III. VISHṆUKUṆḌINS

(Originally in the Śri Sailam region(?), then rulers of Krishṇā, West Godavari and parts of East Godavari Districts. Once ruled upto Rāmatīrtham in the north and a bit south of the Kṛishṇa in the south for some years).

Madhavavarman I (Ac. about 350 A.D. Asvamedhin)

|
son

Devavarman

|
son

Madhavavarman II (donor of Īpūr C. P. II in year 47)

:

Govindavarman

|
son

Madhavavarman III (married a Vākāṭaka, accession to Vengi in 460 or so A.D., donor of Ipur I. C. P. in year 37)

|
son

Vikramendravarman I

|
son

Indravarman (warred with Kaliṅga. Donor of Rāmatirtham C. P. in year 27.) Gaṅga era after year 27

|
son

Vikramendravarman II (donor of Chikkulla C. P.)

|
son

Govindavarman II

|
son

Madhavavarman IV or *Janāśraya* (donor of Godāvarī C. P. in year 48, end of rule in 610)

III. NORTHERN ĀNDHRA

(A small part of Eastern Hyderabad, East Godavari and Vizagapatnam Districts. Kalinga sometimes extended upto the Godāvarī. Later, Vizag District became a part of Kalinga).

Ikshvāku rule ?

:

Mahendra, and Swāmidatta. Kubera (?) 340 A.D.

:

Vāsistiputra Śaktivarman (ruled from Pithāpuram. Ornament of the Magadha family. Donor of Rāgholu C. P.). Any relation with the Ikshvākus or Vākāṭakas ?

:

Chandravarman (donor of Komarti C. P.)

.

Umavarman (donor of Brihatprostha C. P.)

.

Nandaprabhañjanavarman (donor of a C. P.)

.

Indra (opponent of the Vishṇukuṇḍin Indra according to Prithvimūla's Godāvarī C. P., contemporary of Harisena Vākāṭaka, founded the Gaṅga era)

:

Hastivarman (year 80 of the Gaṅgas. Donor of Urlam C. P. Warrior, foe of Pulakesin II ?)

|

son

Indravarman (donor of Achyutāpuram year 87 Tekkali and Parlākimedi C. P. 91

|

grandson

Indravarman (year 128 Chicacole C. P.)

LEADING DATES IN THE BOOK

PART I

B.C.		
413–322	...	The rule of the Nandas.
322–298	...	Chandragupta Maurya.
302	...	Megasthenes at Pāṭaliputra.
272–232	...	Aśōka Maurya.
300–200	...	Foundation of many of the well-known stūpas of Āndhra.
225	...	Śātavāhanas independent.
185–73	...	The rule of the Śungas in Magadha and Vidiśa.
171	...	Accession of Khāravēla of Kaliṅga according to his Hathigumpha inscription.
73–28	...	The rule of the Kaṇwas in Magadha.
A.D.		
II Century	...	Nāgārjuna.
107–128	...	Gautamiputra Śātakarṇi.
128–156	...	Vāsishṭiputra Puḷumāyi II.
120–160	...	Kanishka Kushāna.
225	...	The end of the rule of Puḷumāyi IV (Dr. V. A. Smith).
III Century	...	Āryadeva.
399–414	...	Travels of Fahian.
401	...	Some works of Nāgārjuna translated into Chinese by Kumārajiva.
V Century	...	Dignāga.
VI Century ?	...	Bhāvavivēka.
VII Century	...	Dharmakīrti.
630–644	...	Hiuen Tsang's travels in India.
671–695	...	Travels of Itsing.

PART II

B.C.		
IV Century	...	Dravidian Colonists in Burma.
III Century.	...	Inscriptions of Aśōka near Gooty.
III Century	...	Inscriptions of Bhaṭṭiprolu.

B.C.		
225	...	Simuka founder of Śātavāhana independence.
II Century	...	Khāravēla of Kaliṅga, contemporary of Śātakarṇi of Nānāghāt.
A.D.		
80	...	Pliny.
80	...	*Periplus.*
I Century	...	Inscriptions in South Indian alphabet in Burma.
107–128	...	Gautamīputra Śātakarṇi, contemporary of Śaka Nahapāṇa.
128–156	...	Vāsishṭīputra Pulumāyi II—inscription at Amarāvatī.
128	...	Accession of Rudradāman, Mahākshatrapa of Malwa.
140	...	Ptolemy's *Geography.*
166–195	...	Yajña Srī Śātakarṇi—inscription at the mouth of the Krishṇā.
195–225	...	Śiva Śri—inscription at Amarāvatī (?) Chandra Śri—inscription at Pithāpuram. Vijaya—inscription on a seal at Rāmatīrtham (?) Puḷumāyi IV—Myākadoni inscription.
225	...	End of Śātavāhana rule.
225	...	Fall of the Kushānas.
225–250	...	Śrī Parvata Āndhras. Ikshvākus independent—Chantamūla. Bṛihatphalāyanas independent—Jayavarman. Pallavas independent—Śivaskandavarman's father.
III Century	...	Vocan inscription in Indo-China.
250	...	Chandravarman of Indo-China.
III Century	...	Inscriptions at Nāgārjunakoṇda relating Āndhra to China and Ceylon.
250–275	...	Virapurushadatta, Ikshvāku. Śivaskandavarman, Pallava.
275–300	...	Bahubala, Ikshvāku. Buddhavarman, Pallava. Bṛihatphalāyana kingdom annexed by Śālaṅkāyana Vijayadēvavarman.
340	...	Invasion of Samudragupta.

A.D.		
340	...	Vishṇugopa of Kāñchi, Pallava. Ugrasēna of Palakka, Pallava (?) Hastivarman of Vengi, Śālaṅkāyana. Mahendra of Pithāpuram. Swāmidatta of Kottūru. Mantarāja of Kaurāḷa.
340–360	...	Chōḷa interregnum at Kāñchi. Rise of Mayūraśarman. Prithvisēna I, Vākāṭaka the first to come South and conquer Kuntala. First Vishṇukuṇdin in Śri Śailam region (?) Śaktivarman of Pithāpuram Māhārāja of Kaliṅga.
360	...	Kumāravishṇu Pallava recaptures Kāñchi.
380	...	Accession of Chandragupta II, Gupta.
395	...	Marriage of Prabhāvatī, daughter of Chandragupta II and the Vākāṭaka king Rudrasēna II.
IV Century	...	Fahian in India and Java.
IV Century	...	Mūlavarman in Borneo.
IV Century	...	Buddhist inscription in Malaya.
400	...	Bhadravarman of Indo-China.
V Century	...	Pūrnavarman of Java.
V Century	...	Buddhaghosha and Buddhadatta.
400–425	...	Kumāravishṇu, grandson of captor of Kāñchi and ruler of the country as far as the Kṛishṇa. Raghu, Kadamba. Mādhavavarman II, Vishnukundin in Śri Sailam region (?) Chandravarman, Śālaṅkāyana. Accession of Vijayanandi, Śālaṅkāyana. Chandravarman of Kaliṅga (?)
435	...	Accession of Simhavarman of Kāñchi, Pallava.
425–450	...	Simhavarman of Kāñchi, Pallava—Crowned the Gaṅga. Simhavarman of Nellore and Guntūr who conquered Vēngi. Kakusthavarman, Kadamba. Mādhavavarman III Vishṇukuṇdin who married a Vākāṭaka (450 ?) Umāvarman of Kaliṅga (?)

A.D.	
450	... Invasion of Vēngi by Simhavarman, Pallava (son of Vishṇugōpa).
	Śālaṅkāyana rule ends.
460	... Beginning of Vishṇukuṇdin rule in Vēngi.
	Mādhavavarman III, King of Vēngi.
475–500	... Skandavarman at Kāñchi, Pallava (son of Simhavarman).
	Mrigēśavarman, Kadamba.
	End of Vishṇukuṇdin Mādhavavarman III's rule.
	Accession of Ravivarman, Kadamba.
500–525	... Nandivarman, Pallava at Kāñchi.
	Indravarman, Vishnukuṇdin—Rāmatīrtham C.P. in year 27.
	Indravarman of Kaliṅga.
	Harisena Vākāṭaka.
525–550	... Āndhra and Kaliṅga independent of the Vākāṭaka.
	Gaṅga era.
	Ānandagotra founded (?)
	Bhavavarman of Indo-China.
550	... Accession of Kṛishnavarman II, Kadamba.
	Kadamba-Gaṅga alliance.
	Decline of Kadamba rule.
	Rise of the Chāḷukyas.
	Accession of Pulakēsin I who captured Halsi.
	Gaṅgas in Kaliṅga.
575	... Accession of Simhavishnu, Pallava at Kāñchi, contemporary of Poet Bhāravi.
	Kīrtivarman Chāḷukya who defeated the Kadambas and others.
609	... Accession of Puḷakēsin II and his *dig-vijaya.*
609–610	... Vishnuvardhana, younger brother of Puḷakēsin II, Viceroy of Āndhra, with his capital in the coastal districts.
	End of Vishnukuṇdin rule in Vēngi.
618	... Vishnuvardhana independent.
	Founded the Eastern Chāḷukyan dynasty.

A.D.		
VII Century	...	Harshavardhana of Kanauj (606–647 A.D.)
		Stūpa in Prome Dt. with inscriptions in Telugu-Kannada script.
		Ādhirāja Ādityadharma of Sumatra.
		Hastivarman and Indravarman, Gaṅgas of Kaliṅga (?)
		Jayasimha, Eastern Chāḷukya and his successors in Āndhra.
		Mahēndravarman, Narasimhavarman and their successors in Dravida.
		Puḷakēśin II and his successors in the Deccan.
630–644	...	Hiuen-Tsang in India.
671–695	...	Travels of Itsing.
VIII Century (?)...		Borobudur and Prambanam temples in Java.

INDEX

D

E

L

M

R

T